MONSTERS

Myths, Legends, and Real Encounters

RICHARD ESTEP

Foreword by Dr. Karen Stollznow
Co-host of the *MonsterTalk* podcast

DETROIT

Monsters: Myths, Legends, and Real Encounters

Visible Ink Press®
43311 Joy Rd., #414
Canton, MI 48187-2075

Visible Ink Press is a registered trademark of Visible Ink Press LLC.

Most Visible Ink Press books are available at special quantity discounts when purchased in bulk by corporations, organizations, or groups. Customized printings, special imprints, messages, and excerpts can be produced to meet your needs. For more information, contact Special Markets Director, Visible Ink Press, www.visibleinkpress.com, or 734-667-3211.

Managing Editor: Kevin S. Hile
Cover Design: John Gouin, Graphikitchen, LLC
Page Design and Typesetting: Kevin S. Hile
Proofreaders: Christa Brelin and Suzanne Goraj
Indexer: Larry Baker

Cover image: Shutterstock.

ISBNs:

Paperback: 978-1-57859-877-9
Library Hardbound: 978-1-57859-888-5
eBook: 978-1-57859-889-2

Cataloging-in-Publication data is on file at the Library of Congress.

Printed in the United States of America.

10 9 8 7 6 5 4 3 2 1

Myths, Legends, and Real Encounters

RICHARD ESTEP

Foreword by Dr. Karen Stollznow
Co-host of the *MonsterTalk* podcast

For Erin, Mike, and Ella

About the Author

Photograph by Ali Cotton, Bleu Cotton Photography

Richard Estep is the author of numerous books, ranging from paranormal nonfiction and ufology to history and current affairs. These books include *Serial Killers: The Minds, Methods, and Mayhem of History's Most Notorious Murderers; The Serial Killer Next Door: The Double Lives of Notorious Murderers; Grifters, Frauds, and Crooks: True Stories of American Corruption,* and *The Handy Armed Forces Answer Book*. He is a regular columnist for *Haunted Magazine* and has written for the *Journal of Emergency Medical Services.* Richard appears regularly on the TV shows *Haunted Files, Haunted Hospitals, Paranormal 911,* and *Paranormal Night Shift,* and he has guested on *Destination Fear* and *A Haunting*. He makes his home in Colorado with his wife and a menagerie of adopted animals.

Also from Visible Ink Press

The Afterlife Book: Heaven, Hell, and Life after Death
by Marie D. Jones and Larry Flaxman
ISBN: 978-1-57859-761-1

The Alien Book: A Guide to Extraterrestrial Beings on Earth
by Nick Redfern
ISBN: 978-1-57859-687-4

Alien Mysteries, Conspiracies, and Cover-Ups
by Kevin D. Randle
ISBN: 978-1-57859-418-4

American Ghost Stories: True Stories from All 50 Books
by Michael A. Kozlowski
ISBN: 978-1-57859-799-4

Ancient Gods: Lost Histories, Hidden Truths, and the Conspiracy of Silence
by Jim Willis
ISBN: 978-1-57859-614-0

Angels A to Z, 2nd edition
by Evelyn Dorothy Oliver, Ph.D., and James R. Lewis, Ph.D.
ISBN: 978-1-57859-212-8

Area 51: The Revealing Truth of UFOs, Secret Aircraft, Cover-Ups & Conspiracies
by Nick Redfern
ISBN: 978-1-57859-672-0

Armageddon Now: The End of the World A to Z
by Jim Willis and Barbara Willis
ISBN: 978-1-57859-168-8

The Astrology Book: The Encyclopedia of Heavenly Influences, 2nd edition
by James R. Lewis
ISBN: 978-1-57859-144-2

The Astrology Guide: Understanding Your Signs, Your Gifts, and Yourself
by Claudia Trivelas
ISBN: 978-1-57859-738-3

The Bigfoot Book: The Encyclopedia of Sasquatch, Yeti, and Cryptid Primates
by Nick Redfern
ISBN: 978-1-57859-561-7

Bigfoot Sightings: True Tales from Across America
by Jim Willis and Michael A. Kozlowski
IBSN: 978-1-57859-869-4

Celebrity Ghosts and Notorious Hauntings
by Marie D. Jones
ISBN: 978-1-57859-689-8

Censoring God: The History of the Lost Books (an d Other Excluded Scriptures)
by Jim Willis
ISBN: 978-1-57859-732-1

Conspiracies and Secret Societies: The Complete Dossier, 2nd edition
by Brad and Sherry Hansen Steiger
ISBN: 978-1-57859-368-2

Control: MK Ultra, Chemtrails, and the Conspiracy to Suppress the Masses
by Nick Redfern
ISBN: 978-1-57859-638-6

Cover-Ups and Secrets: The Complete Guide to Government Conspiracies, Manipulations & Deceptions
by Nick Redfern
ISBN: 978-1-57859-679-9

Dark Spirits: Monsters, Demons and Devils
by Richard Estep
ISBN: 978-1-57859-847-2

Demons, the Devil, and Fallen Angels
by Marie D. Jones and Larry Flaxman
ISBN: 978-1-57859-613-3

The Dream Encyclopedia, 2nd edition
by James R. Lewis, Ph.D., and Evelyn Dorothy Oliver, Ph.D.
ISBN: 978-1-57859-216-6

The Dream Interpretation Dictionary: Symbols, Signs, and Meanings
by J. M. DeBord
ISBN: 978-1-57859-637-9

Earth Magic: Your Complete Guide to Natural Spells, Potions, Plants, Herbs, Witchcraft, and More
by Marie D. Jones
ISBN: 978-1-57859-697-3

The Encyclopedia of Religious Phenomena
by J. Gordon Melton
ISBN: 978-1-57859-209-8

The Fortune-Telling Book: The Encyclopedia of Divination and Soothsaying
by Raymond Buckland
ISBN: 978-1-57859-147-3

Ghostly Encounters: Terrifyingly True Hauntings
by Richard Estep
ISBN: 978-1-57859-812-0

The Government UFO Files: The Conspiracy of Cover-Up
by Kevin D. Randle
ISBN: 978-1-57859-477-1

Haunted: Malevolent Ghosts, Night Terrors, and Threatening Phantoms
by Brad Steiger
ISBN: 978-1-57859-620-1

Hidden History: Ancient Aliens and the Suppressed Origins of Civilization
by Jim Willis
ISBN: 978-1-57859-710-9

Hidden Realms, Lost Civilizations, and Beings from Other Worlds
by Jerome Clark
ISBN: 978-1-57859-175-6

The Horror Show Guide: The Ultimate Frightfest of Movies
by Mike Mayo
ISBN: 978-1-57859-420-7

The Illuminati: The Secret Society That Hijacked the World
by Jim Marrs
ISBN: 978-1-57859-619-5

Lost Civilizations: The Secret Histories and Suppressed Technologies of the Ancients
by Jim Willis
ISBN: 978-1-57859-706-2

The Monster Book: Creatures, Beasts, and Fiends of Nature
by Nick Redfern
ISBN: 978-1-57859-575-4

Monsters of the Deep
by Nick Redfern
ISBN: 978-1-57859-705-5

Near Death Experiences: Afterlife Journeys and Revelations
by Jim Willis
ISBN: 978-1-57859-846-5

The New Witch: Your Guide to Modern Witchcraft, Wicca, Spells, Potions, Magic, and More
by Marie D. Jones
ISBN: 978-1-57859-716-1

The New World Order Book
by Nick Redfern
ISBN: 978-1-57859-615-7

Nightmares: Your Guide to Interpreting Your Darkest Dreams
by J. M. DeBord
ISBN: 978-1-57859-758-1

Real Aliens, Space Beings, and Creatures from Other Worlds,
by Brad and Sherry Hansen Steiger
ISBN: 978-1-57859-333-0

Real Encounters, Different Dimensions, and Otherworldly Beings
by Brad and Sherry Hansen Steiger
ISBN: 978-1-57859-455-9

Real Ghosts, Restless Spirits, and Haunted Places, 2nd edition
by Brad Steiger
ISBN: 978-1-57859-401-6

Real Miracles, Divine Intervention, and Feats of Incredible Survival
by Brad and Sherry Hansen Steiger
ISBN: 978-1-57859-214-2

Real Monsters, Gruesome Critters, and Beasts from the Darkside
by Brad and Sherry Hansen Steiger
ISBN: 978-1-57859-220-3

Real Vampires, Night Stalkers, and Creatures from the Darkside
by Brad Steiger
ISBN: 978-1-57859-255-5

Real Visitors, Voices from Beyond, and Parallel Dimensions
by Brad and Sherry Hansen Steiger
ISBN: 978-1-57859-541-9

Real Zombies, the Living Dead, and Creatures of the Apocalypse,
by Brad Steiger
ISBN: 978-1-57859-296-8

The Religion Book: Places, Prophets, Saints, and Seers
by Jim Willis
ISBN: 978-1-57859-151-0

Runaway Science: True Stories of Raging Robots and High-Tech Horrors
by Nick Redfern
ISBN: 978-1-57859-801-4

The Sci-Fi Movie Guide: The Universe of Film from Alien to Zardoz
by Chris Barsanti
ISBN: 978-1-57859-503-7

Secret History: Conspiracies from Ancient Aliens to the New World Order
by Nick Redfern
ISBN: 978-1-57859-479-5

Secret Societies: The Complete Guide to Histories, Rites, and Rituals
by Nick Redfern
ISBN: 978-1-57859-483-2

The Spirit Book: The Encyclopedia of Clairvoyance, Channeling, and Spirit Communication
by Raymond Buckland
ISBN 978-1-57859-790-1

Supernatural Gods: Spiritual Mysteries, Psychic Experiences, and Scientific Truths
by Jim Willis
ISBN: 978-1-57859-660-7

Time Travel: The Science and Science Fiction
by Nick Redfern
ISBN: 978-1-57859-723-9

Toxin Nation: The Poisoning of Our Air, Water, Food, and Bodies
by Marie D. Jones
ISBN: 978-1-57859-709-3

The UFO Dossier: 100 Years of Government Secrets, Conspiracies, and Cover-Ups
by Kevin D. Randle
ISBN: 978-1-57859-564-8

Unexplained! Strange Sightings, Incredible Occurrences, and Puzzling Physical Phenomena, 3rd edition
by Jerome Clark
ISBN: 978-1-57859-344-6

The Vampire Almanac: The Complete History
by J. Gordon Melton, Ph.D.
ISBN: 978-1-57859-719-2

The Vampire Book: The Encyclopedia of the Undead, 3rd edition
by J. Gordon Melton, Ph.D.
ISBN: 978-1-57859-281-4

The Werewolf Book: The Encyclopedia of Shape-Shifting Beings, 2nd edition
by Brad Steiger
ISBN: 978-1-57859-367-5

Werewolf Stories: Shape-Shifters, Lycanthropes, and Man-Beasts
by Nick Redfern and Brad Steiger
ISBN: 978-1-57859-766-6

The Witch Book: The Encyclopedia of Witchcraft, Wicca, and Neo-Paganism
by Raymond Buckland
ISBN: 978-1-57859-791-8

The Witches Almanac: Sorcerers, Witches, and Magic from Ancient Rome to the Digital Age
by Charles Christian
ISBN: 978-1-57859-760-4

The Zombie Book: The Encyclopedia of the Living Dead
by Nick Redfern and Brad Steiger
ISBN: 978-1-57859-504-4

"Real Nightmares" E-Books by Brad Steiger

Book 1: *True and Truly Scary Unexplained Phenomenon*
Book 2: *The Unexplained Phenomena and Tales of the Unknown*
Book 3: *Things That Go Bump in the Night*
Book 4: *Things That Prowl and Growl in the Night*
Book 5: *Fiends That Want Your Blood*
Book 6: *Unexpected Visitors and Unwanted Guests*
Book 7: *Dark and Deadly Demons*
Book 8: *Phantoms, Apparitions, and Ghosts*
Book 9: *Alien Strangers and Foreign Worlds*
Book 10: *Ghastly and Grisly Spooks*
Book 11: *Secret Schemes and Conspiring Cabals*
Book 12: *Freaks, Fiends, and Evil Spirits*

Please visit us at www.visibleinkpress.com

Acknowledgments

When the team at Visible Ink Press offered me the opportunity to write *Monsters: Myths, Legends & Real Encounters,* I accepted without hesitation. I had grown up reading about weird and wonderful creatures, and they hold no less fascination for me as an adult.

I am not the first author to cover this topic for Visible Ink, and I would like to extend my respect and appreciation to Nick Redfern and Brad Steiger, two of the most prolific wordsmiths out there, who have authored more books in this genre than I can easily count. Their work belongs on the shelf of every monster enthusiast.

In addition to thanking Roger and Kevin at Visible Ink Press, I would also like to thank my wife, Laura, for her support; Erin and Mike for being good companions in dark and creepy places; Alan, Jesse, and Anna for arranging my first ever Squatching adventure; and Dr. Karen Stollznow for penning the foreword. Thank you all; this book would not have happened without you.

Table of Contents

Acknowledgments xi
Foreword xv
Introduction xix

Hunting Hodag 1
Hungry Like the Wolf 7
Krampus: The Nightmare before Christmas 29
The Kraken Arises 33
Morgawr 41
Lock, Stock, and Barrel: Nessie 47
Monsters Down Under 81
Creatures of the Night 89
Beyond the Vampire 109
The Fresno Nightcrawlers 135
The Dead Shall Rise 139
The Grafton Monster 157
The Flatwoods Monster 165
Mothman 171
Speak of the (Jersey) Devil 191
The Goat Sucker—El Chupacabra 209
Seeking Sasquatch 219
On the Bigfoot Trail 237
Conclusion 261

End Notes 265
Photo Sources 269
Further Reading 271
Index 273

Foreword

Monsters: Myths, Legends, and Real Encounters shines a light on the creatures under our beds and the things that go bump in the night. Within these pages, Richard Estep takes us on a globe-trotting, time-traveling expedition into the murky world of cryptids, creatures that dwell somewhere between folklore and fact.

Some of the monsters here are familiar fixtures of pop culture such as Bigfoot, the Loch Ness Monster, and Mothman. Others are less well known like the mysterious Morgawr, a sea serpent said to lurk off the coast of Cornwall, or the skinny, leggy Fresno Nightcrawlers. But whether iconic or obscure, each creature is treated with curiosity, an open mind, and a sense of adventure.

We've always had monsters.

The word "monster," dates back more than a thousand years in the English language, but the idea itself is much older. We find monsters lurking in our oldest myths and legends: the ogre Humbaba in the *Epic of Gilgamesh*, the sea-monsters Scylla and Charybdis of Homer's *Odyssey*, and the Mesopotamian demon-goddess Lamashtu, who slew babies and drank the blood of men.

Such creatures aren't just scary bedtime stories. They serve as cautionary tales and cultural mirrors, helping us make sense of the world and the unknown. In this way, monsters are very human. They're reflections of us, our fears, our desires, and our darker instincts.

Often, they are us or versions of us: the werewolves with our rage, the demons with our inner conflicts, and the ghosts with our memories.

Monsters are where we put the things we can't quite name.

And, as Richard reminds us, monsters are everywhere.

From the bunyips of Australia to the chupacabras of Latin America, from the kraken of Nordic seas to the Tommyknockers of Colorado mines, cultures all over the world tell stories of creatures that dwell just outside the reach of science. These beings may be elusive, even implausible, but they persist.

Though over time, monsters change. They adapt to new anxieties, new landscapes, and new technologies. They show up in trail-cam footage and Reddit threads, in drone videos and TikTok testimonials. A belief in the strange is not going away anytime soon. If anything, it appears to be on the rise.

That doesn't mean we're all true believers. Far from it. As someone who's spent much of her career studying language and culture, belief and the psychology of weird experiences, not to mention co-hosting the *MonsterTalk* podcast, I've met my fair share of Bigfoot hunters, paranormal investigators, skeptics, folklorists, and fence-sitters. Richard Estep is a rare kind of writer who manages to speak to all of us.

He's respectful but not credulous. He listens to people's stories without rolling his eyes. And while he doesn't hide his enthusiasm for the unknown, he doesn't brush off inconvenient facts. He does the work: tracing the history, reading the folklore, interviewing the eyewitnesses, and even howling and whooping in the woods, hoping a Sasquatch might call back while half-expecting a black bear or a mountain lion to show up instead.

Yes, Richard has gone squatching (so we don't have to).

His investigations go beyond the page. He's out in the field, not just in the library. Whether he's tracking Bigfoot through the woods or digging into tales of demons and ghosts, he follows the trail wherever it leads—not necessarily to find monsters, but to understand why we look for them.

In this book, Richard presents the evidence and also the counter-evidence. He explores lore, firsthand reports, hoaxes, and the occasional blurry photo. He weaves in history, medicine, and science. When necessary, he challenges the claims, including the ones that believers and skeptics hold dear. But he doesn't insist on a final answer. Like any good investigator of mysteries, he's often more interested in the questions than the conclusions.

And the result is a tour of the monstrous that's equal parts fascinating and fun.

Reading this book, you'll find yourself swept up in the myths of creatures both terrestrial and aquatic, from sea serpents to vampires, zombies, and pop culture icons like the Jersey Devil. Richard delves into theories behind these stories, including the marine reptile hypothesis of lake monsters and the physiological origins of vampirism. Along the way, you might be reminded of a strange encounter on a camping trip or a documentary that made you wonder, "What if some of these tales are more than just fiction?"

You don't have to believe in Bigfoot to enjoy a Bigfoot story. You don't have to accept that Nessie is a surviving Mesozoic reptile to be captivated by the long history of lake monster sightings. You don't have to believe in Mothman to appreciate what the creature meant to a small town on the brink of disaster.

We all love monster stories. We might even need them. They give form to our fears, reflect our anxieties, and bring a spark of mystery to the everyday. Monsters help us test the boundaries of what we think is possible. And they remind us that we don't know everything.

The world still has many mysteries left in it.

So, settle in for the read. There are creatures in these pages. Some are scary, some are sad, some are surprisingly lovable. All are part of the weird and wildly imaginative tradition of monster-making that links us to our ancestors and to each other.

Dr. Karen Stollznow
Author of *Haunting America*
and co-host of *MonsterTalk*

Introduction

The world is filled with monsters. It always has been, and so shall it always be.

Some of them we love; some, we hate and fear.

Some are exciting and magical; others are as banal as they are evil and loathsome.

Let's get the bad and the ugly out of the way first. More often than not, true evil hides behind a human smile. History is replete with examples of the monstrous given human form: Hitler, Stalin, Caligula, Mao Zedong, Leopold II. All wielded supreme power or came as close to doing so as it is possible to get, and they used that power to inflict cruelty upon their fellow human beings on an unprecedented scale.

To cause such widespread death, destruction and abject misery really does take a monster.

Zooming in from the macro to the micro, we have the Jeffrey Dahmers, John Wayne Gacys, and the Jack the Rippers of the world, individuals who are so sick and twisted that they seek pleasure and gratification in the torture and murder of others. We see their faces sneering back at us from the covers of countless true crime books and the splash screens of streaming documentary shows, an ever-present reminder that human monsters sometimes stalk our streets and frequent our own neighborhoods.

Let us not forget the Osama bin Ladens of the world, those who use violence and murder as a means of instilling terror in the population. Their goal is to convert that terror into political capital, which can then be used to leverage ideological goals or to pursue a fundamentalist agenda that brooks no opposition or questioning.

Murder is used as a bargaining chip in a game of fundamentalist religious or ideological brinksmanship.

Although they are ultimately responsible for fewer deaths than oligarchs and heads of state, individuals of this ilk can only be described as being monstrous in nature.

We loathe and shun these vile creatures, finding them repulsive with good reason. Nobody likes to think that men and women who look just like ourselves might be capable of the most gut-churning acts of malevolence and depravity.

That scares us … and it should.

Which brings us to the other monsters.

The creeping undead that stalk unwitting victims in the night to supply them with blood. Giant serpent-like creatures inhabiting lakes, rivers, and the seas, ascending briefly from the depths before plunging back beneath the surface and returning to their underwater world. Winged humanoids with glowing red eyes that soar through the skies, terrorizing those with whom they come into contact. Dragons and devils. Werewolves and water-horses. Chupacabra. Tommyknockers. The list goes on … and on … and on.

These are the monsters that have fascinated many of us since our childhoods. Some of them almost certainly never existed, their stories being folklore rather than fact. Did dragons really soar through the skies, breathing fire and flapping gigantic leathery wings—and if so, why have no remains ever been found?

Others seem a little more credible, while still retaining an air of the fantastical. Millions believe in Sasquatch and Bigfoot. Some people devote many hours of their recreational time to heading out into the boonies "squatching," looking for evidence of the creature's existence. There are scores of equally devoted "Nessie hunters," men and women who have undertaken the perhaps quixotic quest of tracking down and documenting the existence of Scotland's Loch Ness Monster.

Then there are those monsters that are solidly entrenched in folklore and history, things for which science has since provided plausible explanations. We have a rationale for those time-honored classics of the silver screen: vampires, zombies, and werewolves.

It seems that for all the monsters that are explained away more pop up to take their places like the heads of the mythical hydra regrowing and reproducing. A legion of self-professed amateur cryptozoologists has arisen, determined to track down these strange creatures and provide proof of their existence. The creatures in question are referred to as "cryptids," and they are the focus of the book you are now reading.

Why do I say "amateur"? Because cryptozoology is not a science in the commonly accepted sense of the term. It is a pseudoscience—a system of beliefs that, despite being cloaked in the mantel and trappings of science, do not truly adhere to the scientific method.

Before you throw this book across the room in disgust, I should point out that just because cryptozoology doesn't operate within the framework and constraints of the scientific method, it doesn't necessarily mean that there isn't a degree of truth to be found within.

Take the example of ball lightning, an extremely rare weather phenomenon that has been anecdotally reported for centuries. It is spectacular, extremely short-lived, and is seen by numerous credible eyewitnesses. Researchers have repeatedly attempted to recreate the phenomenon without success. Until the 1960s, the prevailing wisdom of mainstream science held that ball lightning didn't exist and that it couldn't possibly exist.

Showing an interest in the study of ball lightning often garnered ridicule and scorn, yet the winds of belief have shifted significantly since then. The existence of ball lightning has come to be accepted, although a definitive explanation for it continues to elude researchers. Eyewitnesses are still coming forward these days, just as they have throughout history. It seems likely that scientists will one day solve the mystery of ball lightning once and for all, and it will find its way into high school science textbooks. The fact that its very existence was once derided and dismissed will be conveniently forgotten.

This is, of course, exactly how science is supposed to work. New evidence comes to light, new hypotheses are formed, and old ways of thinking are discarded.

Who is to say that, someday, the same mindset that laughed at the existence of your favorite cryptid won't be proven wrong?

Perhaps the carcass of a lake monster will wash up on the shores of Loch Ness.

Perhaps somebody will finally obtain a sample of Bigfoot scat and return it to the lab for analysis.

Perhaps a hunter will peer down the scope of their rifle, carefully squeeze off a shot, and realize that the creature within their gunsights was a Chupacabra.

Perhaps.

These things are all unlikely—perhaps extremely unlikely—but they are not impossible.

Monsters thrill us. They chill us. They fascinate us.

We are intrigued by them. Monsters can provide us with a way of engaging our fears in a safe and fascinating manner.

We need our monsters.

Let's go out there and meet them.

Richard Estep
Longmont, Colorado
April 2025

On the morning of September 26, 1918, U.S. Army 1st Lt. Deming "Dick" Bronson shrugged off wounds that had just been inflicted by a detonating hand grenade and led his men in storming a fortified German position. Later that afternoon, he took a bullet in his left arm. Bronson refused to let this wound stop him either. The next day he led another assault on a machine gun nest. For this exceptional heroism and his other gallant actions during World War I, Dick Bronson was awarded the Medal of Honor.

Yet he's still not the most famous name associated with Rhinelander, Wisconsin. That title falls to the Hodag, arguably the state of Wisconsin's most famous exotic beast.

In 1893, the town of Rhinelander was both smaller and far more rural than it is today. It was home to many lumberjacks, or as they were more commonly referred to in the 19th century, loggers. Spending countless hours in the deep, dark woods, loggers loved to tell stories — particularly monster stories. One popular creature was the Hodag, which was basically the zombified, reanimated remains of a dead ox. According to an October 22, 1893, newspaper article printed in the *Leader Telegram* of Eau Claire, Wisconsin,

> ... it is generally well understood among all kinds of lumber jacks that when an ox is butchered or accidentally killed in the woods that its immortal constitution turns into a hodag, and the hodag thus

> formed assumes the same color as the respective ox that he came out of, and he roams about the country formerly occupied by the ox in his summer outings.

The article goes on to state that the Hodag is the most feared of all animals because it is essentially superpowered, possessing "the strength of the ox, the ferocity of a bear, the cunning of the fox, and the sagacity of a Merrill lumberman." A formidable adversary indeed, although the pen-and-ink drawing that accompanies these words looks more like a startled kangaroo with horns than it does a terrifying monster. The image was intended to represent a Hodag encounter that took place the day before the newspaper went to press, in which the beast was found lying atop a log in the midst of a torrential thunderstorm.

More remarkable still, the Hodag actually *spoke,* saying that its name was Berry and claiming to have once been the property of a lumber enterprise based in Rhinelander. The company had branded its initials, B.B. (short for Browns Brothers), into the Hodag's horns. The beast was described as having eyes that were "blood red with yellow eyeballs."

More remarkable still, the Hodag actually spoke, saying that its name was Berry and claiming to have once been the property of a lumber enterprise based in Rhinelander.

Once the newspaper went into circulation, every wannabe hunter for miles headed out into the woods, determined to capture or kill one at any cost. On October 28, a Rhinelander-based newspaper named *The New North* reported in an article titled "Capture of a Hodag" that the hunting parties were armed with not just rifles but also squirt guns filled with toxic water, which were presumably intended to poison the Hodag into submission.

A group of hunters cornered the 185-pound Hodag in a swamp. Hunting dogs were unleashed, which proved to be a mistake; the horn-headed, hook-tailed Hodag reduced them to mincemeat. Taking aim, the hunters let loose with a fusillade of small arms fire, shooting again

A group of armed men surround a Hodag in this photo from 1899.

and again until "their guns got too hot to longer hold in their hands." Their firearms now all but useless, the hunters switched to a combination of knives and dynamite, then followed up by attempting to set the beast on fire.

The Hodag fought back, tearing into the tree limbs and trunks as if they were matchwood. It belched out clouds of black, tarry smoke. Ultimately, the hunters won, burning the cornered Hodag to death and putting its corpse on public display.

The genesis of the Hodag stories can be found with a trapper named Eugene Shepard, who went public with what he said was a Hodag that he had managed to capture in the wild. Scores of credulous customers paid good money to see the creature. The creature was actually carved from wood and covered in an animal pelt. Showing a streak of ingenuity that would have made the Disney Imagineers proud, Shepard even ran wires to the dummy Hodag's limbs in order to make the legs move when they were pulled. It was the closest thing to animatronics in its day.

Perhaps unsurprisingly, considering the nature of the

rather tall story, no convincing photograph exists of the purported Hodag. (A staged picture of a mob of hunters standing around a replica Hodag, which in turn looked as if was about to pounce on a defenseless child, doesn't count.)

Trapper Eugene Shepard hoaxed the residents of Rhinelander, Wisconsin, with a hodag made of wood and covered in fur.

Shepard finally came clean about the hoax once his claims drew widespread attention and inevitable closer scrutiny. Yet belief in the beast remained widespread, particularly in the more rural parts of Wisconsin, and its existence was treated as a matter of fact by many Wisconsinites. Two months after the epic showdown, the December 17 edition of the *Leader Telegram* blithely announced that an Eau Claire barber named John Hurt had left town and ventured out into the woods "to trap hodags." One can only imagine what we would make of such a story today: "Man quits cutting hair to go monster hunting."

In 1894, newspapers reported that a trapper named Mike Ryan lost an ox when it fell into a watering hole and was unable to extricate itself before it drowned. Would the creature remain dead, the paper wondered, or would it return in the form of a fearsome Hodag?

The Hodag legend shares commonalities with much older oral stories told by the indigenous people of Wisconsin, fireside tales of fierce beasts emerging from the water to wreak havoc before returning to the depths once more. It is likely that the trappers who invented the Hodag appropriated elements of those stories and simply added their own spin.

The Rhinelander Chamber of Commerce put its sense of humor and good fun on display by commissioning a hodag statue in front of its office.

Today the Hodag is more popular than ever. There is an annual Hodag music festival and a country festival. In popular culture, it has made appearances in the worlds of *Harry Potter* and *Scooby Doo*. Sports teams have been named after it. It is also a boon to tourism, bringing an influx of Hodag enthusiasts into Rhinelander each year . . . all with their eyes peeled, on the lookout for Wisconsin's most popular (and elusive) fantastic beast.

Since time immemorial, there has been a persistent belief that the baleful light of the full moon is capable of turning susceptible men, women, and sometimes even children into werewolves.

According to Hollywood, the affliction is most commonly passed on when somebody is bitten by a werewolf. The supernatural creature's bite is said to pass on the curse of lycanthropy, causing the victim to transform into a human/lupine hybrid at the next full moon.

Thanks to innumerable horror movies, most people are aware of this method of supposedly becoming a werewolf. Yet it isn't the only way. Some legends maintain that drinking rainwater out of a werewolf's footprint will do the trick just as well. Falling into the bad graces of a witch, warlock, or wizard could mean being magically cursed to become a werewolf, if the practitioner were inclined to cast a spell on the unlucky individual. Evil magic could also be cast upon a pregnant mother, cursing her unborn baby with a most unexpected birth condition.

In some traditions, the curse is passed down through family bloodlines from one generation to the next, so that the child of a werewolf would one day howl at the moon him- or herself.

Not everyone saw lycanthropy as a curse, however, leading some people to actively perform magical rituals in order to deliberately become a werewolf. In some cultures, it was a common belief that one could achieve the

Stories of werewolves go far back into mythology and include the story of the god Zeus turning King Lycaon into a wolf for trying to feed him the entrails of a sacrificed child.

same result by putting on a wolfskin cloak, particularly one that was specially treated and magically warded (protected) for that purpose.

Entering into a pact with the dark side of nature is never something that should be undertaken lightly, yet it's easy to see the appeal of choosing to go down the werewolf route. Trading a relatively feeble human body for the immensely powerful form of a werewolf means adopting immense physical strength. This strength coupled with the innately savage nature of the wolf made for a formidable beast, something that was said to be practically unstoppable — until confronted with weapons made of silver, that is.

Denny Sargent, author of *The Book of Dog Magic* (2016), points out that wolves have always been considered to be powerful totems by those who practice the magical arts. Although prefacing with the fact that belief in shape-shifters long predates the Norse culture — a werewolf transformation appears in the ancient Mesopotamian text *The Epic of Gilgamesh* — Sargent notes that a significant part of the werewolf's origin as we currently perceive it may have its basis in their mystical and mythological traditions.[1]

According to the Norse view, the trickster god Loki sired a giant wolf beast with the giantess Angrboda. Loki possessed the ability to change form whenever the mood took him. Sometimes he became a female; other times, he became an animal such as a fish or a mare. In the latter form, he became pregnant and gave birth to a horse.

The canine offspring of Loki and Angrboda was named Fenrir. Illustrations portray Fenrir as a huge, ravening wolf beast, one who is more than capable of giving the god Odin a run for his money in battle. The Norse loved their wolves; the creatures appear everywhere in Norse mythology, sometimes as helpful allies but just as often as menacing and threatening aids to the heroes of the sagas. This duality of awe and fear still accompanies the werewolf today, a creature that should be equally feared and respected.

Odin himself had a pair of wolves, named Geri and Freki, who stormed into battle alongside him. They were fearsome bodyguards who, once the battle was over, feasted on the flesh of the dead. Norse warriors donned the mantle of the wolf, both literally and figuratively. Viking warriors wore wolf pelts as part of their fighting attire. Such warriors hunted in packs, raiding settlements and chasing down unsuspecting victims in a similar manner to that in which wolf packs hunted their prey. Some even named

The giant wolf Fenrir, son of Loki and Angrboda, attacks the Norse god Odin in a 1909 illustration by Dorothy Hardy.

themselves after wolves, implying that they identified with these predatory animals in some respects.

Nordic berserker wolf warriors would wear wolf pelts—often including the head—to inspire fear in their enemies.

Arguably the most notable were the *berserkrs* or *berserkir,* from whom the English language derives the words "berserk" and "berserker" and the *ulfheonar,* or "wolf skins." These warriors eschewed the use of armor and shields entirely, choosing instead to rush into combat wearing either little to no clothing or, in some cases, trappings made of either bear or wolf skin. "Going berserk" meant fighting like a wild man, heedless of the risks being run and shrugging off all but the most serious, debilitating injuries. The berserker gave no thought to defending himself. They attacked without mercy, hacking and slaying in the midst of a maelstrom of blood and steel.

Such men fought in a trancelike state, channeling the spiritual essence of the wolf, their chosen totemic animal. It has been hypothesized by some authors that the wolf warriors may have used hallucinogenic drugs in order to reach that state of battle lust.

Some of the wolf pelts they wore probably included headgear or face masks that were fashioned from the skinned creature's own head and hide. Picture a heavily muscled, near-naked warrior clad in a wolf cloak and headgear, snarling and grunting as he falls upon his prey in a frenzied attack. The parallels with stories of savage werewolf attacks are clear to see. No wonder that they gained a reputation for being supernatural beasts in tales told around campfires on cold, dark nights by the survivors of such brutal assaults.

The Norse wolf warriors are still with us today, albeit in an unlikely form. The immensely popular *Warhammer 40,000* tabletop game setting from Games Workshop, which has spawned a multitude of novels, novellas, and short stories that are based on the vast, rich background lore written by the game's designers, features a chapter of Space Marines known as the *Vlka Fenryka* — the Space Wolves, or "Wolves of Fenris." These genetically engineered superhuman warriors are far taller and stronger than a human being, and sport wolflike fangs that can tear apart even the toughest meat in just a few bites.

They drape themselves in wolf pelts before going into battle, and fight with a fury that harkens back to the berserkrs and ulfheonar. The Space Wolves hail from the frozen world of Fenris (hello, Fenrir!), which is as icy and inhospitable as the wilds of Norway were. Players build and paint tabletop armies of wolf warriors and use them to fight matches against aliens and monsters of all descriptions. Clearly, the ideal of the man-wolf is here to stay.

Other versions of the legend say that if one is unlucky enough to be born on either Christmas Eve or the following day, December 25, then one is automatically fated to become a werewolf.

Assuming you aren't living in a space fantasy universe that comes with the questionable perk of genetic modification, how else can one become a werewolf? Other versions of the legend say that if one is unlucky enough to be born on either Christmas Eve or the following day, December 25, then one is automatically fated to become a werewolf. Christmas Day is a relatively rare birthday to have; according to statistics, in the United States it is the least common day of the year on which to be born. Yet if this superstition is true, it means that such luminaries as Sir Isaac Newton, Eurythmics singer Annie Lennox, and actor Humphrey Bogart all turned into raging monsters whenever the moon grew full. If that was the case — and it seems odd that no word of it ever leaked out — then one is forced to wonder exactly how they found time to probe the innermost working of the physical universe, record the hit song "Sweet Dreams (Are Made of This)," or shoot classics such as *Casablanca*.

If it seems that my tongue has been firmly in my cheek while writing this section of the book, I intend no disrespect to the time-honored legends and lore that surround the werewolf. Throughout history, cultures ranging from the humans of antiquity all the way up to our own modern-day society have fostered the concept of the werewolf (and other associated were-creatures). It is easy to dismiss such beliefs as being nothing more than folklore, yet even today there is no shortage of people who find the concept of such creatures to be a credible one.

The key question becomes: when it comes to the werewolf, where exactly do we draw the line between fact and fiction?

Clinical lycanthropy — the believe that one either is or can somehow become a wolf — is a genuine psychiatric condition.[2] Consider again the Norse ulfheonar, some of whom are believed to have attained such a mental state that they believed themselves to be literally possessed by the spirits of wolves. It is a belief that, while relatively rare, still arises today. Were those warriors of old simply delusional, a common explanation for clinical lycanthropy in the 21st century, or could something more arcane and mysterious have been taking place?

Lon Chaney Jr. performed what is considered one of the most iconic werewolves in Hollywood history in 1941's The Wolf Man.

Although it is comforting to believe that medical science has all of the answers, this particular condition is poorly understood and tends to be under-studied. What research exists has demonstrated that many of the unfortunate individuals who are afflicted with clinical lycanthropy are also diagnosed with concomitant mental health disorders, such as depression, schizophrenia, or bipolar disorder. Because of its connection with the state of psychosis, the condition is treated with antipsychotic medications — with varying degrees of success.

Researchers have posited that the delusional belief that one can transform oneself into a wolf is further buttressed by the prominent place occupied by werewolves in popular culture. From Lon Chaney's classic portrayal in *The Wolf Man* through the bleak, black humor of *An American Werewolf in London*, to the 21st century's blockbuster *Twilight* franchise and the CGI special effects–laden bonanzas of the *Underworld* series, lycanthropes are ubiquitous.

Everybody knows what a werewolf is. Everybody knows how to kill one — pass the silver, please — and some people are convinced that they literally are one. Setting aside the delicate matter of those individuals who are coping as best they can with mental illness, we come to the question: If somebody truly *were* a werewolf, how would we know?

One old superstition maintains that a werewolf in human form can be identified by eyebrows that meet in the middle, above the bridge of the nose, or palms that are covered with bristly tufts of hair.

There's the obvious, of course — transforming into a ravening beast every full moon. But what about the rest of the time? One old superstition maintains that a werewolf in human form can be identified by eyebrows that meet in the middle, above the bridge of the nose, or palms that are covered with bristly tufts of hair. If so, and assuming that the werewolf wishes to remain anonymous, then these particular problems could be easily fixed in about 30 seconds with the careful application of a shaving razor.

The term for eyebrows that are conjoined in the center is *unibrow*. According to research carried out by the genetic testing and analysis company 23andMe, unibrows are surprisingly common: 29% of people have "a little bit of a unibrow" and 4% of individuals have one that is "moderate to thick."[3]

Scientists estimate that the global population in 2025 is approximately 8 billion people. If 23andMe's data analysis is correct, the implication is that 320 million people — 4% — should have a noticeable unibrow. That's a pretty big background group in which any potential werewolf could hide.

Werewolves don't like to keep banker's hours. They are said to be night owls, more comfortable being up and about during the period of darkness between sunset and sunrise. There are relatively few modern-era sightings of such creatures during the daytime, but once the sun goes down, it is an entirely different story. Rather than occurring in random, widespread places, contemporary werewolf sightings are often localized to a specific geographic area — it's tempting to think of such locations as being hunting grounds for the nocturnal creatures.

Located in Staffordshire, England, Cannock Chase is a national forest encompassing 26 square miles (68 square kilometers) in central England. Popular for its natural beauty, it is visited by some two million campers and vacationers annually.

Great Britain's Cannock Chase is one such location. Nestled in the heart of Staffordshire, the chase is so-called because it was once used as hunting ground by the British gentry. Nowadays the apex predator of Cannock Chase is said to be something entirely different.

Somewhere between 26 and 30 square miles in size (depending on which source one reads) the chase has plenty of room in which something strange could hide. It also has a colorful history. During World War I, it served as a vast military training camp, accommodating tens of thousands of troops as they prepared to endure the horrors of trench warfare. The New Zealand Rifle Brigade made its temporary home there. In World War II, Cannock Chase was pressed into military service again, this time by the Royal Air Force.

There are not one but two military cemeteries located on Cannock Chase. The 5,000 bodies that lie buried in the newer of the two, dating back to the 1960s, are primarily German and Austrian soldiers and civilians who were interned by government order, people who died during each of the World Wars while in captivity in England. It is a peaceful place, well-kept and continuously maintained today by custodians who ensure that the grass around the thousands of headstones is kept neatly trimmed and that weeds are not permitted to gain a stranglehold.

The older cemetery exists to house the remains of Allied service personnel, primarily New Zealanders who died during World War I. A few hundred German soldiers are also buried there—enemies in life, neighbors in death.

Cannock Chase has attained a dark reputation of late with stories of ghosts and other supernatural entities swirling around the place. If there is any truth to the rumors, is it possible that the war dead who were laid to rest there somehow play a part? Some say that the apparitions of those long-dead soldiers have been seen in the vicinity of the cemeteries. Whether they wear the uniform of British, New Zealand, German, or some other nationality is unclear.

Cannock Chase has attained a dark reputation of late with stories of ghosts and other supernatural entities swirling around the place. If there is any truth to the rumors, is it possible that the war dead who were laid to rest there somehow play a part?

One particularly chilling type of encounter involves the Black-Eyed Kids, or BEKs. Although reports of run-ins with BEKs most commonly originate in the United States, Cannock Chase has one of its own: A little girl, dressed in clothing that seems to belong to a time many years before our own, has been seen on the chase. Her eyes contain no sclera (white of the eye) as those of a flesh-and-blood human do; they

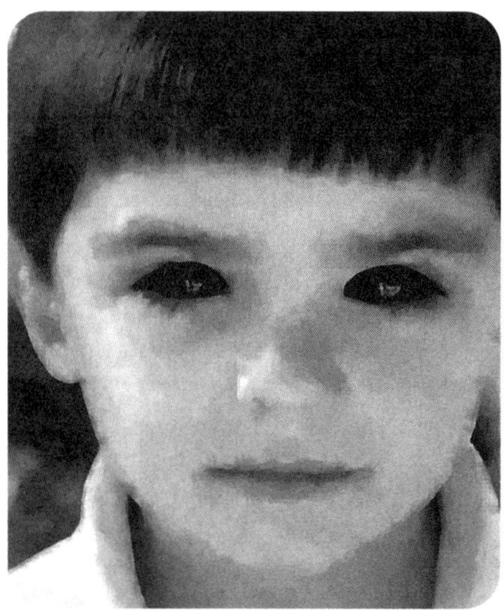

Stories of the Black-Eyed Kids originated in the United States, but there are also tales of encounters with these creepy kids in England, notably in Cannock Chase.

are said to be completely and utterly black, devoid of all life.

BEK encounters tend to follow a similar format. Typically the child, or children, approach an unsuspecting adult and ask for help in some form. Sometimes they may request a ride to the store or to their home. On other occasions, they will knock at a door and all but plead to be allowed inside. (Do vampire rules of entry apply to them? one is forced to wonder.)

In 2022, *Staffordshire Live* recounted the details of encounters. According to ghost hunter Robert Pulme: "We have had lots of reports of a 'black eyed girl' seen walking around. At first, she appears like a normal girl and walkers are worried a little girl is lost in the woods. Then they see her eyes, and she just disappears. It is terrifying."[4]

Terrifying indeed, particularly as the lore surrounding Black-Eyed Kids states that encounters with them can sometimes lead to the living human never being seen again, confined to an unknown fate — but one that presumably is far from pleasant.

Pulme offers the intriguing hypothesis that the Cannock Chase BEK may be the spirit of a child who died of diphtheria, a potentially deadly bacterial infection that sometimes gives the sufferer a sallow, sunken-eyed appearance. One photograph purporting to show the face of a female BEK hovering next to two flesh and blood children playing in Cannock Chase looks suspiciously as if it has been doctored with a ghost picture app. Others have entered blurry pictures taken by drones into the record as potential evidence that BEKs haunt the chase, but while the reports of encounters with these frightening faux children are numerous, there has yet to be a "smoking gun" to prove their existence.

The Hazleslade pub is, naturally, a center of activity for the town that is located within the Chase in Staffordshire. A considerable amount of werewolf activity is said to occur in the area.

If accounts are to be believed, Black-Eyed Kids are far from the only otherworldly thing that's said to stalk Cannock Chase. Author Lee Brickley has researched the bizarre goings-on extensively. Within the boundaries of the chase are a village and a nature reserve both named Hazleslade. There are woodlands that are sufficiently thick to conceal who knows what manner of strange creatures — perhaps even a werewolf.

Writing in *UFOs, Werewolves & the Pig-Man: Exposing England's Strangest Location — Cannock Chase* (2013), researcher Brickley recounts an interview he had with a gentleman whose wife may have had a near miss with such a lycanthrope . . . and lived to tell the tale. One morning while golfing with two companions, their round was interrupted by the sound of the man's wife crying out in distress. They rushed to her aid.

The woman's story was horrifying and fantastical in equal measure. She and her daughter were walking through the woods that bordered the golf course, intent on bringing her husband lunch. What she could only describe as a werewolf appeared seemingly out of nowhere, snatched their daughter, and dragged her off into the undergrowth.

The unfortunate girl was still missing.

Following the deeply shaken woman's direction, the three men immediately gave chase. Fortunately, they were able to locate the missing child, who must have been significantly traumatized by the experience. Any thought that this might have been a hallucination or the product of an overly active imagination vanished when the man saw a creature standing over the girl that did indeed appear to be half man (the upper half) and half wolf.

In his book, Brickley notes that the witness described the beast as

> like a huge dog from the waist down, just two hairy legs, but from the waist up and the neck, it looked like a man — a toned one, at that. Its head, again, was wolf-like, I could see its protruding face, long nose and even the salivating ooze dripping from its big white fangs.

It's unclear whether this is a verbatim quote from the eyewitness himself or whether Mr. Brickley is paraphrasing. Whichever is the case, it paints a florid yet undeniably werewolf-like mental picture of a lycanthrope. Of particular note, this did not occur after dark on the night of a full moon; it happened in the middle of the day, far closer to lunchtime than to midnight. So much for the stereotype. This particular werewolf was prowling around the wooded outer environment of a golf course in broad daylight.

Werewolves are typically described as being aggressive and predatory. Yet not only was the girl unharmed, but the beast fled when the three men happened upon it. The only wound inflicted on her was a gash on her arm, presumably from having been snatched by the creature and hauled off into the woods.

Werewolves are typically depicted as vicious and predatory, but the werewolf that kidnapped the young girl from Cannock Chase was rather easily chased away by a few men and left the girl physically unharmed.

On reading Mr. Brickley's account of what sounds like a very narrow escape, one is struck by the potential aftermath. Having been injured directly by a werewolf, most likely by one of the beast's claws, was the daughter now at risk of transforming into one herself? Werewolf lore certainly suggests so . . . and the account gets stranger still, as the researcher notes the girl quickly developed strange hairs on the back of her hand that doctors were unable to explain.

She also experienced a state of complete amnesia regarding the incident. This is by no means unusual. Sometimes when an individual is subject to a deeply traumatizing experience, the mind responds by blotting those memories out of the conscious recall and sealing them away. It is a protective response, a sort of psychological shield against extreme terror.

Lee Brickley diligently notes that although the husband and wife both insisted they saw a werewolf, and their descriptions of the beast matched, the same is not true of the man's two companions. They saw nothing out of the ordinary that day. Hats off to Mr. Brickley for not simply throwing out this inconvenient part of the story because it doesn't fit the typical werewolf narrative. The incident is puzzling and defies simple explanation.

Neither is this the only werewolf report to originate on Cannock Chase. In 2009, the BBC published an article online titled "Werewolves in Staffordshire." The article claims that there have been numerous recorded encounters with or sightings of werewolves on Cannock Chase over the years. The earliest of them date back to the 1970s, in which multiple eyewitnesses from a ghost-hunting organization ran into "a snarling beast" that "reared up onto its hind legs" before fleeing.

While this doesn't necessarily describe a werewolf per se, similar reports of lupine creatures have risen from Cannock Chase for decades since then. Unfortunately — some might say suspiciously — there have been no compelling photographs documenting the existence of such a beast.

One of the most recent encounters took place in the summer of 2024, as reported in the *Stoke Sentinel* by reporters Hayley Parker and Kelly Ashmore, in the vicinity of the woods close to the German Military Cemetery.

The beast stood about eight feet tall. As it turned to face them, it locked eyes on them and bared its teeth.

A couple was out for a stroll when they began to notice a foul stench in the air, akin to something dead and rotting. The nearer to the cemetery they got, the worse the smell became.[5]

It was then that the pair saw the creature: approximately 8 feet tall, wolflike in appearance, moving in between the headstones marking each German grave. The beast moved quickly, sprinting, and suddenly turned to face them.

"It turned around and instantly locked its eyes on us," stated the male. "They were big and yellow, and the creature had huge teeth, like nothing we'd ever seen before."

Again showing uncharacteristically evasive behavior for a supposed werewolf, the creature bolted, vanishing into the trees before the startled couple could react . . . but not before it had howled at them first.

According to the report by the *Stoke Sentinel*, the male was interviewed by the aforementioned researcher Lee Brickley, who seemed to find him a credible witness. His wife was unwilling to talk about it. Brickley nailed his colors to the mast by saying that he "wholeheartedly believed" the account, adding that "the sheer number of witnesses surely prove there really is something in the woods."[6]

Brickley's point is well taken. The sightings of wolflike entities on Cannock Chase span the course of decades. People are certainly seeing something, and a number of those sightings have taken place in daylight. Fortunately, I could find no record of anybody being seriously injured during these encounters — though that isn't to say that the potential for harm doesn't exist.

Gather together a group of emergency services personnel or healthcare professionals and it's likely that a majority will not only share the belief that the night of a full moon brings an increased volume of emergency calls, but also be convinced that the nature of those calls tends to be more bizarre than on any other day of the month. More behavioral emergencies and psychological crises emerge on such nights, it is claimed, as part of a time-honored superstition that has been passed on from one generation to the next.

The truth is more complicated. A 2006 abstract posted by PubMed notes an eight-year study conducted at San Diego Medical Center during the 1990s. Researchers scrutinized the emergency department admission volume for psychiatric complaints from month to month, paying particularly close attention to the phase of the moon. The study concluded that behavioral emergencies were no more common during the full moon than they were in other phases, no matter what impression the medical personnel on shift might have gotten.[7]

Presumably, no werewolves were brought in by ambulance either.

Between 2009 and 2011, the same study was carried out at a pediatric emergency department to ascertain whether the same principle held true for behavioral crises in children. The result was the same: things were no busier when the moon was full.[8]

Not to be deterred, researchers also investigated the potential link between the full moon and emergency depart-

There are published scientific studies that indicate that behavioral emergencies rise significantly when the moon is full.

ment visits with a complaint of physical trauma. Surely people were more likely to suffer violence and sustain injuries during the full moon?

Stories of werewolves in Great Britain go way back and have continued into the modern age.

No. The same result held true for cases of suicidal behavior as it did for homicidal behavior. Statistically, people were no more likely to be the aggressors or the victims of violent behavior at any particular time of the month.[9]

And yet . . .

There was the time in the 1980s when a werewolf supposedly got into a fight with an entire police station in the United Kingdom.

Stories of werewolves are less common in British history and folklore than they are in Europe, probably because wolves were eradicated from the British Isles hundreds of years ago. Yet some instances do exist, such as the fascinating case of the so-called Southend Werewolf.

On July 30, 1989, the British tabloid newspaper *The Sunday People* published a lurid article titled "Brave Bishop Saves Snarling Werewolf." It was the culmination of a story that began when Bill Ramsey, the werewolf in question, was a 9-year-old boy in the 1950s.[10]

Young Ramsey underwent a very peculiar experience on a warm summer day, during which he was suddenly hit with a gust of freezing air, seemingly out of nowhere. It was accompanied by a noxious odor, which also had no apparent cause. Flying into a rage, he grabbed a sturdy fence post, yanked it out of the ground, and smashed it to pieces. This feat of strength should have been beyond a fully grown man, let alone a still-developing boy.

The youth soon developed an obsession with wolves and all things related to them. They haunted his dreams and stalked his nightmares. His behavior began to change, mimicking that of a wolf, becoming animalistic and savage in nature. As he matured into manhood, the symptoms grew worse. Ramsey became increasingly violent and unstable, even going so far as to attack others, including a nurse who was treating him at a local hospital.

Speaking to the U.S. television show *Sightings*, Ramsey said: "I just had the feeling that ultimately, I would kill somebody." He had gone to the local police station and pleaded to be incarcerated, not only for his own good but also for that of anybody who might cross his path. Bizarrely, he had first picked up a sex worker and brought her to the police station with him. It was during this visit that the 44-year-old Ramsey suddenly sprang at a police officer. Cops piled onto him, got the thrashing man under control, and granted his wish to spend a night in the cells behind a sturdy locked door.

Word of the incident got out. "Werewolf Seized in Southend!" trumpeted *The Sun*, another tabloid, with the subtitle "He fights cops on all fours." Police Inspector Tony Belford recalled that Bill Ramsey's aggression

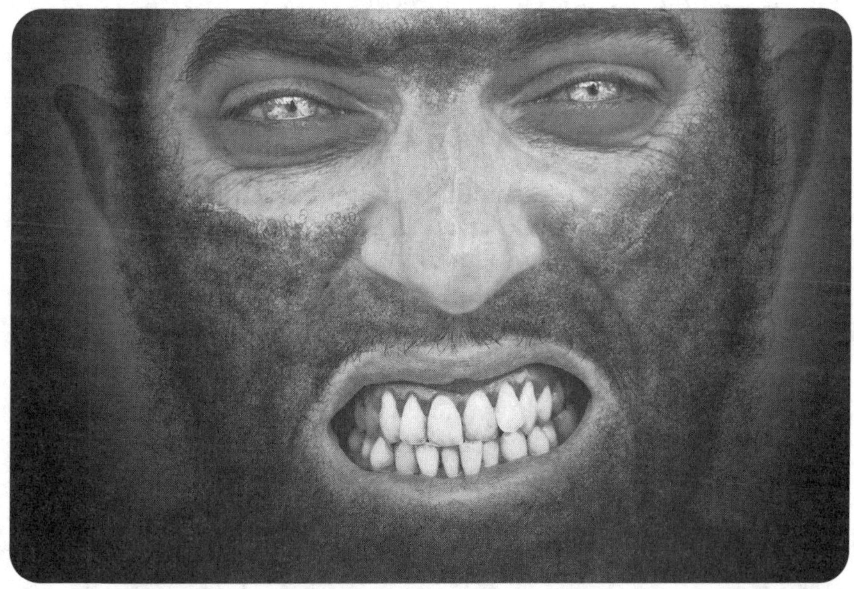

Bill Ramsey felt himself possessed by an aggressive spirit as he attacked the police officers.

was "not something I've ever witnessed before . . . not natural behavior." Understandably, the seasoned officer stopped short of using the term "werewolf." No matter what his personal beliefs were, it would hardly have been conducive to his credibility or to his career prospects.

Terry Fisher, another officer who was involved in restraining Ramsey, quoted him as having growled: "The Devil is in me. When the Devil is in me, I am strong. I am going to kill you. I am strong and you are going to die." True to his word, the would-be werewolf launched himself on top of Fisher and proceeded to strangle him. Were it not for the timely intervention of his colleagues, the officer may well have been seriously injured or killed.

For his part, Bill Ramsey told the same *Sightings* interviewer that he was experiencing thoughts of suicide. "I've suffered public humiliation as the Southend Werewolf," Ramsey told David Alford of *The Sunday People*. He had no idea where to turn next.

At this point, self-described demonologists Ed and Lorraine Warren entered the picture. While operating primarily from their home in the eastern United States, the Warrens heard about Ramsey's case while staying in the United Kingdom and inserted themselves into the matter. They met with the police officers who had been involved in the altercation with Ramsey.

The officers saw "something that very few people have ever seen," Ed Warren later stated on *Sightings*. "The transfiguration of a man into a wolf."

The term "transfiguration" is typically used in a biblical context, referring to the physical transformation undergone by Jesus Christ in which he suddenly erupted in a blaze of blinding light. Transfiguration means a significant change in appearance — and, sometimes, in spirit as well. Police officers recalled that Ramsey bared his teeth at them, and in the words of one, "he took on the appearance of a mad dog."

It seems as though Ed Warren may have been engaging in hyperbole when describing the police encounter

"I don't howl at the moon or turn into a hairy beast at midnight, ... but I do claw, snarl, and bare my teeth at anything that moves."

with Bill Ramsey, because although his aggressive behavior mimicked that of a savage beast, he did not literally change into a werewolf. This raises the question of whether he was experiencing a form of clinical lycanthropy rather than an actual possession by a wolflike entity.

"I don't howl at the moon or turn into a hairy beast at midnight," Ramsey admitted during his newspaper interview, "but I do claw, snarl, and bare my teeth at anything that moves."

We would also be remiss not to consider the fact that the Warrens had a propensity for finding demons and dark entities, case after case. They built a career on it (and later, Warner Bros. built a multibillion-dollar movie franchise on the back of that). Was Bill Ramsey a werewolf, possessed by some kind of lupine spirit — or was he undergoing a behavioral crisis that required professional medical treatment?

The only way to control Ramsey's aggressive behavior was to sedate him. Recognizing the potential threat that he posed to everyone around him — something that he himself acknowledged — the authorities committed Bill Ramsey to a mental health care facility. Although assaulting police officers constitutes a crime, law enforcement personnel were sufficiently enlightened to recognize that they were dealing with a man in dire need of help, rather than a hardened criminal.

Ramsey said that he eventually reached an understanding with his local police department and got into the habit of proactively calling them whenever he felt an episode of lycanthropy was about to erupt. A squad of patrol officers would respond to his home, though the only person capable of controlling him when the wolf persona took over was his wife. All others were confronted with

Denying that he was mentally ill or suffering from alcoholism, Ramsey continued to insist that his behavior was the result of being possessed by a demonic wolf.

increasing aggression and ran the risk of being injured if they got in his way. This included Ramsey's poor dog, which got used to him chasing it around the house while on all fours.

His time in psychiatric care brought little help to Bill Ramsey's troubling situation. Indeed, he was discharged without a clinical diagnosis, meaning that his aberrant and disturbing behavior was not deemed to have been caused by mental illness. It was suggested that alcohol intoxication might be the cause, something that Ramsey vehemently denied.

Rejected by the mental health services to which he had turned for help, Bill Ramsey was left without any form of resolution or closure. The only explanation he felt he could turn to was a paranormal one.

There's an old truism that when you're a hammer, there's a tendency to view and treat every problem as a nail. By the same token, after meeting with Bill Ramsey, the Warrens declared that he was demonically possessed by the spirit of a demonic wolf. They arranged for him to fly to Connecticut to undergo an exorcism.

During the ritual, presideing bishop Robert McKenna was protected by a cohort of security guards. If things got out of hand, they were armed with stun guns and were prepared to use them. Given the bestial manner in which Ramsey had reacted to the British police, this was only prudent.

Photographs of the exorcism show an increasingly distressed Bill Ramsey, his hands twisted into the shape of claws; none of the images that were made public support claims made by Lorraine Warren on *Sightings* that his neck muscles enlarged and his ears grew points.

Ultimately, the exorcism seems to have been a success. Ramsey declared that he felt like "a new person." His symptoms did not return.

That wasn't the end of Bill Ramsey's story, however. As previously mentioned, he sold his story to a newspaper — the same newspaper that paid for him to fly to Connecticut — and cooperated with the Warrens and author Robert David Chase on a book about his lycanthropic experiences, titled *Werewolf* (2014).

Ramsey appeared on the TV talk show *Sally Jessy Raphael* and accompanied the Warrens on the public lecture circuit. While Ramsey certainly isn't the first paranormal claimant to cash in on his alleged experiences, and is unlikely to be the last, the element of financial gain gives cause for some skepticism regarding his story. On the other hand, his stated reason for cooperating with the newspapers also makes sense. Ramsey reasoned that the same reporters who had been trailing him for weeks were going to get wind of developments anyway, so why not have the paper foot the bill for what increasingly seemed like his last hope at freedom from the affliction?

Looking at the bigger picture, it's hard to blame a man who understandably felt that the medical and psychiatric professions had failed him, for turning to what he saw as the only recourse left to him. Although they did make money, both Bill Ramsey and his wife were subjected to ridicule not just locally but at the national level. Their lives were placed in a state of upheaval, with constant intrusion by reporters. If the whole thing was simply a get-rich-quick scheme, there were certainly many easier ways to achieve it than faking lycanthropy.

Looking back with the hindsight provided by 35 years, the case of the Southend Werewolf contains as many questions as it does answers. It all comes down to this: was the mild-mannered Bill Ramsey suffering from an undiagnosed behavioral disorder, or was he possessed by a dark wolf spirit?

That's for you to decide.

We all know the stories. The two lists. One is for the naughty children. One is for the nice. And Santa Claus, a.k.a. Father Christmas, a.k.a. Kris Kringle, a.k.a. Saint Nick, knows which list every single child in the world is on. On December 24th, the nice kids get a nocturnal visit from the jolly bearded man in the red suit, who comes down the chimney somehow — don't ask for details — and leaves presents for them underneath the Christmas tree. He might pause to enjoy some milk and cookies, if the good kids and their parents have been thoughtful enough to provide them, before returning to his reindeer-propelled sleigh and moving on to the next house.

But what about the naughty kids?

In a word: Krampus.

A hairy, goat-legged, curly-horned monster with a long, slavering tongue, Krampus comes out to play on the night of December 5 — also known as *Krampusnacht*. He — for Krampus is usually portrayed as a male, even though he has monstrous characteristics — prowls through the darkness,

The Krampus is a hairy, horned monster that punishes bad children during the Christmas season.

St. Nicholas and a couple of Krampuses share the spotlight at a festival in Austria.

on a mission to find and punish the kids from the naughty list.

Everything about Krampus is terrifying. He represents the dark side of Christmas, the stick to Santa Claus's carrot. Parents who were not averse to injecting a little fear, maybe even terror, into the minds of their children during the holiday season could use the threat that if they weren't good little boys and girls, then Krampus was coming to get them.

(The one flaw in this plan: When December 6 rolled around — the Feast of Saint Nicholas — if there'd been no sign of Krampus roaring and rattling his chains in the darkness outside your bedroom window, then you had made it for one more year. You were, de facto, on the nice list, and could pretty much do what you wanted . . . until the next year, at least.)

Although his origins go back for centuries, probably all the way to pagan times, Krampus reached the peak of his popularity in Central and Eastern European countries such as Austria, Germany, and Bavaria during the past 200 years. His visibility has waxed and waned, but it is only in the 21st century that this pre-Christmas beast has made the leap across the Atlantic to the United States. He is now firmly entrenched in Western popular culture, so much so that in 2015 Hollywood's Universal Pictures released a movie about him: the imaginatively titled *Krampus* is a dark comedy that's relatively suitable for the whole family.

The darker side of Krampus has been depicted in a slew of low-budget horror movies, most of them released direct to streaming, such as *Krampus Unleashed* and *Krampus: The Devil Returns*. These films depict him as a killing machine and, while they pay lip service to the legend, go far overboard with violence and gore.

The Krampus legend is a pretty bleak one. In artistic renderings, he's often shown to have a basket slung across his back. It's a receptacle into which he stuffs naughty children after he kidnaps them (like *Dr. Who*'s TARDIS, the basket seems to be bigger on the inside than the outside) and then runs off to his subterranean lair. That's where the children meet their fate. Depending on which version of the story is being told, Krampus might stuff them in a cage and leave them to languish there for an unspecified period of time; others are beaten with sticks and branches; some unfortunate kids may even find themselves being eaten by the beast, though that would make it difficult for them to straighten out their behavior and earn their way off the naughty list — which is the entire point of Krampus in the first place.

As his renown has grown, Krampus has garnered himself a small army of fans. Krampus runs have been commonplace in Europe for years. Participants dress up as Krampus, sometimes spending thousands of dollars and countless hours on crafting exquisitely detailed costumes, before charging through the streets accompanied by blasts of flame from fire cannons. Scary meets spectacle. Parents often take their children along to watch, and it raises the

Krampus runs have been commonplace in Europe for years. Participants dress up as Krampus, sometimes spending thousands of dollars and countless hours on crafting exquisitely detailed costumes, before charging through the streets accompanied by blasts of flame from fire cannons.

question: If children are encouraged to believe in Santa Claus, is there any harm in having them believe in Krampus as well?

Maybe. A little fear can sometimes be a good thing, but like anything else, when taken to excess it can be harmful. Krampus is, at the end of the day, a terrifying kidnapper and beater of children, and the fact that he is said to target only the wayward kids really doesn't soften that blow. The bottom line: exposing kids to Krampus is probably fine, as long as they know that he isn't real and won't be coming to get them on that cold, dark night of December 5.

Krampus societies and events are spreading across the United States. There are conventions and festivals, usually held in December, that celebrate the Christmas monster. It makes a refreshing change from the constant bombardment of Santa Claus that the holiday season brings each year. Krampus is scary rather than jolly, edgy instead of jovial. This is a monster that excels in extracting the saccharine out of Christmas, bringing some much-needed counterbalance to what has become an increasingly materialistic time of year.

Many people bemoan their belief that the true meaning of the festival has been lost. Krampus stalks the night on cloven hooves, chains rattling, empty basket awaiting the next child, a sinister reminder that not everything about Christmas has to be sweetness and light.

In northern Colorado, a Krampus enthusiast named John Mays is using his alter ego's dark aura to serve a good cause: Dressed in full Krampus regalia, he goes out in public and encourages passers-by to make a charitable donation to Toys for Tots. In exchange for giving cash, donors not only gain the fulfillment of having brought joy into the life of a child, but they are also assured that their name will be taken off the naughty list . . . until next year, at least.[11]

Between 70% and 71% of the Earth's surface is water. The vast majority of that water — around 96.5% — comprises the oceans, of which there are five: the Atlantic, the Pacific, the Indian, the Arctic, and the Southern or Antarctic.

In actuality, the situation is much simpler. There is only one ocean, spanning the entire globe. All of the named oceans are contiguously interconnected. Their names are evidence of the way in which the human mind works; we love to divide and categorize things in an attempt to understand them.

The oceans are mysterious and fascinating. As of 2026, fully 80% of Earth's oceans remain unexplored and uncharted. In fact, it can be argued that humanity has done a better job of exploring outer space than we have of charting the deep domains of our own home world.

Who knows what lurks in those cold, inky black depths?

Sailors do.

As I noted in *Ghostly Encounters* (Visible Ink Press, 2025), early mariners believed wholeheartedly in sea monsters, the great dragons of the deep, and in the danger of sailing so far that one could fall off the edge of the world.

Sailors were, and still are, superstitious individuals. That goes with the territory when every day at sea is a day in which the sea might kill you. From storms to ship-

An early-sixteenth-century drawing by Olaus Magnus depicts frightening sea monsters rumored by sailors to lurk in the northern Atlantic.

wrecks to sea creatures, the oceans are hazardous. And for thousands of years, sailors lived with the iron-clad conviction that monsters prowled beneath the waves, waiting for the chance to pounce on unwary seafarers.

That might sound quaintly amusing today, in what we like to think of as more enlightened times, but before we get too self-congratulatory, let's remind ourselves that until very recently it was commonly accepted that anybody sailing or flying through an area of the Atlantic Ocean nicknamed the Bermuda Triangle ran an increased risk of vanishing without a trace. This is primarily thanks to the work of an author named Charles Berlitz, who posited that the region bordered by Bermuda, Puerto Rico, and coastal Florida formed some sort of mysterious disappearance zone that was responsible for swallowing ships and aircraft whole.

In 1974, Berlitz wrote a book on the subject that became immensely popular, selling tens of millions of copies and launching a pop culture phenomenon that still reverberates today. In the 2022 TV documentary film *Ghosts of Flight 401*, psychic medium Cindy Kaza investigated the crash of an airline into the Florida Everglades to uncover the "truth" about what brought the passenger jet down. She concluded that a form of energy that tied into the Bermuda Triangle could have been partly to blame. No scientific evidence was presented to support this claim.

It is true that ships and planes have disappeared and indeed still *do* disappear in the Bermuda Triangle. However, they disappear in other parts of the world's oceans too. It is statistically no more hazardous to travel through the Triangle than it is to traverse other shipping lanes, a fact that is borne out by the maritime insurance rates being no higher there than elsewhere.

On its web page, the U.S. Coast Guard, the military service that bears primary responsibility for rescuing those who are lost or in distress at sea, sets forth its official position clearly:

> The Bermuda Triangle or Devil's Triangle is a mythical geographic area located off the southeastern coast of the United States. It is noted for an apparent high

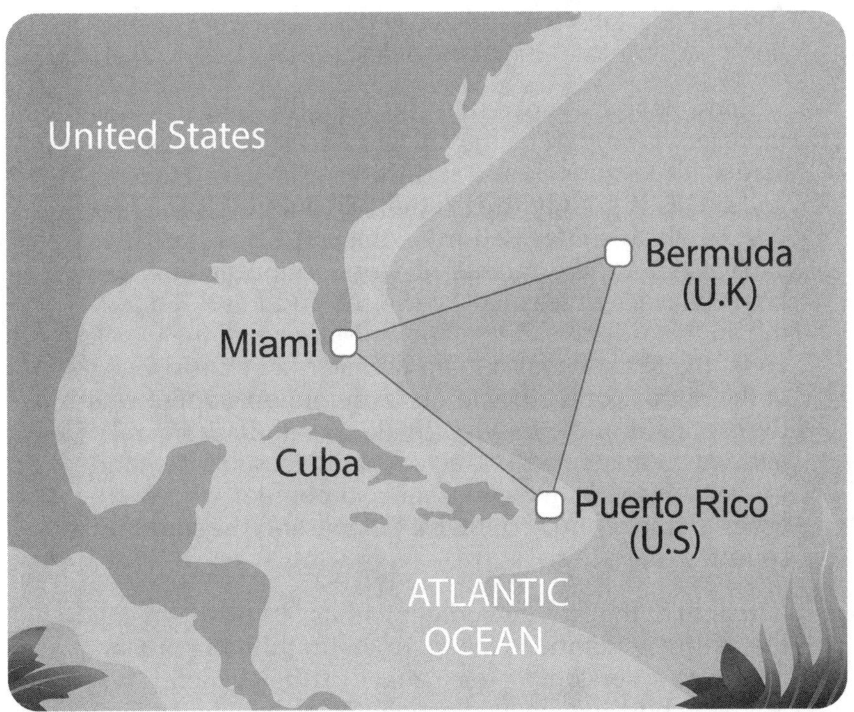

The mysterious and dangerous waters of the Bermuda Triangle extend from Florida to Puerto Rico to Bermuda.

> incidence of unexplained losses of ships, boats, and small aircraft. The Coast Guard does not recognize the existence of the so-called Bermuda Triangle as a geographic area of specific hazard to ships or planes. In a review of many aircraft and vessel losses in the area over the years, there has been nothing discovered that would indicate that casualties were the result of anything other than physical causes. No extraordinary factors have ever been identified.[12]

Yet still, the belief persists. Viewed in that context, 21st century humans haven't come all that much further from our oceangoing forebears who believed that at the far corners of the world, "here be dragons."

The question then becomes: *So, were there?*

Mythology has been the basis for many monster stories and legends, tales that have been passed on from generation to generation. One of the oldest is that of the Kraken.

Many people believe that this massive, tentacled sea monster was a part of the ancient Greek myths, associated with Perseus, Zeus, and the pantheon of Hellenic gods. This is mainly due to the 1981 movie *Clash of the Titans,* which showcased mythological Greek creatures as realized by the talents of stop-motion genius Ray Harryhausen. Unleashed by the sea god Poseidon, acting on the orders of Zeus, supreme among all the Greek gods, the Kraken was a giant monster kept imprisoned at the bottom of the ocean. Its stop-motion puppet was the highlight of the movie's finale. When *Clash of the Titans* was remade in 2010, actor Liam Neeson's demand to "release the Kraken!" became so popular with audiences that it became an internet meme and the source of countless parodies.

In light of the Hollywood depictions, it's unsurprising that entire generations have grown up thinking of Harryhausen's version of the Kraken as being definitive. Many a child has opened a book on Greek mythology only to be surprised to find the Kraken is absent. That's because tales of the creature really come from 18th century Scandinavia (Denmark, Norway, and Sweden). Contrary to Ray Harryhausen's creation, this Kraken was more akin to a giant squid or octopus.

An 1801 illustration by Pierre Dénys de Montfort depicts the giant Kraken wrapping tentacles around a doomed ship near the coast of Angola.

Although Norse culture contained tales of giant sea monsters for centuries, the Danish author (and also the Bishop of Bergen) Erik Pontoppidan brought the Kraken to popular attention in his seminal work *The Natural History of Norway,* which was published in 1753. In the mid-18th century, seafarers claimed to have encountered enormous tentacled creatures on their voyages, some of which were so massive and powerful that they were capable of enfolding ships in their tentacles and dragging them beneath the surface, never to be seen again.[13]

Pontoppidan described the beast as "a devil." Based on the accounts of fishermen he interviewed, Pontoppidan noted that the creature was so large that when submerged, the parts of its body corpus and tentacles that appeared above the waterline were often mistaken for islands rather than parts of a single, huge creature. It was only when the Kraken surfaced and revealed its miles-long form that sailors were alerted to immediately steer clear, for when the monster submerged again, its plunging mass was capable of dragging their boats and ships down with it into the ocean depths.

Monsters rarely find themselves to be the subject of poetry, but such was the case in 1830 when Alfred, Lord Tennyson waxed lyrical in *The Kraken:*

Below the thunders of the upper deep,
Far, far beneath in the abysmal sea,
His ancient, dreamless, uninvaded sleep
The Kraken sleepeth: faintest sunlights flee
About his shadowy sides; above him swell
Huge sponges of millennial growth and height;
And far away into the sickly light,
From many a wondrous grot and secret cell
Unnumber'd and enormous polypi
Winnow with giant arms the slumbering green.
There hath he lain for ages, and will lie
Battening upon huge sea-worms in his sleep,
Until the latter fire shall heat the deep;
Then once by man and angels to be seen,
In roaring he shall rise and on the surface die.

We should note that the Kraken of mythology was a single beast. There was only said to be one iteration of the creature; however, the word "Kraken" can also be used to refer to a species of sea creature, as a plural term. Accounts exist of ships running afoul of *a* Kraken rather than *the* Kraken, such as the case of the French warship *Alecton*, which tangled with a large sea monster in 1861.

The corvette's captain, Frederic Bouyer, ordered his crew to open fire on the unsuspecting animal with everything they had, including a weighty harpoon. The creature was less than 20 feet long, far less than the Kraken was purported to be, and much too small to pose a credible threat. Bouyer's goal was to capture, rather than kill, the beast. In this, he was unsuccessful, taking only a chunk of its flesh back with him as evidence of the encounter.

In reality, the closest thing to an actual Kraken (and what the *Alecton* almost certainly fought) would have been the giant squid, or *Architeuthis dux*. When it came to the existence of such creatures, opinion among the finest minds of the time was divided. There was a wealth of anecdotal information concerning them, going all the way back to the time of the ancient Greeks.

Scientists measure an Architeuthis dux (giant squid) that has washed ashore on a Norwegian beach. The squid species has been known to grow up to 16 feet (5 meters) in length.

In 1870, Jules Verne published the timeless classic *20,000 Leagues Under the Sea*. In it, a giant squid-like creature attacks the submarine *Nautilus*, under the command of Captain Nemo. The *Alecton* incident was public knowledge, having occurred just nine years prior, and would have provided ample fodder for Verne's already fertile imagination. The giant squid was formally named in 1856 by the Danish zoologist Japetus Steenstrup. Prior to that, many of the attacks by giant squid had been laid at the feet (well, the tentacles) of the Kraken, and had helped to fuel the legend of that leviathan. Whenever body parts from the carcass of a giant squid washed up ashore, they were attributed to the Kraken, which provided a simple and handy explanation for many years.

It was only in the mid-to-late 19th century that, thanks to the efforts of researchers such as Steenstrup, fact and fable would finally begin to diverge and the truth become clear. The giant squid is so large, achieving lengths of around 13 meters (about 43 feet) in some cases, that the only other creatures big enough to pose a threat to them are whales. Marine biologists continue to study these most enigmatic sea creatures, which are much easier to find now that we know where to look for them.

Of the Kraken, however, there is still no sign.

Watery mysteries are not restricted to the ocean depths. Moving to the coastal waters closer to shore, for hundreds of years the rivers, tributaries, and lakes of the world have given rise to monster sightings aplenty.

Off the southern coast of Great Britain, the English Channel has its own sea monster named Morgawr. In addition to breathtaking scenery, the historic town of Falmouth is best known for its bay, which has the distinction of being the third biggest natural harbor in the world. That may be why generations of Cornish folk, sailors and landlubbers alike, have reported sighting the strange beast in and around the waters off the coast near Falmouth.

The name *Morgawr* translates to "sea giant" in the old Cornish language, which dates back to around 600 B.C.E. It is a fitting description of the large creature, which has been described as having a long, sinuous neck and several humps on its back. Comparisons with its more famous relative, Nessie, are inevitable. Yet there are subtle differences; according to the lore, the Loch Ness Monster has relatively smooth, unblemished skin (one has to wonder what Nessie's skin care routine is!) whereas its Cornish cousin supposedly has spiky spines running down the length of its back.

Another difference is that Morgawr has a pair of stubby horns jutting up from the top of its head, above its eyes — an interesting touch, as it makes little evolutionary sense for a sea creature to need such protuberances.

The Morgawr has been described as a sea serpent with horns and a humped back.

The Cornish have always been seafarers. The county's history is replete with fishermen, smugglers, merchant seamen, and every type of mariner imaginable. Sailors are superstitious, and as a breed they have always loved a good monster story; we have them to thank for spreading tales of mermaids and mermen, giant squid and octopi, plus all manner of sea serpents and even dragons. ("Here be Dragons" was once used on maps to indicate the presence of potential danger in uncharted, unexplored lands and waters.)

Sightings of Morgawr have been sporadic over the last two centuries. The creature has often been spotted near the entrance to the Helford River, relatively close to the shore. Locals christened the region the Morgawr Mile. Although sightings of *something* monstrous and serpent-like in that area go back to at least the 1870s, a number can be explained as having been large fish and other known objects of marine life. The first truly compelling Morgawr encounters began in the 1970s, when a cluster of sightings was reported to the press.

This streak of Morgawr sightings peaked on March 5, 1976, when a correspondent known only as "Mary F" mailed photographs of what was claimed to be the monster to the *Falmouth Packet* newspaper. The so-called Mary F pictures show what appears to be a creature with a large body and a long, curved neck that slopes down toward the water in the second photograph relative to the first.

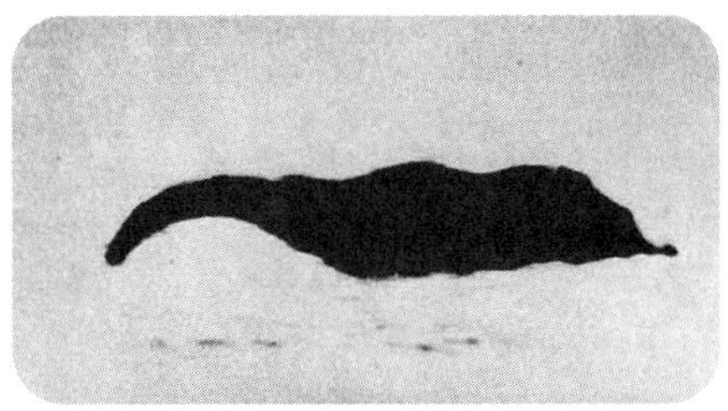

One of the Morgawr photos published in the Falmouth Packet *newspaper in 1976. The person who provided the photo was known only as "Mary F."*

As with so many alleged monster photos, the true scale is impossible to make out, not least because the resolution is poor and the focus too blurry. The "monster" in question could be something large seen from a distance, as the mysterious Mary F claimed, but could equally be something relatively small that was photographed close-up. Predictably, when the photos went public, there was significant interest. In pubs not just across Cornwall but through the entire British Isles, drinkers debated whether the monster shots were genuine or not.

Today, the Mary F photos are generally believed to have been a hoax. The identity of Mary remains unknown. She never came forward into the limelight, either to offer up more detail on her sighting or to cash in on it. Unless fresh information comes to light, the pictures are likely to remain one of the many tantalizing "what ifs" that have plagued the field of cryptozoology for years.

Other pictures of Morgawr have popped up over the years. Much like the better-known photos purporting to show the Loch Ness Monster, none of them are particularly convincing. One of the more colorful characters connected to both the story of Morgawr and Nessie was Tony "Doc" Shiels. An artist by profession, Shiels somehow fell into the world of cryptids and became a self-professed "raiser of monsters." In other words, using occult techniques and mystical powers, he sought to psychically induce the Nessies and Morgawrs of the world to manifest on demand — and thereby give him the opportunity to take their picture.

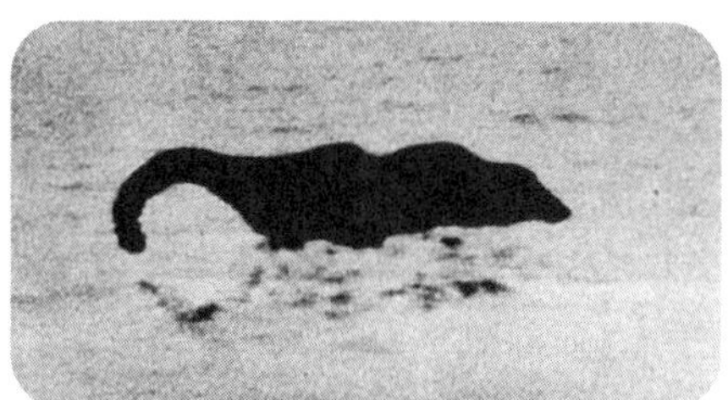

A second photo from "Mary F" published in the Falmouth Packet *shows the humps and sinewy neck a little better.*

Shiels was a showman by nature, a true larger-than-life bohemian who had a huge streak of P.T. Barnum, Charles Fort, and John Keel running through him. Considering himself to be something of a wizard, he had a love of publicity that was matched only by his fascination for the arcane. Living in Cornwall at the height of the 1970s Morgawr flap, Shiels is strongly suspected by some of being none other than the elusive Mary F; he has been accused of mailing the photographs to the *Falmouth Packet* in an attempt to generate publicity (though this was never proved).

The more Shiels inserted himself into the growing Morgawr imbroglio, the more his credibility was questioned by the journalists who were covering the story. Some saw him as a fraud, a description with which Shiels himself sometimes agreed — albeit with a mischievous twinkle in his eye. Although he went by the nickname "Doc," Shiels was far from a genuine academic. The "doctorate" in question had been purchased from a company in the United States for the princely sum of $5.

Fanning the flames of publicity even further, Shiels arranged for a small group of witches to visit the shore near one of Morgawr's favorite haunts and attempt to summon the creature to the surface. The ritual was conducted with the female participants completely naked, which may or may not have explained why reporters from the national press made the journey to Cornwall in order to cover the event. Nudity and monsters made for good newspaper copy, after all.

Despite the group's claims that Morgawr was close by, the monster neglected to rear its horned head in response to the witches' attempts at conjuration. Predictably, the press coverage was lurid in tone and mocked their efforts savagely.

Months later, Shiels had a Morgawr sighting of his own, witnessing the creature's humps and head emerge from beneath the water. As evidence, he produced two monochrome pictures that were even blurrier than the Mary F photographs. Shiels claimed that they depicted Morgawr's head and neck; it would be tempting to simply dismiss this particularly sighting out of hand, had it not been corroborated by Shiels's companion, magazine editor Dave Clarke. Clarke wrote a piece for *Cornish Life* in which he recalled seeing some kind of long-necked aquatic animal that may have been a seal but seemed to be a better fit for Morgawr in appearance.

Much of the Morgawr story, and its associated controversy, centered on Doc Shiels. There is no shortage of those who believe that he whipped the whole thing up for his own amusement, manipulating the beliefs of the public and to an extent the desire of the press for a good story in order to breathe life into a fictitious sea monster. Other eyewitnesses came forward to report Morgawr sightings of their own, independent of Shiels.

Falmouth Bay is a popular coastal town attraction in Cornwall, but not because of the Morgawr, which seems to have vanished.

His supporters claimed that the magical rituals conducted by Shiels and the witches, who were members of his own family, may actually have succeeded in bringing Morgawr up from the depths. They point to the rather indistinct and absolutely inconclusive photographs as being evidence of the creature's existence.

Hoax . . . or sea monster?

The heyday of Morgawr seemed to be the mid-to-late 1970s. Once the large influx of sightings that occurred when the story was making headline news had dissipated, significantly fewer encounters were reported — but there were a handful. Skeptics explained the "humped sea monster" reports as likely having been misidentified seals or eels, both of which call the waters of Cornwall home; couple this with the fact that Morgawr's name had become firmly embedded in the weft of Cornish cultural life, and you have an almost surefire recipe for a monster sighting.

Falmouth Bay remains a popular tourist destination, particularly in the summer months, yet in the 21st century, Morgawr seems to have all but disappeared . . . if, that is, it was ever there in the first place. Yet a strange coda to the story took place in 1999, when museum worker John Holmes filmed the head and long neck of a strange beast poking up from the waters of Gerrans Bay, which is located to the east of Falmouth — well within easy swimming distance for any sea monster worth its salt.

Barring one further potential sighting in 2002, Morgawr has now gone radio silent. The only man who can say with certainty whether this was simply one giant hoax was Tony "Doc" Shiels. He died on July 12, 2024, and if he truly did invent the Morgawr legend lock, stock, and barrel practically all by himself, then he took the secret with him to his grave.[14]

LOCH, STOCK, AND BARREL: NESSIE

We now move from the southwestern part of the British Isles up to the far north. No discussion of sea or lake creatures would be complete without mentioning Nessie, the infamous Loch Ness Monster. For almost a century, Scotland's best-known aquatic beastie has delighted, thrilled, and fascinated generations of people. Nessie draws tens of thousands of visitors to the loch each year, each hoping to catch a glimpse of the elusive cryptid.

Those glimpses are few and far between, but they do happen. The loch is under constant camera surveillance, and those who would dismiss the possibility of it harboring a monster (even a large creature, as Nessie is purported to be) use the dearth of photographic evidence for its existence as a means of buttressing their case. While there is some merit to this point of view, the flip side of the coin is the vast size of the loch — 22.5 miles long, 1.7 miles wide, and 755 feet deep. This means that the hunt for the Loch Ness Monster is the proverbial search for a needle in a haystack. So much surface area, not to mention subsurface area, needs to be covered that the relative lack of compelling photographs and video footage should come as no surprise.

The water in Loch Ness can be distinctly chilly, but no matter how cold it gets, the loch never freezes. It is composed of freshwater not salt water, which means that any creature living there must be suitably adapted to that specific type of environment.

It's fair to say that the appearance of the Loch Ness Monster is so well-known that it has become iconic; even its silhouette, the long, curving neck tipped with a tapering head, is instantly recognizable. Those who say they have seen the creature in its entirety — i.e., out of the water, on the shores of the loch — typically claim that it has four diamond-shaped flippers and a relatively short tail. This tracks closely with the description of a type of plesiosaur, a classification of marine reptile that was ubiquitous during the Mesozoic era, which spanned 252 million to 66 million years ago. There's a commonly held misbelief that plesiosaurs were dinosaurs, perhaps because of the "saur" in the name. "Giant marine reptile" is the currently accepted classification for these fascinating creatures of the deep.

Loch Ness is a huge lake at 22.5 miles (36.2 km) long, 1.7 miles (2.7 km) wide, 433 feet (132 m) deep, and covering 21.8 square miles (56 km^2).

Meals for the plesiosaur typically depended on their environment and on the part of the world in which they lived. It's believed that some plesiosaurs ate a diet that was heavy on fish and mollusks, whereas others trawled the bottom of the ocean for food such as clams. Loch Ness is home to numerous potential food sources, such as salmon, trout, eels, and many others. This might seem like a lot, but even a single plesiosaur living in its depths would require tons of food each year in order to survive. Despite the diversity of food on offer, for a great marine reptile, hunting down other animals would be the equivalent of a never-ending scavenge for crumbs.

The presence of eels in the loch may even provide an explanation for some of the monster sightings, according to some researchers. In a September 5, 2019, article ("Loch Ness Monster may be a giant eel, say scientists"), the BBC reported on efforts of scientists from New Zealand who were conducting a study attempting to definitively catalog every single species of animal resident in Loch Ness. Their chosen methodology involved using DNA samples to identify and categorize the loch's inhabitants. It was conceivable that any unknown DNA might possibly belong to the elusive Nessie.[15]

We don't have plesiosaur DNA samples in storage to test for a potential match. Unfortunately for Loch Ness Monster enthusiasts, no such anomalous DNA was found. The closest match to something that at least *looked* somewhat like a plesiosaur was the DNA of a giant eel. Loch Ness is absolutely teeming with eels. Some giant eels can reach lengths of up to 10 feet and weigh the same as a fully grown human adult — or even heavier, in rare cases. Could this be what people are *actually* seeing when they encounter the Loch Ness Monster?

A classic form of Nessie sighting involves seeing only a hump or two protruding above the surface of the loch. However, eels do not have flippers, though some do

A completely restored fossil skeleton of a plesiosaur is on exhibit at Paleo Hall at the Houston Museum of Natural Science in Texas.

have dorsal fins. They tend to be wormlike or snakelike in appearance, moving sinuously through the water.

Scientists who focus on plesiosaur research are working primarily from fossil-based evidence and are limited in the amount of data available to them. Their current best educated guess is that the average plesiosaur had a lifespan from somewhere between 25 to 100 years, though the possibility of a violent death must also be factored in. Although plesiosaurs were predatory and occupied a spot high up in the food chain, as the old saying goes, "there's always a bigger fish." This included other, larger plesiosaurs. The oceans were dangerous places back then, with hunters sometimes becoming prey in the blink of an eye.

Clearly, any plesiosaurs that may be living in Loch Ness in the 21st century must be descendants of their Mesozoic forebears. According to studies conducted on fossils by scientists at the Natural History Museum of Los Angeles County, it has been hypothesized that pregnant plesiosaur mothers carried and gave birth to a single baby at a time, and that those babies reached a significant size by the end of their gestation. (Up to 40% of the mother's body mass — the same as a human mother giving birth to a 6-year-old child!)[16]

So, what happened to the masses of plesiosaurs with which the Earth's oceans once teemed? They were wiped out, along with 80% of the other species, some 66 million years ago in the Cretaceous-Paleogene mass extinction. There are several different hypotheses seeking to explain exactly how and why this happened, but the most likely involves a giant asteroid striking the Earth. The resulting environmental upheaval annihilated the dinosaurs completely, along with their oceanic cousins, the giant marine reptiles, and most — though not all — of the mammals too. Bird species fared better, but they did not escape unscathed either.

Lending weight to this hypothesis is a massive crater located both in the seabed off the coast of Mexico and beneath the Yucatan Peninsula. The Chicxulub Crater is 93 miles in diameter, which is indicative of its parent asteroid having been somewhere between 7 and 10 miles wide. When this planet-killer struck, enormous

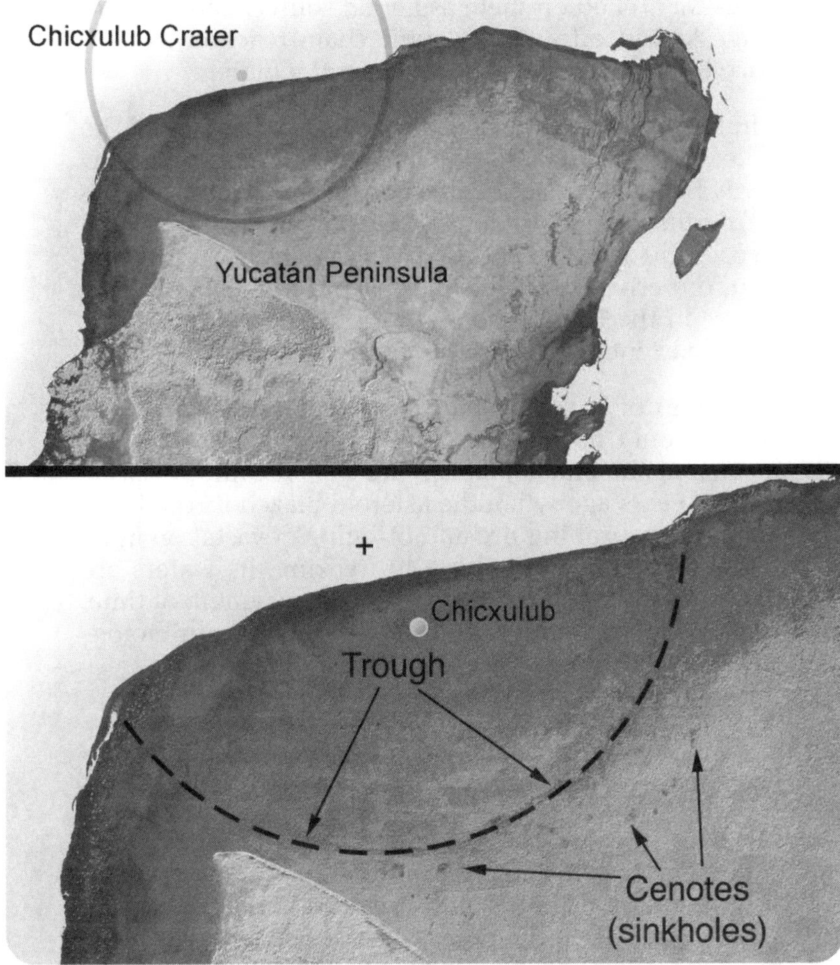

A combination of research by geologists and NASA scientists uncovered the Chicxulub Crater off the coast of Mexico's Yucatan Peninsula. It is now considered by many scientists be evidence of a meteor impact that occurred around the same time as the last mass extinction.

tidal waves and tsunamis swamped the coasts. Huge clouds of dust and ash rose into the atmosphere, creating a smog-like blanket that partially blocked out light and heat from the sun and caused temperatures to cool to levels that would have been fatal to many of those creatures that survived the initial incident.

Plant life also died out, which meant there was little food left for herbivorous creatures to eat. As the herbivores died out at an increasing rate, so too did the carnivores that relied on them as a food source. The asteroid strike kicked off a catastrophic chain reaction that induced mass extinction across the entire globe.

In the oceans, the level of water acidity increased. The water also became less rich in oxygen. This almost certainly had a detrimental effect on the survival prospects of marine life, which included the plesiosaurs. Some Nessie aficionados believe it was possible that a plesiosaur, or perhaps multiple plesiosaurs, were able to take refuge in the Loch, essentially riding out the mass extinction event that killed the rest of their species.

There's one major problem with that contention. Loch Ness is only approximately 10,000 years old, having formed at the end of the last ice age. It didn't exist 66 million years ago when the asteroid blazed through the atmosphere, trailing fire and bringing devastation in its wake. Although not subject to freezing, its waters are too cold for a reptile to survive in for any length of time. A plesiosaur certainly could not live there, if our biological understanding of them is correct.

Despite there being folklore and vague legends relating to some kind of strange, possibly large creature in Loch Ness, sightings didn't really come to widespread attention until 1933.

One of the better-known photographs purporting to show Nessie was taken on November 12 of that year by a man named Hugh Gray, as he was taking an early afternoon walk along the side of the loch. When he noticed a significant disturbance in the waters of the otherwise serene loch, Gray had the presence of mind to snap several photographs of what he believed to be some kind of "object of considerable dimensions," as he later told a reporter from the *Scottish Daily Record*. Only one of them survived the development process, and it has been the object of much controversy ever since.

When considered carefully, one can definitely see an eel-like quality to the object captured in the monochrome photograph. Yet skeptics rightfully point out that one can just as easily see the face of a dog swimming in the water, clutching a curving stick in its jaws as though playing a game of fetch. Indeed, once one sees the face of the dog, it is almost impossible to unsee it — much like seeing the "Man in the Moon" for the very first time. The eye naturally fills in the gaps and wants to attribute meaning to the jumble of light and dark colors, turning a chaotic mess of splotches into the face of a paddling canine . . . or the writhing body of a lake monster.

Those who knew Hugh Gray described him as having been an honest man of good character. It is unlikely that he would have sought to prank his friends, much less an entire country (once the story reached the national press) for his own amusement. He not only stuck to his guns for the remainder of his life, but he also claimed to have sighted the monster on several subsequent occasions.

Even if we rule out intentional hoaxing on Gray's part,

The 1933 Hugh Gray photo of Nessie was taken near Foyers. The picture is so blurred that it has been speculated to be everything from a swan to Gray's swimming labrador retriever. In 1963, Maurice Burton showed it to be an otter rolling in the water.

as I believe we should, it is still certainly possible that he misinterpreted one of the loch's entirely natural denizens for something monstrous.

Writing in the *Journal of Scientific Exploration* ("Empirical Analysis of the Hugh Gray 'Nessie' Photograph," August 2022), researcher Roland Watson conducted an exhaustive assessment of Gray's photograph and alleged Nessie sighting. Watson does not buy into the swimming dog explanation, on the basis that the dog would have to be missing half of its face. The researcher used reference photographs of an actual dog as a control method to support his case. Equally damning for the dog hypothesis is that Gray's picture was touched up prior to its reproduction in 1934, which means that most versions of the photograph in current circulation are contaminated. They therefore provide a poor basis for formulating an opinion. A side-by-side comparison of the earliest available version of the photograph alongside the darker variant that is most prevalent today starkly emphasizes Watson's point. He does an excellent job in demolishing the "swimming dog" explanation.[17]

That doesn't necessarily mean the image depicts a monster of some sort, however. Closer examination of the higher-quality version of Gray's picture has led some to believe that it actually shows the side-profile head, face, and open mouth of some kind of creature — potentially a seal, or even a whale. It seems unlikely that somebody who lived and worked in the vicinity of Loch Ness would make such a mistake, but floating logs and biological life are frequently mistaken for the monster.

Watson also notes that Hugh Gray was no stranger to Loch Ness. He lived close by, which gave him the opportunity to become familiar with the way it behaved in all manners of weather and throughout the seasons of the year. By extension, he would also have gotten to know the wildlife, particularly that which swam in and on the waters of the loch. It seems unlikely that a man so well-versed in his surroundings would misidentify a turtle or a fish as being something much larger.

Debate still rages about the photograph. Sadly, with the original picture and its negatives long since lost and therefore unavailable for analysis with sophisticated

21st century techniques and technologies, it is unlikely to be settled conclusively any time soon — if ever.

The monster stories drew the interest of sightseers, who came to visit the loch equipped with picnics and cameras. It is a tradition that continues to this day, no matter how wet and blustery the weather.

Whatever it was that Hugh Gray saw and photographed that day, more sightings of similar ilk were to follow. A local newspaper, the *Inverness Courier*, dutifully published some of the accounts. The monster stories drew the interest of sightseers, who came to visit the loch equipped with picnics and cameras. It is a tradition that continues to this day, no matter how wet and blustery the weather.

Since late 1933, the Loch Ness Monster story has enthralled not just British newspaper readers but also those on the other side of the Atlantic.

On January 5, the *Cleveland Press* trumpeted: "Giant Sea Monster Shows Self Again to Crowds of Watchers at Loch Ness." The article declared that a crowd of tourists "saw him" — not only an assumption of the monster's gender, but a sexist one at that — "far out, his long tapering neck arched like a swan's." Unfortunately, no reckoning of the distance from the observers to the creature is given in the article. The farther out into the loch the object was sighted, the more likely it was that their eyes were simply playing tricks on them — or that the sighting was the product of suggestion, expectation, and the climate of Nessie-mania that blanketed Inverness and its surrounding regions at the time.

On the other hand, perhaps the witnesses — unfortunately, we do not know how many there were — truly did see something monstrous on the waters of the loch.

Something else that remains unknown is the origin of a nickname given to the creature by local residents. Around the same time that it was christened Nessie, the Loch Ness Monster was also known by a substantially less monster-like name: Bobby. Unsurprisingly, the moniker never really caught on.

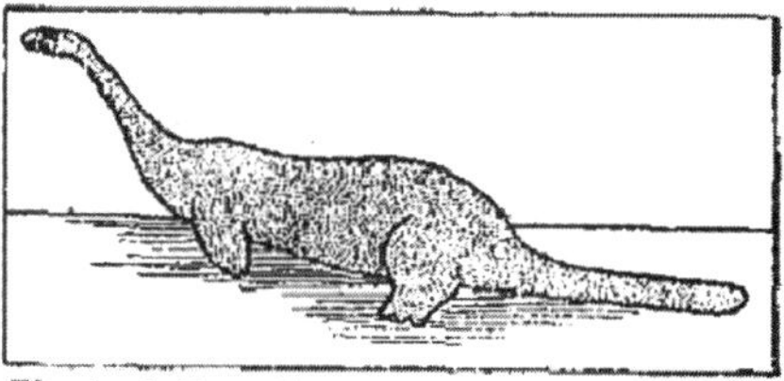

The Loch Ness Monster, As Sketched by Mr. A. Grant From Lieut.-Commander Gould's Interesting Monograph Upon the Subject.

This sketch of Nessie based on Arthur Grant's sighting appeared in the October 5, 1941, issue of the San Antonio Light *newspaper.*

January 5, 1934, was apparently a very active day for the creature. In the wee small hours of the morning, as the Scottish like to say, a motorcyclist named Arthur Grant was riding by the loch when he encountered the beast on dry land. Although several writers have claimed that the moon was full that night, thereby casting the creature in bright moonlight, the phase was actually waning gibbous, when the amount of visible lunar surface dwindles from 100%. Astronomical records show that 86% of the moon was shining down on Loch Ness that night, and on the huge animal that Grant claimed was lumbering along the side of the road.

Grant said that he almost hit the creature, so unexpected was its appearance. He described the characteristically long neck, small head, and flippers, estimating the creature's length as being somewhere between 15 and 20 feet from head to tail. It's worth nothing that Grant was a veterinary student and should therefore have possessed more than a passing familiarity with the various different species of animals that lived in and around Loch Ness. On the other hand, the eyes do like to play tricks on the mind, particularly at night. The fact that he was moving fairly quickly could also have increased the likelihood of misidentification.

The monster may have been spooked by the sound of Arthur Grant's motorcycle engine, as it immediately made a beeline for the shore of the loch and plunged into the water.

There have been other sightings of the Loch Ness Monster on the shore over the years, but they are relatively rare. The great majority relate to anomalous objects and creatures swimming in or surfacing from the waters of the loch, rather than ambulating along its shoreline.

During the previous summer, on July 22, 1933, a married couple from London named the Spicers were driving along the eastern fringe of Loch Ness when they claimed to have seen a "dragon or pre-historic animal" move downhill before crossing the road directly in front of their car. It was a Saturday afternoon in broad daylight. Mr. George Spicer estimated in a letter to the *Inverness Courier* that the creature was 6 to 8 feet in length. The newspaper article detailing the Spicers' account was headlined: "Is it the Loch Ness 'Monster'?"

Adding further intrigue was the Spicers' belief that the creature was carrying something akin to a deer or a sheep along with it, perhaps a snack that it had snatched from somewhere nearby.

Whatever it was that the Spicers saw seems to be too small to be the commonly reported Loch Ness Monster, based on this first account. That would change with later retellings of the story, however, as both the tail and the size of whatever it was the Spicers claimed to have seen would grow in the telling.

Could the anomalous creature perhaps have been a child of the larger creature? The Spicers caught only a relatively brief glimpse of the beast, recalling that it had dark, elephant-like gray skin, but it was noteworthy that there was no clearly visible tail or flippers (later, George Spicer would opine that there probably was a tail, but angled away from his line of sight).

The thing then rushed off in the direction of the shore. Although George Spicer assumed that the creature dived into the waters of the loch, neither he nor his wife heard a splash, which would be expected when something large and heavy hit the surface of the water. The thing simply vanished, apparently into thin air.

Had the Spicers mistaken a more conventional animal, such as an otter, for being the monster? Large otters may reach sizes of around 4 feet, which is notably shorter than the 6 to 8 feet described by George, who later said the creature was about 5 feet high. (As noted, the Spicers changed their story over time concerning such things as the size of the otters, which has subjected them to some criticism.) To further complicate matters, over subsequent retellings, he increased his estimation

More than once, an otter, a common species found all over Scotland, has been said to have fooled photographers reporting to have snapped a picture of Nessie.

of the beast's length significantly, to somewhere between 20 and 30 feet, thereby adding an additional frisson of beastliness and danger to the story.

Were the Spicers hoaxers? If so, it is difficult to fathom their motive for doing so. They reaped little in the way of money or fame in exchange for sharing their experience. If anything, the reverse was true; as happens to so many of those who report encountering a cryptid, they were publicly ridiculed and branded as liars. Writing to the newspaper to detail their experience and request further information turned out to be a bad move for the couple, bringing as it did notoriety and tarnishing their personal reputations. George Spicer was a respected tailor on the London scene. On the face of it, he had far more to lose than to gain by sharing his story with the world at large.

While it is true that some pranksters do what they do simply for the joy of putting one over on their fellow human beings, there is no evidence to suggest that Mr. and Mrs. Spicer were so inclined.

Some believe that the couple enjoyed the fame and notoriety that the alleged monster sighting brought their way, yet it is equally possible that the Spicers wished they had never come forward with their story in the first place. Whichever was the case, despite the malleability of George's public testimony, they both stuck to their guns and never recanted, even in the face of some very vocal skepticism.

The stakes were raised even higher a few days after Arthur Grant's January 5, 1934, encounter when it was claimed that the creature had killed a man. On January 10, the *Lancaster Daily Intelligencer Journal* ran a story titled "Loch Ness Monster Claims a Victim, Dodges Reporters." It noted that the body of a "well-dressed" 50-year-old man had washed up on the shore of the loch, and implied that the monster had just claimed its first human victim — that we knew of, at least.[18]

No monster-shaped tooth wounds were found on the deceased's body. Parts hadn't been bitten off or chunks ripped out, as one would expect from a monster attack. The rationale given for blaming Nessie for the unfortunate man's death was both simple and tenuous. The site at which John Doe's body was discovered was in the same vicinity as at least one previous Nessie sighting — therefore, the monster was probably to blame. QED.

The rationale given for blaming Nessie for the unfortunate man's death was both simple and tenuous. The site at which John Doe's body was discovered was in the same vicinity as at least one previous Nessie sighting — therefore, the monster was probably to blame.

It has long been said that Loch Ness never gives up the bodies of those who drown in it. Although a long-standing superstition, it is also one that makes good sense. The exceptionally cold water temperature means that a dead body would sink more quickly than in warmer waters, and once submerged was likely to remain on the bottom of the loch rather than float back up to the surface again. A recent tragedy occurred on the evening of July 9, 2020, when a Polish sailor fell into the loch while urinating over the side of his boat. Despite the best efforts of the rescuers, which included the police and the coast guard, the missing man's body was never recovered.

Given the loch's reputation for holding on to the bodies of any who drowned in it, the mysterious arrival of the unidentified male on its shore understandably caused speculation concerning the monster being responsible. This was compounded when reporters from the *Daily Mail* claimed to have seen a dark hump traveling at high

The deep, dark waters of Loch Ness are said to not give up the dead who have drowned there easily. Once submerged, bodies tend to stay in the murky cold rather than float up again.

speed through the waters of the loch that same morning. According to the *Intelligencer Journal* story:

> W. R. Turner, staff photographer of the *Daily Mail*, declared the creature created a wash which rocked their boat violently when the "thing" disappeared into the depths of the lake. M.A. Wetherell, a Central-African big game hunter, asserted the object appeared to be twelve to fifteen feet long at the surface of the water, and moved at a terrific rate of speed, leaving bubbles in the water when it disappeared.
>
> "I am satisfied it was the monster," Wetherell said. "It was a most large, powerful creature."

Other eyewitnesses claimed to have seen something similar traversing the waters of Loch Ness later that same day. If the big game hunter's assessment of the anomalous object's size was correct — some 12 to 15 feet — then it is reasonable to assume that more mass lay unseen, submerged beneath the surface of the water.

However, there is something fishy about this account — not least the fact that Marmaduke Wetherell, the big game hunter who went on record with the *Mail* to say that he'd seen a "most large, powerful creature" in the loch, was also an actor and a flamboyant showman. He also happened to be on the *Daily Mail*'s payroll, having been hired for the express goal of tracking down the monster. An impartial and unbiased eyewitness, he most certainly was not.

In December of the previous year, he had struck gold . . . or so it seemed. Wetherell found tracks along the shore of Loch Ness that looked to have been made by some gigantic creature. Indeed, they had been — but once plaster casts of the footprints were made and submitted to expert zoologists in London for scientific analysis, that creature turned out to be a hippopotamus, not a giant marine reptile. To make matters worse, the footprints were all of the *same* foot, as opposed to four different and distinct feet.

Clearly, it was a hoax. The question now became: by whom?

Suspicion fell on Marmaduke Wetherell himself.

After trumpeting the initial discovery of the tracks in its headlines, the *Daily Mail* did an about-face and swept the whole affair under the rug. Marmaduke Wetherell, on the other hand, was left with egg on his face. If he had been a party to what could only be seen as a hoax, as some have alleged, then it backfired spectacularly. If not, he was made to appear overly credulous and incompetent. Having lost major credibility because of the Loch Ness farrago, the *Daily Mail* wasted no time in cutting ties with its monster hunter for hire, lest it be tarnished by association.

Marmaduke Wetherell would not take this lying down.

It was this same *Daily Mail* that would soon after pay one Dr. Robert Wilson handsomely for an alleged photograph of the monster and publish it to broad acclaim. This turned out to be a huge milestone in Nessie photographic lore, becoming what is inarguably the best-known, most iconic picture associated with the Loch Ness Monster. Even the picture's name — "the Surgeon's Photograph" — carried an aura of mystique and gravitas. It depicted the silhouette of a long, curved neck rising up out of the waters of the loch. At the end of the neck was a tapering head matching descriptions of that belonging to the monster.

Surely, given the pedigree and respectability of the photographer — a doctor, an officer, and a gentleman — this had to be a genuine capture of the Loch Ness Monster on film . . . didn't it?

Surely, given the pedigree and respectability of the photographer — a doctor, an officer, and a gentleman — this had to be a genuine capture of the Loch Ness Monster on film . . . didn't it?

Making its first of many appearances in the April 21, 1934, edition of the *Daily Mail,* the picture immediately ignited a firestorm of public interest. To this day, whenever an article is written covering the Loch Ness Monster, the Surgeon's Photograph is usually the picture that accompanies it.

Most of those articles now contain the caveat that the picture is a hoax.

Dr. Robert Wilson should, by all accounts, have been an impeccable witness. Wilson would serve his country in the British Army during not just one but both world wars, attaining the rank of colonel. He took time out in between to attend medical school and graduate as a physician, specializing in gynecology and becoming a Fellow of the Royal College of Surgeons. By 1934, five years prior to the outbreak of World War II, he was a respected professional whose word carried considerable weight.

In other words, he was just the man to sell a monster story to the public.

The story associated with the picture went that Dr. Wilson and a companion were driving alongside the

An unabashed hoaxster created this image of Nessie that emulates the Surgeon's Photograph, although this image was taken near Fort Augustus at the southern end of Loch Ness.

loch when they suddenly caught sight of the monster's head and neck breaking through the surface of the water. Pulling the vehicle over, Wilson quickly deployed his camera and fired off a sequence of four pictures in rapid succession. Of the four, only one showed anything meaningful — the one that became front page news around the world.

In exchange for publication rights to the picture, the editorial team at the *Daily Mail* wrote him a hefty check on the spot.

It took 60 years, and a newspaper exposé, for the lid to finally get blown off the case, thanks largely to the diligent detective work of researchers Alastair Boyd and David Martin.

Unsurprisingly, Marmaduke Wetherell had not been happy with his treatment at the hands of the *Daily Mail* in the wake of the hippo-print imbroglio. He allegedly set out to get his own back on the newspaper, and in order to do so, it is claimed that he enlisted the help of his son and his stepson, along with a friend named Maurice Chambers and Dr. Wilson. Between them, they would create the infamous "Surgeon's Photo" — or so it is said, for when it comes to determining the truth behind this picture, the waters become truly murky indeed.

The story broke publicly on March 13, 1994, in Britain's *Sunday Telegraph* newspaper. The expose was fittingly titled "Nessie and a Big-Game Hunter's Monster Ego: Clockwork Submarine and Plastic Wood Fashioned a Legend."[19]

Wetherell's son, Ian, and his stepson, Christian Spurling, were both inducted into the plot to hoax the *Daily Mail*. In 1992, Spurling, then in his 90s, confessed to researchers that he had used a model submarine purchased from the toy department at Woolworths to serve as the mobile base for a monster head and neck that they put together themselves. Spurling crafted the head and neck from plastic wood, a favorite of model-makers, and built it around the conning tower of the toy sub.

In 1992, Spurling, then in his 90s, confessed to researchers that he had used a model submarine purchased from the toy department at Woolworths to serve as the mobile base for a monster head and neck that they put together themselves.

Once it was finished, the fake Nessie-submarine was pushed out onto the surface of Loch Ness, where it was carefully photographed, surrounded almost entirely by water, but with a small strip of coastline at the margin of the uncropped picture.

Considering the fallout that had ensued from what it is increasingly tempting to call "Hippogate" in January, it is surprising that the *Daily Mail*'s editor was willing to take the chance on another Nessie-related story, but the paper had a vested interest in keeping the Loch Ness affair alive. Despite what the newspaper had essentially brushed off as being nothing more than a minor hiccup, its readership was still fascinated with all things monster-related.

Dr. Wilson's standing in the community was a major factor behind the paper's decision to publish. It is debatable whether the same would have happened if Robert Wilson had fixed toilets for a living — "the Plumber's Photograph" just lacks gravitas and credibility. Nobody at the *Mail* had the slightest inkling that the real photographer was Marmaduke Wetherell — a man who wanted to get back at the paper for the way it had treated him in January.

Dr. Wilson, it was alleged, was simply helping Wetherell and his boys out by participating in a practical joke . . . a prank that was meant to be harmless, he believed, but which quickly blew up into a genuine phenomenon. Once the so-called Surgeon's Photograph was front-page news, confessing that he had been part of a hoax would almost certainly have negatively impacted his career. He quickly backed away from the story, never actively disavowing the veracity of the experience but leaving sufficient room for doubt as to what he and his unidentified companion had supposedly seen.

In reality, he may never even have gone near Loch Ness at all. Rather, if Spurling's story is true, he was simply the front man for a mean-spirited joke that got out of hand.

By the time the story broke in April 1994, everybody involved — including Christian Spurling — was dead. Marmaduke Wetherell died in 1939. Robert Wilson died in 1969. The world's press picked up the story and ran with it, decrying the Surgeon's Photograph as one of the greatest hoaxes of the 20th century.

While it is commonly accepted as being a hoax by researchers today, a word of caution is needed. The toy submarine story is certainly feasible, and Marmaduke Wetherell did indeed have a motive to fake the monster picture — getting revenge on the *Daily Mail*. But just as the 1934 claims of the picture's authenticity rested on the word of one man, Dr. Robert Wilson, so too do the 1994 claims of a hoax rest on the word of another . . .

A recreation of Nessie can be seen outside the Loch Ness Centre and Exhibition in Drumnadrochit, Highlands. There are still some researchers who believe the Surgeon's Photo could be legitimate.

Christian Spurling. There are still Loch Ness Monster researchers today who find the claims that the Surgeon's Photograph was fabricated to be questionable.

As far as physical evidence goes, Spurling claimed that after the notorious picture was taken, the conspirators disposed of it beneath the waters of the loch. All that remains is the testimony of the now-dead witnesses, the photograph itself . . . and a decades-long controversy.

In the end, the mystery of the Surgeon's Photograph simply boils down to a case of "he said, he said."

Nessie mania continued long after the release of the Surgeon's Photo. Tourists continued to flock to Loch Ness, either paying a premium for boat tours or taking the cheaper option of standing on the shore and watching for the elusive beast to put in an appearance. The steady flow of cash provided a reason for keeping the stories alive and in constant circulation. Nessie-related merchandising tourism continues to be a powerful economic force to this day.

In September 1934, Terence McGrath, an executive for the Cunard White Star Line of passenger ships, dismissed the monster stories after visiting the loch in person. He declared that after Royal Navy divers had been dispatched to Loch Ness at the behest of the government, the explanation for the monster sightings was a simple one: a German blimp dating back to World War I, which had crashed into the loch, was behind it all. The wreckage was poking up above the waterline at low tide and was being misconstrued as a giant reptile.[20]

McGrath's explanation may indeed have accounted for a small percentage of Nessie reports but fails to explain those that took place on dry land. Zeppelin wreckage is incapable of moving across the ground under its own locomotion, as the creature is said to have done. McGrath claimed that the Loch Ness Monster was always reported at the same specific location, when the water in the loch was low. This was demonstrably untrue.

A German Zeppelin like the one pictured, reasoned Terence McGrath, could have crashed into Loch Ness during World War I, where its remains would be mistaken for the lake monster.

In October 1941, Nessie made its first appearance of the Second World War years when it surfaced in close proximity to the MacFarlane-Barrow family, a father and three of his children, who were enjoying a boat outing on the loch. The astonished family watched for 10 minutes as the creature, which had a "long, snaky neck and 15 to 18 feet of body," zoomed back and forth through the water. Despite the subsequent sensationalized newspaper headline — "Loch Ness Beast Comes Up for War" — nobody was harmed by the creature's high-speed antics.[21]

Nessie was by then already a global phenomenon; so much so, in fact, that the creature was drawn into the ongoing propaganda war between the Axis Powers and the Allies. In 1940, the head of the Third Reich propaganda arm, Joseph Goebbels, declared that the monster was nothing more than a fairy tale, and he used the widespread belief in its existence as a stick with which to beat on the stupidity of the British people. He authored newspaper articles to this effect.

The Nazi regime, not particularly known for either its rationality or its stability, then reversed course and stated that Nessie *was* in fact real — but that the monster was now dead, blown to smithereens after coming into contact with a rogue mine. Exactly how an explo-

Italian dictatory Benito Mussolini declared that Nessie was real, but that his air force had bombed that area in Scotland, killing the monster. It was a patently absurd statement.

sive mine had gotten deployed in a Scottish loch that contained no major shipping to speak of was left to the imagination. After all, why spoil a good propaganda tale by introducing logic?

Not one to be outdone by his fascist Nazi allies, the regime of Benito Mussolini, the dictator of Italy, also jumped on board the Nessie train. Although the German Luftwaffe is rightfully cast in the role of villain during the Battle of Britain today, the Italian air force, the Regia Aeronautica, also launched bombing sorties against the British mainland. It was during one of these sorties, Mussolini wrote, that an Italian bomber pilot overflew Loch Ness and dumped his plane's deadly payload right on top of the hapless monster.

Regio Aeronautica 1; Nessie 0.

The story was printed in the Italian newspaper *Popolo d'Italia*. In order for this patently ludicrous story to be true, Goebbels had to have been lying. Mussolini apparently didn't care that he was insulting his more powerful ally.

Despite having been beaten down by two years spent at war, the British public took these stories with both a huge grain of salt and also their characteristic good humor. Brits laughed off the notion of Nessie being dead, noting that although sightings of the Loch Ness Monster had declined since their mid-1930s glory days, the creature was still rearing its head from time to time. With its tongue firmly in its cheek, on November 22, 1941, *The World's News* remarked that "the [British] Admiralty did not deny the claim, which remained until the other day as one of Italy's very few undisputed naval victories."

The MacFarlane-Barrow encounter was cited as evidence that Nessie was still alive and flipping. In addition to being fascinated with the possibility that such a creature might exist in Loch Ness, the propaganda skirmish demonstrated that the British people had grown decidedly fond of their elusive Scottish lake monster.

After the war ended in 1945 and a semblance of normalcy returned to the British Isles, Nessie continued to put in appearances. As the decades passed, technology steadily improved. Cameras became capable of taking pictures in increasingly higher resolutions. All things being equal, it should have gotten easier to capture solid evidence of the Loch Ness Monster's existence. There were a number of intriguing candidates, but nothing truly convincing ever surfaced — if you'll please pardon the pun.

In 1955, a bank manager named Peter MacNab claimed to see something huge cutting through the water close to one of the loch's most recognizable features: Urquhart Castle, which juts out into Loch Ness on an outcrop of land. The castle was the object of MacNab's photograph. It was only as he set about framing the picture that he noticed something strange breaking the surface alongside it. A pair of large humps was visible, and McNab took a photograph of them quickly before the creature submerged. It did not resurface.

The resulting photograph is one of the most intriguing of the numerous images that purport to show the Loch Ness Monster. Whatever the object captured by MacNab is, it is BIG. Using the castle as a yardstick for comparison, the long, dark anomaly could be greater than 50 feet long. No natural denizen of the loch could grow to such a length — if, that is, the picture truly shows what MacNab claimed that it did.

Fearing mockery, MacNab said he was reluctant to release the image to the public. He finally did so three years later, in 1958. His photograph lives on, as does the controversy surrounding it. Skeptics have dismissed the MacNab picture as being either outright fakery —

something for which there is no conclusive evidence — or as the misinterpretation of something as innocuous as the wake of a boat (or multiple boats, for the anomaly is considerable in size) motoring across the loch. By all accounts, Peter MacNab appears to have been a man of good character, one who lacked good reason to perpetrate a hoax. On the other hand, with no disrespect intended to the late Mr. MacNab, the same appeared to be the case with Robert Wilson.

Despite the progressive improvement in camera technological development, the validity of other Nessie pictures tends to be questionable. The use of underwater cameras has been equally unproductive.

Despite the progressive improvement in camera technological development, the validity of other Nessie pictures tends to be questionable. The use of underwater cameras has been equally unproductive. Many of the resulting images are little more than incomprehensible messes, thanks to the inky black nature of the water in Loch Ness.

On May 21, 1977, Tony "Doc" Shiels (he of Morgawr fame) took a color photograph of a reptilian head sticking out of the water on a long, serpentine neck. The image is so impressive that it falls under the category of "almost certainly too good to be true," even before one factors in Shiels's colorful personal history with regard to lake and sea monsters. The picture made it onto the front page of the popular British tabloid newspaper *The Daily Mirror*, causing quite the sensation, but many critics dismissed it out of hand, giving it the derogatory nickname of "The Loch Ness Muppet."

Shiels documented his version of the story in his autobiographical book *Monstrum! A Wizard's Tale*. He went so far as to fill out and sign an affidavit, which was witnessed and signed by a lawyer, under the constraints of the 1835 Statutory Declarations Act. This meant that, should the information turn out to be false — i.e., if it should be proven that Shiels had faked the Nessie photograph, which he now legally declared to be genuine — then he could be charged with a crime.

According to Shiels, he was exploring the remnants of

Artist and musician Tony "Doc" Shiels (1938–2024) was an artist and later magician who, beginning in the 1970s and through the 1980s, performed "monster raisings" of the Morgawr and, later, Nessie.

Urquhart Castle at around 4:00 in the afternoon when he suddenly noticed the creature's head having popped up some 4 or 5 feet above the surface of the loch. Roughly six seconds later, the monster turned away from him and quickly submerged, though not before Shiels had the opportunity to take a couple of photographs of it.

Researcher Tim Dinsdale — about whom we'll learn more later — submitted the pictures to a photographic expert for analysis. Dr. Vernon Harrison concluded that the picture had not been tampered with in any way, ruling out double exposure or attempts to physically manipulate the image. Harrison had been president of the Royal Photographic Society and was also a member of the Society for Psychical Research, which made him well-qualified for the task of examining an alleged photo of Nessie.

"The obvious explanation is that the photograph depicts a living creature strongly resembling a Plesiosaurus," Harrison observed, before cautioning that " . . . it could be a hoax. For example, a diver might have made a model of the head and neck and be holding it above the water while he himself was submerged."

If this was indeed the case, then there were shades of the Surgeon's Photograph. Clearly, Shiels could never definitively prove that the picture hadn't been faked in exactly this way.

To add a layer of additional strangeness to the whole affair, Shiels was working with a group of self-professed psychics as part of an experiment dubbed "Monstermind." Its purpose was to raise what he referred to as

British paleontologist and author Darren Naish has published books about dinosaurs, but he also cowrote Cryptozoologicon: Volume 1 *(2013) and* Hunting Monsters: Cryptozoology and the Reality Behind the Myths *(2017).*

dragons from the deeps, as was detailed earlier in this chapter's section pertaining to Morgawr. This lent an air of performance art to the affair, which some felt was beginning to seem like a media circus.

In his book *Hunting Monsters: Cryptozoology and the Reality Behind the Myths* (2017), paleontologist Dr. Darren Naish comes out against the authenticity of the picture, stating that it "is certainly not an image of a real animal but more likely shows a model, as are the two additional photos that show the same subject but in slightly different poses and stages of submergence."

Tim Dinsdale, the researcher who submitted the so-called Muppet Photo for photographic analysis, had captured video footage of what he believed to be Nessie on April 23, 1960. While driving along the side of the loch, something out on the water caught Dinsdale's eye. Stopping the car, he took a closer look with binoculars.

His mission in life was to capture evidence of the creature's existence, so Tim Dinsdale had come prepared. He quickly deployed a tripod-mounted camera and began to shoot footage as what he took to be the monster started moving through the water.

"It looked like the back of a huge animal," Dinsdale recalled to a BBC journalist during an interview conducted at the same location several years after. "It stood 2 or 3 feet out of the water, 4 or 5 feet across . . . and then it approached the far shore, and then under the surface, throwing up a wave that has since been measured on the film, at a height of about 2 feet."[22]

Tim Dinsdale devoted much of the remainder of his life to an effort to capture more footage, patrolling the loch daily in a boat specially outfitted with mounted cameras and other equipment. He was unsuccessful, although he did claim two more sightings of Nessie's head and neck in subsequent years — neither of which were photographed. He died in 1987, having lectured extensively and authored a number of books on the Loch Ness Monster. The film recording he made in 1960 remained his most solid piece of evidence.

The footage itself is relatively unremarkable at first glance, looking like a motorboat filmed from a distance, speeding across the loch. Indeed, some skeptics believe that a motorboat is exactly what the object is. Footage taken by Dinsdale of a boat in the same place does look similar, it must be said, but there are noticeable differences between the two. Another problem with the boat explanation is that it depends on Tim Dinsdale being unable to tell the difference between a piloted boat and something entirely different, after having scrutinized it carefully through binoculars. There is also the fact that boats do not submerge. Dinsdale developed a solid reputation among the cryptozoological community, with nary a whiff of hoaxing ever emerging.

Of course, just because the subject of the film may not have been a boat doesn't necessarily make it the Loch Ness Monster, and the debate concerning its identity continues to this day.

The 21st century heralded the arrival of Photoshop and other computer software capable of digitally manipulating imagery. Photographs taken of alleged cryptids must now be considered even more questionable than they were before, due to the lack of a physical negative that can be examined and analyzed by photographic experts.

There are, broadly speaking, two schools of thought concerning the nature of the Loch Ness Monster. The first, which has already been discussed, is that the sightings are of a biological creature — some sort of remnant or throwback to a much earlier period in the Earth's history, such as a plesiosaur. We have already discussed this explanation at some length. As a potential solution, the plesiosaur/biologic angle simply has far too much more going against it than for it. The lack of physical evidence and the fact that the loch didn't even exist when the last such creatures died out are, in this author's view, insurmountable obstacles.

Photoshop and AI-generate art can easily create faked images of Nessie, so "photos" of the monster are getting more and more dubious in the modern tech age.

The second hypothesis may seem either far stranger or, conversely, easier to accept, depending on one's worldview. As an umbrella term, one that encompasses several different hypotheses, we'll refer to this as the paranormal explanation: the notion that although the creature may indeed exist, it does so in a manner that is completely inconsistent with the laws of nature as we currently understand them.

A colorful and diverse array of myths and legends has been associated with Loch Ness for hundreds of years. The loch is an isolated and sometimes lonely place, one that has a distinctly haunted feel about it. Tales of monsters such as kelpies — shape-changing water spirits, usually of malign intent — long predated sightings of the Loch Ness Monster. Although Loch Ness wasn't the only loch in Scotland to attract such stories, it did seem to garner more than its fair share.

In 1899, this mystical atmosphere drew the attention of the occultist Aleister Crowley, famously dubbed "the wickedest man in the world" by the British magazine *John Bull* in 1923. It should be noted that Crowley's tenancy at Boleskine House, a historic estate situated on the shores of the loch, began some 35 years before stories of the monster gained widespread circulation. It was the region itself, not the Loch Ness Monster, that attracted Crowley to such an extent that he paid double the market value of the property. He owned the place for almost 15 years, selling up and moving on in 1913; yet that didn't stop rumors from spreading in later years that Nessie was Crowley's magical familiar. Some stories even claimed that the eccentric self-professed "Laird of Boleskine" regularly slaughtered sheep and tossed them into the loch for it to feed on.

Other rumors claim that Crowley had tangled with dark and malevolent forces during his time at Boleskine — forces that remained behind when Crowley left. Even decades after his departure from Loch Ness, stories of a curse have surrounded the place. In 1970, the guitarist of Led Zeppelin, Jimmy Page, purchased Boleskine House, fulfilling a long-standing fascination with the life and works of Aleister Crowley. Page spent relatively little time there, leaving friends to play the role of custodians. These house sitters reported experiencing an unnerving amount of poltergeist activity at Boleskine. Jimmy Page subsequently sold the property in 1991.

Aleister Crowley, an occultist who founded the Thelema religion, the basic tenet of which was that one should do what one wishes to discover their True Will. His residence at Boleskine House near Loch Ness was said to emanate supernatural powers.

Two significant fires at the house in 2015 and 2019, which all but destroyed the property, only served to strengthen the perception that Boleskine House was blighted with some sort of evil supernatural presence.

Could Nessie be a manifestation of those malign supernatural powers — if, that is, one believes in such things? One hypothesis holds that the creature (or creatures) was conjured from another plane of existence and may have the capacity for traveling back and forth between that realm and our own, either at will or at certain times when circumstances permit.

Others believe that the monster may be the ghost of a plesiosaur, or some similar creature from far back in the mists of time. They point to those accounts in which the monster is said to have disappeared into the waters of Loch Ness without making a sound — no splash, no disruption of the water's surface at all. Yet this viewpoint ignores those instances, which are very much in the majority of reports, in which Nessie *has* disturbed the water, sometimes to a significant extent. Indeed, there are many sightings in which some kind of subsurface disturbance is the primary characteristic. Whatever people are seeing in those cases, it does indeed appear to have physical mass.

The Nessie-as-a-ghost story was popularized by the 2009 movie *The Men Who Stare at Goats*, starring George Clooney and Ewan McGregor and based on the book by Jon Ronson. Purporting to tell the true story of a U.S. military psychic spy unit, Ronson's book includes one Major Ed Dames, who "had taken to spying on the Loch Ness Monster during the fallow months, when there wasn't much official military psychic work. He determined that it was a dinosaur's ghost."

The psychic spy program did indeed exist. Although the broad sweeps of Ronson's book and its movie adaptation are true, it's fair to say that there is also much exaggeration for the purposes of dramatic effect. Whether the Nessie-related findings of psychic remote viewer Major Dames is one of those exaggerations remains unclear.

Alternatively, it's entirely possible that the Loch Ness Monster doesn't exist at all.

The influence of the media and popular culture on the way that we as human beings perceive things and think about them must always be factored in when assessing claims of cryptids and monsters. It is a theme that crops up time and again and runs through the stories in this book as an ever-present skein.

Nessie skeptics rightfully point out that in 1933, when the monster sightings really began to gain traction, the Hollywood motion picture *King Kong* was making big money at the box office, not just in the United States but also in British cinemas. The movie premiered in London over Easter 1933 and went on general release on June 23. It was wildly popular. Moviegoing audiences were thrilled by the exotic locale and the — for the time — cutting-edge special effects, which not only brought to life the titular Kong, but also pitted him against giant dinosaurs and other monstrous creatures.

Nessie skeptics rightfully point out that in 1933, when the monster sightings really began to gain traction, the Hollywood motion picture King Kong was making big money at the box office, not just in the United States but also in British cinemas.

It hardly seems coincidental that *King Kong* and the Loch Ness Monster both enjoyed a surge in popularity at the same time. Nor is it much of a leap to suggest that some of the eyewitnesses who turned in Nessie sighting reports had already seen the film when they did so. This implies that, far from attempting to deliberately create a hoax, they were instead psychologically primed by the intense and visceral moviegoing experience. The film contains stop-motion animated images of long-necked, sharp-toothed prehistoric monsters that made quite an impact on viewers of the film; an impact that, while entirely subconscious, could possibly have contributed to their interpretation of otherwise entirely mundane and natural items or animals they encountered in and around Loch Ness. This effect became even more pronounced when the stories of Nessie grew into a widespread phenomenon, as they had by 1934, when it seemed that anybody and everybody was talking about the creature.

Considering that social and cultural environment, how could somebody living in those times *not* be influenced toward thinking about monsters? The bias was ever-present and pervasive, particularly in the vicinity of the loch itself. Most of those who went to visit did so with the express intention of seeing the creature for themselves. Is it really so unlikely that a log bobbing on

A scene from the 1970 movie The Private Life of Sherlock Holmes *in which Nessie makes an appearance. During filming, the prop monster sank to the bottom of the lake, where it was rediscovered by a submersible robot in 2016.*

the surface or an otter glimpsed for just a second or two could be transformed in the observer's mind into something monstrous?

Awareness of the Loch Ness Monster is even more pervasive today. One would be hard-pressed to find anybody who was unaware of the creature or fail to identify its classic profile and silhouette of humps and long neck arching up out of the water.

In 2016, a monster truly was found beneath the surface of the loch. A submersible robot was capturing underwater images when it detected the presence of a 30-foot anomaly. Unfortunately, there was an entirely prosaic explanation. This particular Loch Ness Monster was a giant prop, constructed for the 1970 movie *The Private Life of Sherlock Holmes,* which starred Sir Robert Stephens in the titular role and Sir Christopher Lee as his brother, Mycroft.[23]

Shot on an expensive (for the time) $10 million budget, the movie production spared no expense in creating Nessie in the waters of the loch itself. A pair of humps concealed the flotation devices that kept the faux monster buoyant. The director, Billy Wilder, disliked the way the humps looked on camera and had the film crew remove them . . . at which point, Nessie promptly sank, never to be seen again.

(The monster did make it into the final cut of the movie, albeit in a different form. A head and neck prop were fashioned and shot in the controlled environment of a water tank in a movie studio.)

When all is said and done, at least one monster has been found in Loch Ness. Will there be others? Only time will tell.

The Moolyewonk

Lake and river monsters are not unique to the United Kingdom; indeed, many countries have them. On the opposite side of the globe, the Hawkesbury River flows to the northwest of Sydney, in New South Wales, Australia. The river is said to be the home of a Nessie-like creature that modern-day locals refer to as the Hawkesbury River Monster. The Aboriginal people have legends of a large riverine creature that go back thousands of years. Known to them as the *Moolyewonk* (lurking water monster), it has been depicted in their ancient rock carvings.

In 2009, cryptozoologist Rex Gilroy told journalist Justin Vallejo of the *Daily Telegraph* that for Moolyewonks to exist in modern times, "we'd have to have a breeding population of no less than 300 to 600. We're dealing with ocean creatures coming into the river to breed."[24]

Gilroy claimed to have personally spotted a long-necked creature swimming in the river. Most eyewitnesses describe the monster as having leathery gray skin; a long, arching neck; four flippers; and a tail. These descriptions of the Moolyewonk mirror those of the plesiosaur, an aquatic dinosaur, the fossils of which were first discovered in 1823.

It was long believed that plesiosaurs lived in the ocean, with salt water being their natural habitat. Doubt

Australia's Hawkesbury River is located not far north of Sydney, a somewhat surprising location for a river monster such as the Moolyewonk.

was cast on this hypothesis when plesiosaur fossils were found in a Moroccan river system that dates back to the Cretaceous period. Many critics of the "Loch Ness Monster as a plesiosaur" hypothesis have pointed to the fact that, although it ultimately connects to the North Sea, Loch Ness is a freshwater body. The evidence now strongly suggests that plesiosaurs were capable of living in freshwater under certain circumstances and were not restricted to the seas and oceans.

Being some 75 miles in length, the Hawkesbury River flows directly into the sea. Believers in the Moolyewonk suggest that the creature (or creatures) may live in the ocean and would then venture up the Hawkesbury on occasion — in order to mate, if Rex Gilroy is correct. It now looks as if plesiosaurs were not simply marine animals, living exclusively in the ocean, but rather were capable of existing in both freshwater and saltwater environments.

Whatever the Moolyewonk may be, white settlers were warned of the dangerous creature by the Aboriginal inhabitants of the land when they first arrived. The monster was said to prey on unsuspecting women, children, and even fishermen who were sailing on the river, snatching them out of their boats, which were then sometimes damaged or sunk. When no human beings were within chomping range, the Moolyewonk was willing to settle for farm or domestic animals that wandered a little too close to the riverbank.

In a letter to the editor of the *Sydney Morning Herald* published on August 9, 1980, Gilroy related an unsettling incident that took place in 1979, which saw a family hurled around inside their boat as the creature clumsily attempted to surface underneath it. The author of numerous books, Rex Gilroy spent decades documenting sightings of the Moolyewonk. Unfortunately, at the time of writing, no definitive evidence has emerged to prove that the so-called Hawkesbury River Monster is anything more than a long-standing bit of folklore.[25]

Yowie!

Move over, Bigfoot; Australia has its own version of the shaggy, brown-haired humanoid, a creature known as the Yowie. Typically described as between 7 and 8 feet tall, covered in thick, bristly hair, Yowies stand upright and have generally humanoid characteristics. It is said that they are heavily muscled and possess a set of powerful jaws, and are more than capable of killing and eating a human being.

One theory about the origin of the Yowie is that it comes from the legend of the Aborigine monster known as the Yaroma, also known as the Yahoo, a man-eating creature resembling a horrifying giant.

A question that is equally pertinent with regard to every creature covered in this book would be: Why has a Yowie never been captured or killed and subjected to examination? Australia certainly has plenty of space in which humans rarely set foot, even today; over a million square miles of wilderness remain undeveloped, though most of it has at least been mapped and charted. Some of the more isolated rural areas could conceivably be home to Yowies, and potentially other cryptids too.

Yowie sightings go back for centuries, originating with indigenous Aboriginal people, and the accounts share an impressive consistency. Speculation regarding the creature's origins runs the gamut from it being a flesh-and-blood creature, albeit one that has become exceptionally skilled at avoiding contact with human hunters, to it being some kind of supernatural or trans-dimensional entity, capable of phasing into and out of our material reality at will. In this respect, there are comparisons with the Mothman stories, which feature elsewhere in this book — and indeed, some of those who have claimed to encounter the Yowie say that it also has glowing red eyes, just as Mothman does.

There are greater parallels between the Yowie, Sasquatch, and Bigfoot than there are with Mothman, however. The hefty, shambling hairy humanoids seem to look and behave similarly in both the northern and southern hemispheres. Their favored terrain seems to be forests and wooded areas, offering a degree of protection and shelter not only from the elements but also from intrusive humans.

Whatever it may be, the creature appears to have a definite physical presence. Tracks have been found in the vicinity of Yowie sightings: primate-like footprints, larger and heavier than those of a human being. Some of the tracks have only three or four toes. Another relatively common finding is a foul stink that the Yowies leave in their wake.

Sightings continue to be reported in the 21st century. The website yowiehunters.com.au maintains a database of such sightings, which are available for anybody to read. It also contains interviews with Aboriginal people in which they explain their own cultural beliefs concerning the Yowie; it is a concept with which they are very familiar, as it has been part of their tradition for so long.

There are accounts of Yowies causing property damage, tearing up fences and tossing around or eating animals and livestock. However, despite their fearsome appearance and aggressive roar, there is little in the way of testimony suggesting that the beasts are inclined to harm humans. On the other hand, there are some that attribute the disappearance of individuals in the outback and remote regions of Australia each year to abduction by Yowies.

Monster or myth? Opinion is divided. As if the snakes, spiders, and crocodiles weren't terrifying enough, the Yowie gives visitors to Australia one more reason to keep their head on a swivel.

Bunyip

Nor is the Yowie the only strange creature reputed to stalk the Land Down Under. There's also the Bunyip, a creature so strange in appearance that it makes some other cryptids seem positively ordinary by comparison. To illustrate this point far better than words ever could, take a moment to open up a browser window, and point it to a search engine such as images.google.com (or any other that takes your fancy). Enter the word "bunyip" and hit Search.

An 1890 illustration of a Bunyip, the Australian beast that hunts in bogs, swamps, and creeks.

What comes up is remarkable not just for the sheer weirdness of each image, but also the inconsistency between them. Some of the pictures are AI-generated, whereas others will have been sketched by human artists. All show a creature that moves about on all fours. Most have a tail. Some have claws, others long, curved fangs like those of a saber-toothed tiger; in others, there are tusks or tentacles. Legs or flippers serve as a means of locomotion.

Some of the few things that the artists seem to agree on are that the Bunyip lives in swamps and pools — most of the pictures depict the creature emerging from a body of water — and that it has a distinct appetite for human beings, based on the many variants that show Bunyips clenching a helpless child within its jaws. The creature can look like anything from a tiger to a giant toad to the horned, savage Terror Dogs from the *Ghostbusters* movies.

Legend has it that the Bunyip's favored habitat is any form of swamp, marsh, or wetland. As with the Yowie, tales of the Bunyip long predate the arrival of white settlers, being firmly rooted in the folklore and mythology of the indigenous people. One of the few things that those first storytellers agreed on was that the Bunyip was best avoided. Not only might it gobble up any errant children who strayed too close to its lair, but even the creature's cry was supposedly capable of causing injury or disease.

As with the Yowie, tales of the Bunyip long predate the arrival of white settlers, being firmly rooted in the folklore and mythology of the indigenous people. One of the few things that those first storytellers agreed on was that the Bunyip was best avoided. Not only might it gobble up any errant children who strayed too close to its lair, but even the creature's cry was supposedly capable of causing injury or disease.

Bunyips could be found on or near riverbanks, it was believed. The same is also true of the far more tangible crocodile and alligator, making it doubly wise to tread warily in the vicinity of rivers and watering holes. Belief in Bunyips was widespread for centuries, and many unusual moans or creature calls were attributed to them. Stories abounded of Bunyips prowling abroad at night, searching for an unsuspecting victim to snatch and eat. They were the stuff of nightmares — cautionary tales told to children and adults alike in order to scare them into staying safe.

The Bunyip's dark image has undergone some significant rehabilitation. It became less a figure of fear and more a lovable, if not downright cuddly, creature. It's now possible to buy plush Bunyips as toys for children. The year 1987 brought an animated TV show for kids titled *Bunyip,* in which the titular monster was now friendly, welcoming, and helpful to other animals. For many years, Australians have regarded the Bunyip with a sense of affection, not fright.

Be that as it may, if I ever should find myself in the wilds of Australia, I would still be inclined to keep my distance from the water's edge — just in case.

Creatures of the Night

Everybody loves a good vampire story. Whether it's Béla Lugosi, Gary Oldman, or Christopher Lee portraying the iconic Count Dracula or Robert Pattinson's moody, sparkling-in-the-daylight vessel of vampiric angst Edward Cullen in the blockbuster *Twilight* saga, vampires have always meant big box office.

Readers and moviegoing audiences alike have long been fascinated by these creatures of the night. There is something deeply seductive about the vampire, something that seems to be both timeless and undefinable — in its literary and silver screen versions, at least. Perhaps it is the sheer romanticism of the tortured soul who is gifted, although some would say cursed, to live forever, unless its existence is snuffed out by the cruel rays of the sun or by a wooden stake being pounded violently through its heart.

Depictions of vampires in many recent Hollywood movies have romanticized the bloodthirsty creatures, making them increasingly appealing to audiences.

Equally romantic are the other trappings of cinematic vampirism: sleeping in a coffin secured in an underground lair, usually lined with soil from the vampire's homeland;

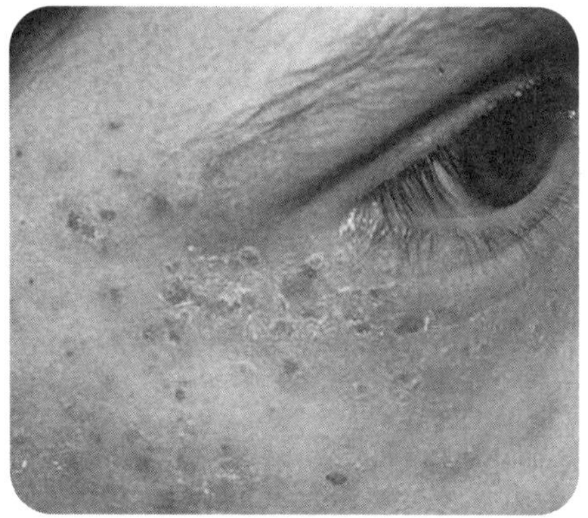

One of the symptoms of porphyria is a skin rash and sensitivity to light. Other symptoms include hypertension, vomiting, and abdominal pain.

gothic mansions, castles, and ruined abbeys; the silky black apparel, ranging from flowing capes to silken dresses. Many of these are clichéd stereotypes, admittedly, yet they are indelibly burned into our minds as essential parts of vampiric lore.

The reality, needless to say, is somewhat different.

Human beings have always excelled at creating heavily fictionalized narratives in order to explain things we don't understand. It is highly likely that our belief in vampires can be attributed to an ignorance regarding certain clinical conditions and pathologies at a time when medical science was considerably less advanced than it is today.

Porphyria is known informally as the "vampire disease." This family of blood diseases derives its name from porphyrins, compounds within the body that play a key role in the creation of hemoglobin. Within human blood cells, hemoglobin is the protein that carries oxygen and carbon dioxide throughout the bloodstream. (The red color in human blood comes from the iron-rich hemoglobin.) Without porphyrins, hemoglobin would not exist. Porphyrins create the heme (the iron molecule that is a core component of hemoglobin), and when we have either too little or too much, the symptoms can look a lot like vampirism.

Those afflicted with the disease could appear pale and sallow of complexion. They often had the tendency to stay indoors during the daytime, leaving their homes during the hours of darkness because direct sunlight was physically painful to them when it came in contact with their skin. The pain could be so severe that the skin actually burned, turning red, swelling, and even blistering if the exposure was sufficiently long.

In this lay the genesis of Hollywood movie vampires screaming and writhing as they burst into flame whenever a shaft of sunlight struck them; the advent of computer-generated imagery took this to the next level, with stricken vampires disintegrating into clouds of ashes. The intense fear of the sun is just one way in which a genuine medical symptom has permeated the vampire mythology.

Some forms of porphyria manifest with anemia, a pathologically low level of hemoglobin or red blood cells within the body. In certain cases, the sufferer's teeth are stained a reddish-brown color, which would only serve to add fuel to the fire in the days when such unfortunates were suspected of being vampires. Gum recession is another consequence. As the gums shrink in size, it can give the impression that the teeth are enlarging and lengthening. Couple this with relatively pointed canine teeth, as some individuals have, and the result is the appearance of a human being possessing fangs.

The disorder can also cause the urine to turn either brown or red, which could easily be mistaken by the untrained eye for the urination of blood.

Effects of porphyria on the brain and on the central nervous system can cause irrational behavior and altered mental status, which might include aggression and combativeness — and the perception of a vampire attacking its victim. In the 1960s, it was commonly believed that Britain's so-called mad king, George III, was suffering from porphyria; the idea has since been discredited, however, and contemporary clinical thinking holds that the king was most likely beset with a mental illness such as bipolar disorder.

Porphyrias are not infectious. They cannot be transmitted from one person to another in the way that some diseases can. They are passed on in the genes, from one generation to the next. Despite the many advances made by 21st century medical science, porphyrias cannot be cured. They can, however, be treated — and not by driving a stake through the heart, as happened in bygone days. Bone marrow transplants, which were unavailable in most clinics and hospitals until the 1960s, may be used in severe cases. Blood transfusions are a mainstay of porphyria treatment today.

Despite porphyria's reputation for being the "vampire disease," another malady can make an almost equally strong claim. Tuberculosis, formerly known as consumption because of the cadaverous, wasted appearance of those who contracted it, is commonly believed to be a disease of the lungs and the respiratory system. This perception comes mainly from movies such as *Tombstone,* in which the gun-slinging dandy John Henry "Doc" Holliday (played in a career-defining performance by actor Val Kilmer) frequently coughs up bright red blood throughout many scenes in the movie.

The reality is more nuanced. It is true that the infectious bacteria that cause tuberculosis primarily affect the lungs. However, once the disease has become firmly entrenched within the chest, it may also spread throughout the body. The brain, spinal cord, liver, kidneys, and heart can all be damaged or altered as the disease progresses. It may also spread into the lymph system.

In the late-nineteenth-century American West, such unfortunates were nicknamed "lungers" due to the pulmonary symptoms of the disease. The term "consumptive" applied primarily because of the effects of tuberculosis systematically ravaging the body, eating it away from the inside. Sudden and unanticipated weight loss is a hallmark indicator of TB, and to this day is a sign that physicians look for when considering it as a potential diagnosis.

At the turn of the twentieth century, the United States was hit hard by tuberculosis. Many sufferers took the advice of physicians and relocated to areas with dry climates and clean air, such as the Rocky Mountains of Colorado or the deserts of Arizona. Dedicated sanatoriums were established for the infected, places for them to convalesce — or die. Less fortunate individuals were consigned to camps, isolated from everyday society in remote locations that placed the problem out of sight and out of mind . . . a similar approach to that which Victorian-era medicine took toward mental health.

It is not difficult to see why cadaverously thin, pale sufferers of tuberculosis sometimes were accused of

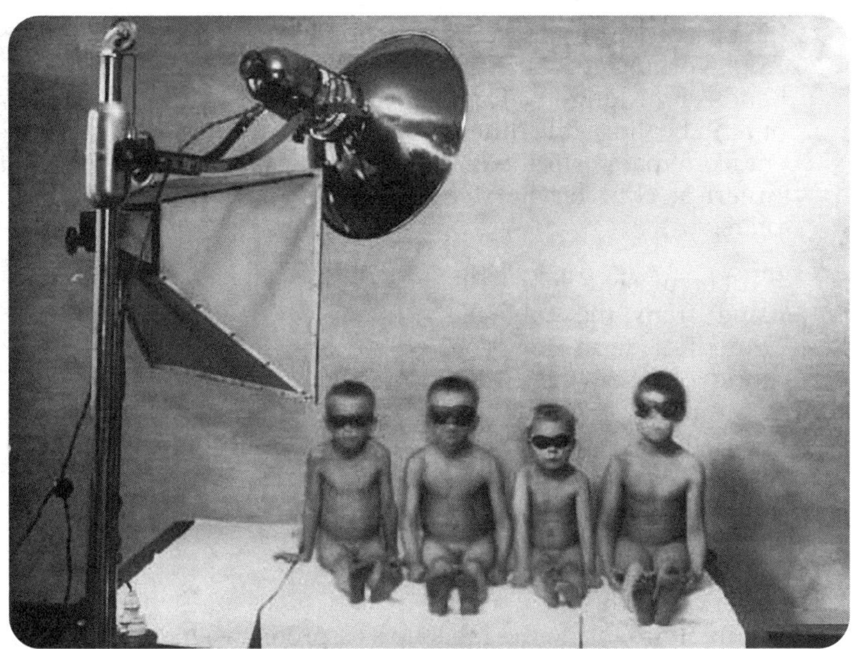

Finnish children are shown here receiving phototherapy for tuberculosis. The UV light in particular has been shown to kill the bacteria that causes this disease.

being vampires, particularly when their teeth and lips were stained with bright red blood. Not the blood of victims from whom they had attempted to suck the life, but rather their own blood, coughed up from within their own traumatized, infected lungs.

Such beliefs were more common in relatively isolated rural communities, the kind of settlements that remained mostly untouched by the latest thinking in contemporary medicine. Tuberculosis has blighted humanity for hundreds of millions of years. In the Middle Ages, it was referred to as "the King's Evil" because of the commonly held belief that the touch of a king could cure it. Sometimes the infected were brought into the presence of the king, who would lay hands on them directly. On other occasions, in order to protect themselves from direct exposure to the ailment, monarchs would sometimes touch medallions, coins, or other artifacts, which would then be given to the sufferer in the belief that these would effect a cure. Known as "touch coins," they were considered to be extremely special, the physical manifestation of God working through the hands of the king — a form of faith healing little different from that performed in American churches in later years.

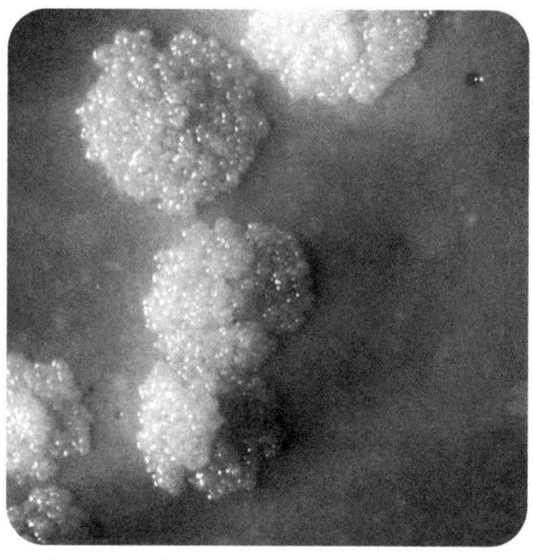

Tuberculosis bacteria are shown in a lab culture. The bacteria infect body parts with round outgrowths called tubercles.

Tuberculosis gets its name from the tubercle, a medical term for tiny round outgrowths within the body. In relation to bones, they can be perfectly normal. When found within infected lungs, tubercles are not normal; each one contains the tuberculosis bacteria, with the body walling it up inside the tubercle as a protective measure, like a prisoner kept confined within a jail cell by the immune system. This is latent tuberculosis, a disease that remains surprisingly common today. The Centers for Disease Control (CDC) estimates that around 13 million Americans may have the latent version of the disease. That figure includes the author of this book, who contracted tuberculosis while working as a paramedic.

Latent tuberculosis is rarely a problem. Once the disease activates within the body, it becomes life threatening. The sufferer begins to suffer night sweats, waking up drenched in sweat, with chills running through them that set their teeth chattering. Next comes a fever, as the body kicks the immune system into high gear in an attempt to stave off the worsening infection. As the lungs begin to bleed, there comes the iconic bloody cough, which may start out as pink-tinged spittle and progress to become active, frank bleeding.

The appetite is suppressed. Dark circles form around the eyes, a consequence of far too many sleepless nights. The tuberculosis sufferer becomes scrawny, reduced to a pale, hacking, shuddering version of their former self. Until the arrival of life-saving medications such as streptomycin during the 1940s and 1950s, tuberculosis earned a reputation for taking lives on a massive scale.

By 1950, the heyday of the sanatorium in the United States was over.

In the late 18th and throughout the 19th century, a time of great scientific progress across numerous fields of endeavor, the belief in vampires was nonetheless widespread. European tradition was steeped in vampiric folklore, particularly in the region of Transylvania, but the New World wasn't immune to such beliefs. In few places was the fear of vampires more prevalent than it was in rural New England.

Tuberculosis had brutally ravaged the East Coast of the United States. Few communities went unaffected by the disease. It is no exaggeration to state that almost everybody knew somebody who had contracted the disease, many of whom died as a result. Humans like nothing better than knowing where to place the blame for our misfortunes, and vampires made for a convenient scapegoat. Medical science and faith were at odds with one another as to how best to deal with the epidemic of deaths that were taking place throughout Vermont, Rhode Island, Connecticut, and their surrounding regions.

The poster child case was that of the unfortunate Mercy Brown, who died at the age of 19 on January 17, 1892, in Exeter, Rhode Island. Even considering the high mortality rate of the time, the Brown family had seen a disproportionate amount of death. In the span of 10 years, Mercy's sister, Mary Olive, had died at the age of 20; their mother, Mary, was also dead. In each case, the cause of death had been an ailment that caused them to sicken and grow weak before dying in great pain. That ailment was, of course, tuberculosis, but not everybody in the community was willing to buy the explanation offered by the physicians. A combination of faith and ignorance led them to the conclusion that the Brown women had been killed by vampires.

It's easy to see why they would think that. As if George Brown, the widowed father of Mercy and Mary Olive,

The grave of Mercy Brown can be viewed at the Baptist Church in Exeter, Rhode Island. People of her day thought that she was a vampire because her body, when exhumed, had not decayed, but this can be explained by the fact she died in winter and the cold preserved the remains.

hadn't suffered enough heartbreak already, it was now the turn of his son Edwin to fall ill with what looked like the same affliction.

Up until then, Edwin Brown had been a robustly healthy young man. Now, just as his mother and sisters had, he began to grow weak and frail. Suspicion grew among the Browns' neighbors that a vampire was preying on their small community. Either this undead creature had killed Mary Olive, Mercy, and their mother . . . or perhaps, the whispers said, it was even one of them.

There was only one way to find out.

In March 1892, matters came to a head. With the courage that comes when a mob is formed, the graves of Mercy, Mary, and Mary Olive were dug up, and the bodies of the dead women were exhumed. Once the coffin lids were pried open, it became clear that neither Mary Brown nor her daughter Mary Olive could be the vampire. Their remains were both in a state of advanced decomposition, which was suited to the length of time they had been dead.

Mercy's body was a different story entirely. Despite having been dead since January, her corpse showed no signs of decay. In addition to the presence of blood, which the exhumers found to be particularly damning, it also appeared as though Mercy's fingernails and hair had continued to grow after her death.

Clearly, Mercy Brown was the vampire who had

plagued their village. She was rising from the grave after nightfall and was somehow drinking the blood of her own brother, Edwin. The fact that her corpse seemed extremely well-preserved despite spending months in the ground left no room for argument. While we don't know exactly what was said at the time, it is troubling that nobody could answer the question of exactly how Mercy the Vampire managed to get in and out of her grave without leaving a trace. There are no records of the soil being disturbed prior to the time the exhumation party dug down to Mercy's coffin. It was one thing to accept that a vampire, which was said to possess superhuman strength, could force its way out of its coffin and up to the surface; but returning there before sunrise and somehow contriving to pull the earth back on top without any hint of disarray was another question entirely.

Perhaps this was airily dismissed as being some sort of occult vampire magic.

At any rate, the people of Exeter reasoned, the only way to save young Edwin from meeting the same horrific fate as his sisters and mother was to destroy the vampire utterly in order to free him from its thrall. This they did by cutting out Mercy's heart and setting fire to it. Once the organ was burned to ashes, those ashes were collected and mixed into a medication, which Edwin was instructed to drink.

The fact that her corpse seemed extremely well-preserved despite spending months in the ground left no room for argument. While we don't know exactly what was said at the time, it is troubling that nobody could answer the question of exactly how Mercy the Vampire managed to get in and out of her grave without leaving a trace.

Drink it he did. It made no difference. He died anyway, which horrified the villagers but should come as no surprise to us. The ashes of cardiac tissue have no curative effect on tuberculosis. The condition of Mercy's remains makes complete sense, given what we know about the normal postmortem changes that the human body undergoes after death. The blood that welled from beneath the skin when it was punctured or cut was not fresh. The ground in Rhode Island is cold between the months of January and March. This would have had the effect of preserving Mercy's body. Had she died in the heat of July instead, the condition of her body would have been quite different. The notion that the perfectly innocent 19-year-old was a vampire would have been much harder to accept, and the subsequent desecration of her remains most likely avoided.

The situation in Exeter was far from unique. To many people, it was considered entirely plausible that the corpses of the dead might hunt members of their own family if they became vampires. Cutting off their heads was seen as an effective countermeasure. This probably didn't take place before the burial. Rather, when the blight of tuberculosis struck a community, suspicions of vampirism would fall on one of the recently deceased. Their grave would then be dug up and the body beheaded in its coffin. For good measure, the limbs might also be severed, to prevent the vampire from walking or crawling its way out of the grave.

At the dawn of the twentieth century, vampires drew less blame for what, it became increasingly clear, were actually symptoms of infectious disease. Ironically, this was the era of Bram Stoker's *Dracula,* published in 1897 and the subject of numerous theatrical productions and motion pictures. Of the many performers who have portrayed the vampire count on the big screen, the most iconic must be the Hungarian actor Béla Lugosi. His love-hate relationship with Dracula began when Lugosi, having immigrated to the United States, played the role on stage in a popular theatrical run on Broadway. He trod the boards as Dracula for the first time in 1927 and would play the titular role more than a thousand times in his career.

Lugosi famously grew to resent his association with Dracula, but like many actors who find themselves in a much-loved, iconic role, he could not escape it. Upon his death following a heart attack in 1956, Béla Lugosi was even buried in Dracula's signature costume, including the flowing black cloak. As a final irony, his gravestone in Culver City in Los Angeles County bears the sign of the cross, the religious icon that Lugosi's fictional alter ego found so repulsive.

Many argue that director Tod Browning's 1931 movie adaptation reigns supreme over all other screen depictions of Dracula. Even today, almost a century after its release, the film has the ability to impress. It exudes eeriness and suspense from practically every frame, despite it having been shot on a shoestring budget at a time when special effects were in their infancy. Bats flit around Castle Dracula, and in Stoker's novel, it was explicitly stated that the count had the ability to transform into such a flying creature. The author was not the first to advance the idea that vampires could change their form into that of a flying rodent (and other animals), but the notion of vampire-as-bat is now firmly entrenched in both popular culture and folklore.

The 1931 film Dracula *brought fame to the actor Béla Lugosi, who would sadly find himself typecast for the rest of his career.*

The existence of vampire bats as an entirely real species of animal was already well-known by the time *Dracula* reached the bookshelves. Vampire bats survive primarily on the blood of farm animals and livestock, not that of human beings. Once the vampire bat has bitten into its prey, its saliva seeps into the puncture wound made by the bat's fangs. This saliva contains a glycoprotein that acts as an anticoagulant, ensuring that the victim's blood does not clot; it continues to flow, enabling the bat to feed more easily. Showing a fine sense of appreciation for the vampire's popularity, scientists have officially named the glycoprotein Draculin. Research is currently underway to investigate Draculin's potential as part of a blood-thinning medication. Such drugs are prescribed to patients with irregular heartbeats and other risk factors for stroke and heart attacks to prevent them from forming blood clots. If Draculin does indeed turn out to be a benefit to humanity, the irony of its association with the Prince of Darkness himself, Count Dracula, is difficult to overstate.

Bats — of both the vampire and the garden variety — are carriers of rabies. Although relatively rare, the rabies virus is a particularly nasty and virulent disease that, if left untreated in an exposed human or animal victim, typically results in a lingering and excruciatingly painful death. It is estimated that a person dies of rabies every nine minutes somewhere on Earth.

Rabies is another disease that has helped to fuel stories of vampirism over the centuries. The signs and symptoms of rabies start out as being relatively subtle. Patients lose their appetite and develop headaches. They become nauseous, and as the body recognizes and then reacts to the presence of a virus, a fever is generated in order to make the environment as inhospitable as possible to the invader. This is easily mistaken for a flu or the common cold, unless the victim makes the connection between their new illness and having recently been bitten by an animal.

In the majority of patients, symptoms then progress to the next level. They become subject to mood swings, often trending toward belligerence and aggression. This can result in the rabid individual physically attacking others, even biting them in vulnerable places such as the neck. Those who are bitten are likely to develop rabies themselves.

Vampire bats, which survive by sucking blood from prey, are also feared as potential carriers of rabies.

As the disease begins to fester within the central nervous system, the sufferer may froth at the mouth and convulse. Hallucinations begin, causing them to thrash and claw at things that are not really there. Seizures are not uncommon in the later stages of the disease, which is likely to end with the death of the victim.

As the disease begins to fester within the central nervous system, the sufferer may froth at the mouth and convulse. Hallucinations begin, causing them to thrash and claw at things that are not really there.

It is easy to see why the out-of-control behavior of a rabid person could be misconstrued as being that of a vampire. The tendency to attack and bite, thereby passing on the infection to others, is a standout link between the two conditions. Pale, drooling, drenched in sweat, lunging at potential victims with teeth bared and hands clawing — the parallels are both obvious and striking. Rabies outbreaks certainly occurred in eastern and southeastern Europe during the times at which the vampire myth was gaining steam.

A rabid human may result from the bite of a rabid bat. If the two had been seen in close proximity to one another, it was an easy conclusion to later reach that the human was a vampire that had assumed the form of a bat . . . particularly when both reacted in a similarly aggressive way.

In today's world, medication exists to protect those who either have been bitten by a rabid animal or run a risk of being bitten by one (e.g., because they work with them). Rabies exposure prophylaxis isn't given routinely, but it is effective and readily available throughout the Western world.

Louis Pasteur pioneered rabies treatment in 1885, when he injected fluid containing dead rabies virus extracted from the spinal cord of a rabid rabbit into a nine-year-old boy. This seemed barbaric at the time, but Pasteur stuck to his guns and kept up the injections for two weeks. The child had been savaged by a rabid dog, and it seemed clear that without some sort of medical intervention (or an act of God), he was going to die.

Pasteur wasn't making this up as he went along. He had already experimented with this technique, using dogs as his basis for study. His confidence that it would also work in a human was proved well-founded. So effective was it that Pasteur's method is still used today.

It makes one wonder why the scientist heroes of some vampire movies don't try reversing the process by injecting the victim with doses of inactivated vampire blood. Food for thought, perhaps.

Thus far, we have examined medical aspects of the vampire phenomenon, examining historical instances of vampirism through the lens of disease. There is also a psychological component to be addressed. It is easy to overlook the fact that, depending on the perceptions of the individual, being a vampire could be a whole lot of fun.

There are basically two sides to the vampire coin. On the first side, the vampire gets to live forever — that is, assuming that its life is not cut short by stake, blade, or sunlight. The suave, sophisticated, and downright sexy vampire made popular by the film and TV industry is immensely attractive. Perhaps the tagline for the movie *The Lost Boys* (1987) said it best: "Sleep all day. Party all night. Never grow old. Never die. It's fun to be a vampire."

French microbiologist, chemist, and pharmacist Louis Pasteur (1822–1895) created the process of vaccination, which he used to find a treatment for rabies.

The Lost Boys introduces us to a gang of teenage-appearing vampires living the beach bum lifestyle in fictional Santa Carla, California. Clad in leather, riding motorcycles, flying through the air, and feasting on the blood of their enemies—the titular Lost Boys have an absolute blast when not sleeping the day away in their lair, where they hang from the ceiling like nesting bats.

An eternity of wine, song, and fun sounds great — at least until the vampire hunters get the better of them.

Bullying is a problem that has plagued generation after generation of children and teenagers. In 1985's *Fright Night*, we meet a character nicknamed "Evil Ed" (played by actor Stephen Geoffreys), who begins the movie aligned with its hero and protagonist, Charlie Brewster (William Ragsdale). Bullied for being a nerd, Evil Ed is a lonely, outcast kid whom many find to be relatable. This is the hook that the vampire Jerry Dandridge (Chris Sarandon) uses to turn Ed, convincing the teenager to become his familiar and accept the dark gift of vampirism.

"You don't have to be afraid of me," the vampire practically purrs when he traps Evil Ed with no possibility of escape. "I know what it's like being different. Only, they won't pick on you any more. Or beat you up. I'll see to that. All you have to do is . . . take my hand."

Ed does indeed take Dandridge's hand. By becoming a willing minion of the vampire, the teenager gains almost limitless power and security, something that almost every victim of bullying, no matter their age, would love to have.

The flip side of the coin is the view that vampirism is a curse, rather than a gift. Eternal life sounds great until you factor in the sheer loneliness that comes with it, living year after year and watching everybody that isn't also a vampire age and die while you remain the same. Then there's the boredom. Once a vampire has done everything and tried everything there is to do, living forever becomes an exercise in tedium and monotony. Even those all-night parties get old after a while.

Living in constant fear of the sun, which would burn you to a crisp, has to be an anxious backdrop to living for centuries. Also to be feared are those who hunt down and try to kill vampires. All it takes is one unlucky moment for the vampire, and it's a wooden stake through the heart and an agonizing death.

It seems that vampires have never been more popular, not just in the literary sense or in their dramatized version on screens both large and small; there is a large,

Immortality and immense strength might be benefits to being a vampire, but there are drawbacks, such as never being able to see the sun again without burning into a pile of ash.

thriving subculture of individuals who bring the vampire ethos into the everyday world. This community is steadily growing, as an increasing number of people reject the trappings of the 21st century and choose instead to embrace the realm of the undead.

As with any culture, different degrees of commitment and a broad range of approaches characterize those who choose to adopt the vampire lifestyle (should that be "undeathstyle" perhaps?). Some sleep all day and go about their lives only during the hours of darkness. Others hold down day jobs and careers, looking no different from anybody else, until they put their 9-to-5 on hold and adopt the mantle of their alternative life.

Many elect to dress in suitably dark and gothic garb, and the majority have fangs. These range from affordable over-the-counter prop fangs, at one end of the scale, all the way up to expensive, individually customized fangs that are meticulously crafted by artists or dental professionals. Many dentists will make fangs to fit over the would-be vampire's actual teeth only with the caveat that they will return shortly afterward to have them removed. These fangs are really little more than casual affectations, suitable for Halloween costumes, rather than for the true vampire aficionado.

For those who take the vampire lifestyle seriously, long-term caps can be sculpted from porcelain or composite resin. They fit over the underlying canine teeth and are to all outward appearances indistinguishable from the other teeth. Expensive to sculpt and to fit, once these fangs are emplaced, they are for all intents and purposes permanent — only a dentist can safely remove them.

Another key part of the vampire mythos is the consumption of human blood, and there are those self-professed vampires (termed *sanguinarians*) who follow this practice. By no means do all members of the subculture do this. Although screen vampires are known for pouncing on their victims and biting into their neck, in reality the vast majority of vampires act in accordance with a proper code of ethics. They only consume blood that has been voluntarily offered by willing donors who share similar beliefs.

It is important to note that many if not most sanguinarians do this because they are convinced that they have a genuine need for the blood of others; they are driven by the conviction that without it, they will grow weak, sicken, and possibly even die. Blood holds a great significance to them, which cannot be understated; some sanguinarians base the entirety of their lives and belief systems around the need for it.

Some self-professed vampires go so far as to be sanguinarians—that is, they will actually indulge in the practice of drinking blood, although the source of the blood is likely to be animal rather than human.

Rather than biting the donor, their blood can instead be extracted with a needle or sucked directly from a small, carefully made incision in the skin. There is a ritualistic aspect to such feedings that is based on mutual respect, something that the vampires that stalk the pages of novels and across the movie screen usually lack.

The 2014 movie *What We Do in the Shadows* spawned a television series of the same name (it ran from 2019 through 2024). Both incarnations of *WWDitS* are built around the conceit that a TV documentary crew is given access to film the daily — well, nightly — existence of a small group of vampires, who

The cast of the award-winning TV series What We Do in the Shadows *included (left to right) Harvey Guillén, Mark Proksch, Natasia Demetriou, Matt Berry, and Kayvan Novak. The dark humor of a show about a bunch of real vampires (and their assistant) living together in a house and being filmed for a documentary was full of gruesome laughs.*

are living together in a suitably gothic mansion. It offers an entertaining and creative slant on the world of vampires. In a talented cast, one standout is the character of Colin Robinson, played by actor Mark Proksch.

Rather than being a classic bloodsucker like his housemates, Colin Robinson is an energy vampire. He drains the life out of his victims not by sinking fangs into their veins and arteries but by sapping them of their life energy, leaving them listless, sleepy, or just plain bored. As a comedic character, Colin is pure gold; we've all met somebody like him at one point in our lives, the sort of person that is draining simply to be around. Turning him into an emotional vampire is a clever move on the part of the showrunners, yet it is not a truly novel idea. For decades, there have been those who believe that something similar exists in reality: the psychic vampire.

Sanguinarian vampires subsist on blood, a substance that has been irrefutably proven to exist. Nobody doubts its existence. The same cannot be said of the indefinable "life" or "life energy" on which psychic vampires claim to feed. Some psychic vampires believe they are able to consciously feed on the life energies of others, making a deliberate choice to do so — preferably with a consenting donor partner or partners — whereas other unwitting victims are unaware that any kind of energy transfer is taking place.

Once the psychic vampire has fed, their donor (the term "victim" becomes inaccurate once consent has been granted) often feels drained to the point of near exhaustion. No permanent harm seems to be done, however, and after resting for an appropriate period of time, the donor usually returns to their normal state of health and well-being.

It might be easy to leap to the conclusion that self-professed vampires are somehow emotionally imbalanced or may even have a degree of mental illness. The truth of the matter is very different. They are simply people, no more or less equal to any other members of society, who happen to adhere to a discrete, specific set of beliefs and culture norms that lie far beyond the mainstream. For those who adopt the vampire lifestyle, it goes far beyond the activities of LARPers (Live Action Role-Players) and cosplayers who like to dress up and attend events. It truly is a chosen lifestyle. Theirs is a community that is as valid and as deserving of respect and tolerance as any other. Its members believe unquestioningly that they are vampires, though it should be noted that the word "vampire" has a multitude of different interpretations.

The vampire community is a mixture of not just individuals but also of vampire collectives comprising those who share common values and beliefs. Such collectives are variously known as houses, courts, clans, temples, or covens (to list just some of the more prominent names) and can be found globally. As one might expect, New Orleans is a popular home for vampires — thanks in no small part to the fiction of Anne Rice, whose *Interview with the Vampire* (1976) and subsequent novels in the *Vampire Chronicles* series gave a much-needed shot in the arm to the literary vampire, which has been riding that wave of popularity ever since. Atlanta, Georgia, is also a vampiric hub. On opposite coasts of the United States, many vampires call New York City home, whereas, by comparison, Los Angeles barely makes the list.

The vampire organizations vary in the degree to which

they are willing to share with the outside world. Many are insular and guard their secrets. Others are willing to answer the questions of non-vampires with relative frankness, presumably with the intent of allowing for better understanding of who they are and what their values may be. Most have their own rules, regulations, and codes of ethics to which members are expected to adhere.

At the time of writing, their membership shows little sign of waning. Whatever anybody else may think, the "reality" of these self-proclaimed vampires is something in which they believe wholeheartedly, whether they are sanguinarians, psychic vampires, or a combination of the two. At the end of the day, their beliefs determine their reality.

Yet what of the traditional vampire? If we leave aside the explanations of disease, illness, and simple misinterpretation, how has the vampire stalked its way through the annals of history? To answer these questions, let's go back in time some 900 years to medieval times.

One of the great chroniclers of twelfth-century life was William of Newburgh (1136–1198), contemporarily known as William de Newburgh, whose writings gave future generations great insight into life in medieval England. He was a keen collector and documenter of stories; we have William to thank for some early accounts of vampires on Shakespeare's sceptered isle in his manuscript *Historia rerum Anglicarum*.[26] While fancying himself something of a historian, in many respects William of Newburgh could also claim the title of folklorist.

Located in the far north of England, the county of Northumberland lies on the border with Scotland. Within it is the market town of Alnwick, which is today known for its castle, a fortification and seat of power that dates back more than 900 years. In William of Newburgh's day, however, Alnwick Castle was said to be the hunting ground of a vampire — one that was created because of an accidental death.

Suspecting his wife of having an affair with another man, a powerful and influential retainer of the lord of the castle set out to catch her in the act one day. To that end, he sneakily climbed up to a concealed vantage point on a wooden beam in the roof of their bedroom, from where he could spy on his wife and her supposed lover. Perhaps he might finally obtain proof of his suspicions, and if so, woe betide them both.

Unfortunately for the retainer, not only did his suspicions prove to be correct — he caught his unsuspecting wife and her lover red-handed in the marriage bed — but the outraged cuckold slipped and fell from his perch, breaking his neck when he hit the ground. It remains unclear whether the fall is what ultimately killed him; William's account simply tells us that "being much shaken by the fall, and his whole body stupefied, he was attacked with a disease," and "the next night, destitute of Christian grace, and a prey to his well-earned misfortunes, he shared the deep slumber of death."

With the benefit of hindsight — not to mention hundreds of years' advancement in the medical sciences — a number of potential reasons for the man's death seem reasonable. The most likely explanation is that he sustained a closed head injury during the fall, resulting in an intracranial hemorrhage, bleeding inside the skull or the brain that killed him within 24 hours. If he struck his head on the ground, the possibility of a brain bleed is high.

Despite the severity of his injuries, the retainer nevertheless turned down the opportunity to make a confession and receive the Eucharist, a Christian's way of making things right with God. William tells us at the outset of his account that this was a man of "evil conduct" and "evil propensities." Perhaps this is the chronicler's way of explaining how it was that the retainer came to rise from the grave as a vampire. There is nothing in the source manuscript concerning the dead man being bitten by a vampire or having had any form of contact with such a creature.

As a servant of the castle's lord, the dead man was accorded the courtesy of a proper Christian funeral and the attendant rites — yet it was too late. He came back from the dead, wandering about Alnwick after night had fallen, and set about feasting on the blood of any hapless farm animals he could find. The vampire's next target would surely be the people themselves.

Terrified of the undead monstrosity that haunted them, the local populace made sure to be inside their homes before nightfall and stayed there until the sun rose the following morning. There was always ample warning of the vampire's approach, as it brought with it a foul and pungent stink that was redolent of death and

Alnwick Castle was built in the 11th century and is home to the current 12th Duke of Northumberland, Nathan Percy, and his family. The castle and its adjacent garden are host to over 500,000 visitors annually.

the grave. Even when the locals were cowering behind locked doors, there was no mistaking the arrival of the Alnwick Vampire. A pack of dogs ran behind the vampire, barking and howling.

The efforts to evade the attention of the vampire were only partially successful. People began to die, it is said, of what was most likely the plague. It should be noted that plague outbreaks were relatively common occurrences in medieval England, but to the people of Alnwick, the vampire must have appeared to be a harbinger of doom, in the same way that a comet in the night sky was believed to herald disaster and destruction. Afraid of what would happen if they fell afoul of either the vampire or the plague, some of the townsfolk decided that discretion was the better part of valor and left the town permanently to set up home in pastures new.

For those who remained behind, there was but one solution: the vampire must be destroyed. To that end, the townspeople plucked up their courage (and likely picked up a few sharpened farming implements as well) and made their way to the graveyard. The identity of the suspected vampire was well known to them. It was Palm Sunday, considered an especially holy day, and therefore an ideal day to do God's work.

With a priest leading them, they unearthed the grave of the former retainer and were greeted with a repulsive sight: the bloated, swollen corpse that seemed fattened on blood. The corpse bled profusely when the skin was punctured, which was all the evidence the people of Alnwick needed to confirm their suspicions. They also noticed that, rather than being buried the traditional six feet deep, the body was just a short distance beneath the ground.

Plagues were a recurring problem throughout Europe and the British Isles throughout the Middle Ages and into the Enlightenment, as this painting from 1665 depicts. Back in William of Newburgh's day, it was not uncommon to blame such tragedies on witches or, in this case, a vampire.

The destruction of a vampire can be a messy business. Rather than contaminate their own community any further, the mob dragged the blood-swollen corpse to the very edge of town, where they quickly gathered a large stack of wood to serve as kindling. Using a blunted spade, a particularly motivated individual smashed open the vampire's ribs until its heart was exposed within the now-gaping chest cavity. Reaching inside, he forcibly ripped the organ out of the vampire's chest.

Many believed — and some still do — that the heart of a vampire is where its power lies. The people of Alnwick tore apart the heart of what they believed was their undead tormentor. Only then did they consign the body to the burning pyre they had built for that purpose. Their fears and apprehension went up in flames alongside the remains of the Alnwick Vampire.

The term "vampire" didn't exist at the time and doesn't feature in Historia rerum Anglicarum, *but the term fits an undead or reanimated corpse that thirsts for the blood of the living, be it from livestock or humans.*

If William of Newburgh's account is to be believed, the plague deaths stopped, further cementing the belief that the vampire had been responsible for them.

A fascinating point of debate regarding the Alnwick Vampire case is the manner in which it all got started. The term "vampire" didn't exist at the time and doesn't feature in *Historia rerum Anglicarum,* but the term fits an undead or reanimated corpse that thirsts for the blood of the living, be it from livestock or humans. Folklore has long held that someone who dies by their own hand has the potential to become a vampire. It was also thought in some parts of the world that being buried without a formal funeral rite being performed could have the same effect, although this belief was by no means universal. The source for William of Newburgh's story appears to have been a clergyman, and it is therefore unsurprising that so much emphasis is placed on the mortally injured retainer not only being an evil man by nature but also dying without adequately preparing his soul in the traditional Christian manner.

It's clear from his writing that William had no idea why the dead man supposedly became a vampire either. His account is prefaced with the following:

> It would not be easy to believe that the corpses of the dead should sally (I know not by what agency) from their graves, and should wander about to the terror or destruction of the living, and again return to the tomb, which of its own accord spontaneously opened to receive them, did not frequent examples, occurring in our own times, suffice to establish this fact, to the truth of which there is abundant testimony.

In other words, twelfth-century England was a time and a place in which stories of vampires were not unheard of.

The vampire legend has accompanied the human race throughout its history. At times, usually when there was a spate of unusual deaths, claims began to circulate that a specific individual was to blame. These people were accused of being vampires.

One such story dates back to 1725–1726 and comes to us courtesy of a 1732 account titled *Visum et Repertum* by Johannes Flückinger, a military surgeon whose testimony should be considered credible. This type of report was commonly filed following official inquiries, and as we shall come to see, this particular case of vampirism would be investigated by the governmental authorities themselves.

It involves an Austrian soldier named Arnod, Arnold, or Arnont Paole, depending on which translation or version of the account one is reading. (We will stick with Arnod here.) While serving with the army overseas, Arnod is said to have encountered a vampire and to have been bitten. After his term of service was complete, he returned to his home in the Serbian village of Meduegna

Paole was a Serbian hajduk, a foot soldier common in Central, Eastern, and Southern Europe from the sixteenth through nineteenth centuries.

and set about exchanging a life of war for one of farm work. For a time, life was good. Arnod was his own boss, and although the labor was challenging, he got to enjoy the proceeds. The only thing missing was someone to share it with. That was remedied when Arnod asked a local girl to marry him. She said yes. It should have heralded the beginning of a happy life together.

A shadow hung over that life, however. Try as he might, since his return to civilian life, Arnod Paole was unable to shake the conviction that he was going to die before his time. This belief stemmed from a terrifying encounter he had with a vampire. After surviving the attack, he claimed to have tracked the creature back to its grave and, in an effort to protect himself from becoming a vampire, he ate dirt from the grave itself and then daubed his skin with the undead creature's blood.

That should have been the end of the matter, but the incident still haunted Arnod long after he had sailed away from Greek shores. His wife doubtless listened sympathetically but also reassured her husband that he no longer had anything to fear. After all, the vampire was now nothing more than charred ash. It no longer had the ability to harm him, and so it disappeared from the narrative into the mists of uncertainty.

Yet bad luck did indeed find Arnod Paole, who fell from a moving cart and broke his neck while working on his farm one day. The injury was fatal. His wife mourned. After an appropriate funeral, he was buried in the local graveyard. That should have been the end of it.

The sightings began a few weeks after his death. Villagers who knew Arnod well by sight claimed to have spotted him in and around town. Claims of a dead man walking were alarming, but matters took an even greater turn for the sinister when some of those same eyewitnesses began to die off under strange circumstances. Their deaths, four in total, involved no obvious injuries, and none of them were said to have been sick prior to meeting their unexpected and untimely ends. The only factor linking the deaths was their run-in with the shade of Arnod Paole.

Word began to spread around the township and its surroundings: Arnod Paole had risen from the dead as a vampire and was preying on those whom he encountered during his nocturnal wanderings. He was also seen feasting on sheep and other livestock. The decision was made to dig up his grave and to settle the matter once and for all. Once the last shovelful of earth was scraped from atop the dead man's coffin and the lid pried open, what they found inside came as no surprise. The corpse of Arnod Paole was suspiciously well-preserved, showing no signs of decomposition. The tinge of blood stained not only his mouth — a mouth that the men who now stared down into the grave suspected had been feeding on the blood of their neighbors — but had also streamed from every visible orifice. The casket interior was encrusted with it. Arnod's shroud had been soaked in it.

Not only had his fingernails and toenails grown, but the old sets were lying on the bottom of the casket. The dead man had somehow grown replacements.

Clearly, he was a vampire. There was only one remedy, the tried and trusted method of finishing off a vampire for good. A sharpened wooden stake had been brought along for exactly this purpose. With its pointed end resting directly beneath Paole's breastbone, it was hammered home into the vampire's heart, under the direction of a medical doctor who had accompanied the party to the graveyard. According to the written account, Paole's chest cavity gushed blood when the tip of the stake penetrated it. The ostensibly dead man was said to groan or to scream when the stake entered his body.

While the idea might have worked in previous centuries, vampire killing kits such as this one displayed at the Royal Armouries Museum in Leeds, United Kingdom, only date back to the last half of the twentieth century. This particular kit includes a pistol, wooden stakes, a mallet, and a crucifix, but no holy water.

For good measure, the vampire hunters set fire to Paole's remains and reburied them in the same grave. The four dead villagers who were believed to have been victims of Arnod Paole, and who were therefore considered to be at risk of turning into vampires themselves, received the same treatment. The locals were determined that never again would any of these dead rise from their graves to stalk unsuspecting members of their community.

For a while, these drastic measures appeared to have been successful. This wasn't the end of the story, however. Even with Paole long gone, five years later even more suspicious deaths began taking place. The townsfolk recognized the signs immediately. Yet again, they were being set upon by vampires. All of the deaths were mysterious and involved otherwise healthy individuals suddenly falling into a rapid state of decline and dying in great pain. There were even claims by those who were dying that they had been paid late night visits by their already dead neighbors. The stepdaughter of a military officer was found screaming late one night, claiming that she had just been attacked by a young man who had died months before. Weeks after the attack, she sickened and died.

No less an authority than the monarch himself ordered an inquiry, dispatching soldiers and physicians to investigate in his name.

As soon as this official vampire-hunting posse was hastily assembled, the cemetery was searched, grave by grave. In all, 17 recently deceased villagers were dug up and examined. Although a minority of corpses had decomposed appropriately, this time multiple bodies were found in the same condition that Arnod Paole had been in when his coffin was opened: they appeared to be freshly dead, and to be filled with blood that had not yet coagulated. They ranged in age from children to the elderly. According to those who

This 1851 lithograph shows villagers exhuming a vampire in order to kill it permanently. This was done by a stake through the heart or by beheading the creature.

had known them previously, some of the corpses actually looked healthier in death than they had during their lifetimes.

Each of those bodies met the same fate: staking, beheading, and burning. Rather than rebury the ashes in their graves, they were instead consigned to the fast-flowing river. It seemed to work, because the spate of strange deaths immediately stopped, never to resume again, as far as historians are aware.

At first glance, this account is a challenging one to explain away skeptically, not least because of the pedigree of the investigators. If the mysterious ailment that claimed so many lives was an infectious disease such as tuberculosis, why did it suddenly stop as quickly as it began — and moreover, why did it stop only when the graves of the alleged vampires were opened up and their bodies disposed of in the traditional manner?

Each of those bodies met the same fate: staking, beheading, and burning. Rather than rebury the ashes in their graves, they were instead consigned to the fast-flowing river. It seemed to work, because the spate of strange deaths immediately stopped, never to resume again....

At the Emperor's behest, the inquiry was attended by trained physicians and surgeons. These medical professionals would not only have been familiar with the signs and symptoms of the diseases that were prevalent at the time but also would have been as skilled at assessing the state of a corpse as anybody could possibly be. It is unlikely that they would have mistaken the cause of the spate of deaths for something they had dealt with many times before in their careers — or so one would think. Yet there are fundamental problems with some of their findings.

A case in point: one of the victims found to be in a state consistent with that of being a vampire was an infant just 8 days old when it had died. (No gender was documented in the report.) It had been buried for three months when the investigators opened its coffin. No matter how active one's imagination might be, it is difficult to conceive of how a vampire baby would be able to escape its coffin, claw through several feet of earth, and then hunt down a victim. How would it walk, let alone attack? Eight-day-olds have no teeth. The idea is patently ridiculous and should lead us to question the validity of the other medical observations that accompany it.

Although Johannes Flückinger was a meticulous scribe, the account of Arnod Paole's case was based on information told to him by the alleged vampire's neighbors. It was not something Flückinger witnessed himself. Tales do have a tendency to grow in the telling, so it is tempting to dismiss that particular case as being the product of deeply frightened and superstitious villagers who were living in fear for their lives. It was no minor thing to dig up the body of another human being — especially someone who was familiar to them — before staking and immolating it . . . and then to do the same to four others. Clearly, the townsfolk were sincere in their convictions that vampires were among them.

Harder to explain are the fingernails and toenails that dropped away from the hands and feet of several of the burials, only to be replaced with new ones. As mentioned previously, it is a fallacy that nails grow after death; they only appear to because the tissue surrounding them constricts and retracts. Once they fall off, however, there is no possibility that new nails could grow. There is no cellular activity in a dead body whatsoever in terms of growth. Assuming that Flückinger's observations are accurate, then he had a genuine mystery on his hands. The man was the chief medical officer of an infantry regiment. Unless evidence to the contrary should arise, then posterity owes him the presumption of professional competence.

Was Arnod Paole a vampire — and by extension, were those on whose blood he fed? What caused the second outbreak of apparent vampirism, years after Paole's "second death"?

Finally, were Johannes Flückinger and his fellow medical officers simply mistaken, or was something mysterious and sinister at work — something that could only be brought to an end by burning, decapitation, and a wooden stake?

A primary inspiration for Bram Stoker's seminal *Dracula* was the Wallachian prince Vlad Tepes, more commonly known as Vlad the Impaler because of his propensity for skewering captives on enormous wooden stakes. If you were an enemy of Vlad, it didn't pay to be taken alive. He was said to be so ruthless that he once ate dinner among a mass of writhing, screaming victims. One version of the story, most likely apocryphal, has Vlad casually dipping chunks of food in the oozing blood of dying men as though it were ketchup.

Vlad was, by all accounts, a butcher, in the days when butchery was practically a prerequisite for rulers and military commanders — the fifteenth century. Still, even by the savage standards of the time, he was reputed to be unnaturally brutal and cruel. Impalement was just one technique in his sadistic repertoire. When the mood took him, he might order victims to be burned alive or boiled to death in cast iron cauldrons. Stabbing, strangling, suffocation . . . Vlad enjoyed it all, and even his own subjects were not immune from his bloodthirsty attentions. He was no respecter of age or gender. Nobody was safe when the lust for violence was upon him.

A portrait of Vlad Tepes can be viewed at the Forchtenstein Castle in Burgenland, Austria.

Vlad proudly bore the soubriquet of Draculea, or "Son of the Dragon." (His father, Vlad II, was known as the Dragon.) In the language of Wallachia, the word *Dracula* meant "devil" — which was almost certainly why Stoker chose it for both the name of the central character in his novel and its title.

The Son of the Dragon met a predictably violent end, as such men often did, taken by surprise, cut down by his enemies, and immediately decapitated. Vlad's reign of terror may have been over, but his legend was eternal. The connection between this Wallachian warrior and vampirism is extremely tenuous, to say the least, but that hasn't stopped it from becoming firmly entwined in the Dracula mythos. Director Francis Ford Coppola made this theme a central focus of his 1992 retelling of the story, *Bram Stoker's Dracula,* starring Gary Oldman in the titular role.

The fictional Count Dracula and his real-life historical counterpart are now inextricably linked in the mass consciousness, to such a degree that it is no longer possible to separate them. Yet in reality, as monstrous a human being as Vlad Tepes was, he was certainly no vampire.

Countess Elizabeth Báthory of Ecsed was a Hungarian noblewoman who was accused and convicted of the horrific abuse and murders of hundreds of young women from 1590 to 1610. She spent the last four years of her life imprisoned in Castle Csejte in Slovakia.

Sometimes known as the female Dracula, Elizabeth Báthory had a similar predilection for human blood. Her motives for acquiring it, however, were very different from those of the Son of the Dragon. The Hungarian noblewoman sought to preserve her beauty by bathing in the blood of younger women, many of whom are said to have died in order for her to maintain her flawless complexion.

Born in 1560, Báthory was accused of sacrificing hundreds of innocent victims in order to satiate her desire for blood. If she had only confined her attentions to commoners and servants, the countess might have gotten away with it; yet when the daughters of other nobles began to go missing too, questions were asked, and fingers were pointed squarely in her direction.

The blood had been used to fill washbasins and bathtubs, in which the countess was alleged to have bathed, hoping to absorb the vitality and life energy of her victims.

In 1610, justice finally caught up with the so-called Blood Countess. When the authorities came for her, Elizabeth immediately threw her own servants to the wolves, arguing that they bore as much responsibility as she did for the deaths of the missing girls because they were the ones who had procured them for their mistress. It was Báthory's own loyal servants who had lured the girls in with false promises and had either stood by as she tortured and then killed them or actively participated in the murders and abuse. The countess was far too regal to sully her hands with body disposal, so that unpleasant task fell to the servants as well.

The court that was convened to judge the case was sympathetic to this argument. The servants were all put to death. Their mistress got off lightly, her punishment being simple confinement to her castle for the remainder of her days. Elizabeth Báthory died there, aged 54. History has not been kind to her reputation, and perhaps deservedly so . . . and yet some historians have made the argument that she might have been framed, the victim of a smear campaign artfully orchestrated against her by powerful and influential rivals. It is unlikely that the truth will ever be known.

Indian Vampires

Many other cultures have their own equivalent of the vampire. In India, there has long been a belief in female vampires known as *Chedipe*. Think of them as a cross between an undead witch and a vampire. According to

A Chedipe is an undead woman who, in Indian folklore, often rides a large tiger. She sneaks into houses and sucks blood out of men's toes.

lore, the Chedipe is the result of a woman dying a death that was considered to be premature or unnatural, such as suicide or while giving birth to a child. Some versions added the possibility that "unclean" or "impure" women, such as sex workers or those considered to be promiscuous, also had the potential to return from the grave as a Chedipe.

Taking a closer look at the Chedipe legends, it is difficult not to view them through the lens of a patriarchal tool of oppression against women. By incorporating elements of a morality tale into Chedipe lore, storytellers could weave tantalizing and terrifying stories of tiger-riding, blood-sucking undead women that were meant to scare girls and younger women onto what was considered to be the straight and narrow. (*"Be a good and pure girl or else you might end up becoming a Chedipe . . . "*)

There are also similarities between the vampire and the succubus, a type of female demon that was thought to engage in sexual intercourse with unsuspecting males when the men were asleep. (The male equivalent would be the incubus.) The Chedipe was believed to magically gain access to homes after dark and would choose a male victim from whomever she found within. The creature would then feast on his blood while he slept and, if she felt so inclined, would have sexual intercourse with him. Why? Because, some versions of the story maintain, this would cause great friction between the husband and wife involved, and the Chedipe was also capable of feeding on those negative emotions — the more intense, the better. The parallels with the concept of a psychic vampire are obvious.

If this sounds like every man's dream, it should be noted that the Chedipe made return visits, always at night, and drank the blood of her chosen victim until he finally died. For some unfathomable reason, rather than go for the juicy jugular vein in the man's neck, the Chedipe instead chose to feed on blood from his feet.

There are two ways to look at the Chedipe story. On the one hand, they can be seen as one of many means by which a male-dominated society could control females — a cautionary tale spun with the purpose of keeping women "in line." On the other hand, especially when viewed from the perspective of the 21st century, the Chedipe might alternatively be seen as a means of female empowerment. These literal ladies of the night rode into town *on a tiger*, stark naked, kicked down the doors (either metaphorically or literally), and then set about preying on the male authority figures of the household. Chedipe were also thought to possess super strength and magical powers. That sounds like a much more attractive proposition than the life of quiet subservience that was imposed on most females at the time.

As for the Chedipe seducing the aforesaid male and having sex with him, with the intent of creating inter-marital strife and distress, one is forced to wonder how many men blamed these vampire-witches for arguments with and possibly abuse of their wives. The Chedipe would have made for a convenient scapegoat at a time when men ruled the roost and women were often made to take the blame for things that were not their fault.

Lilith

Hollywood, horror fiction, and long-standing myth have offered up several candidates for the identity of the very first vampires. Ancient Greeks, Egyptians, and even denizens of the lost city of Atlantis have all been proposed for the role by different creators. Tossing out the traditional origin story of the world's most famous vampire, the Patrick Lussier–directed movie *Dracula 2000* (2000) revealed that Dracula was in fact Judas Iscariot, doomed to restlessly wander the Earth forever as a punishment for having betrayed Jesus Christ. It's a fresh and interesting take on the Dracula mythos, but it wasn't the first time that vampires were connected with biblical times.

This dubious honor goes to Lilith, regarded by some (though by no means all) as having been the first wife of Adam. *Wife* may, in fact, be too formal a word; it may be more accurate to say that the two of them were mates.

Stories of Lilith predate the writing of the Bible, in which she is only referred to once, and even then with minimal detail. In the early accounts, she is depicted as having been created at the same time as Adam, made from the same dust God used to make him, and she therefore quite rightly regarded herself as being on an equal footing with him. Adam did not agree. Apparently, neither did God, because Lilith was either cast out of the Garden of Eden or left of her own accord, depending on which version of the story you're reading. At least one instance of the myth has Lilith being punished for refusing to lie submissively beneath Adam during sexual congress.

After leaving paradise, she set about fornicating with a host of demons, bearing many demonic offspring as a consequence. Unwilling to tolerate Lilith's disobedience, God sent three of his angels after her. Their message to Lilith was unequivocal: go back to Adam and toe the line or face the consequences — those consequences being the cold-blooded murder of her children.

Lilith was unrepentant, and the angels were uncompromising. They set about killing her children by the hundredfold. Driven into a fury, Lilith set out for revenge, hunting for newborn babies, swooping down on great bat-like wings and killing them in their cribs. She was said to strike only at night, usually when her victims were sleeping. It is a mission of vengeance that, tradition holds, continues to this day, and protective amulets are still placed above the cribs of children in order to ward off Lilith's vengeance.

A fresco in the basilica of Santa Maria Novella in Florence, Italy, depicts Adam protecting a child from the evil clutches of Lilith.

The bat wings are only part of Lilith's connection with vampirism. Mythology variously claims that she either feasts on helpless babies or sups their blood. Her bad rap doesn't end there; other legends cast Lilith as a demoness and introduce a sexual component into the mix by bestowing succubus-like characteristics and behavior upon her. Her intention is to procreate with the hapless male victims while they sleep, becoming inseminated and birthing half-human, half-demon offspring to replace those who were slaughtered by God's trio of angels.

As with the Chedipe, it takes little imagination to see the story of Lilith as being anti-female propaganda, and her horrific story as another morality tale, a story that demonstrates the dangers of being disobedient to one's husband. "Be more like Eve [Adam's second wife]," seems to be the lesson. As written in biblical scripture, Eve was far more agreeable and less willful than her predecessor. Of course, that didn't stop Eve and her husband from ultimately being cast out of the Garden of Eden anyway, so perhaps a little disobedience at the correct time could be a good thing.

Fortunately, Lilith's tarnished reputation has undergone something of a renaissance in modern times, and there are now adherents to some belief systems that treat her as a goddess rather than a vampire-succubus-demon, actively praying to her and making offerings in Lilith's name.

To some, she remains a vampiric creature of darkness; to others, a source of inspiration, free-spirited and independent, unwilling to bend the knee when threatened.

Flying Vampires

Vampiric creatures don't necessarily have to adopt a human form on a 24/7 basis. Take the *Wakwak*, a huge flying creature of the night that hails from the Philippines. By day, Wakwaks can appear to be regular human beings, walking, talking, and acting exactly like us. They have no fear of sunlight and are said to fit in easily with the general population, going undetected during the daytime hours.

Once the sun goes down, it's a different story. The Wakwak grows a set of enormous bat-like wings and takes to the night skies in search of prey. Mirroring both Lilith and the Chedipe, Filipinos perceive the Wakwak to be female and believe that in its human form, the creature will appear in the guise of a woman.

Swooping out of the darkness, Wakwaks are messy eaters. The somewhat refined method of sucking blood from the neck is not for them; instead, the Wakwak will use its talons and fangs to shred its victim and consume their blood and innards in a savage feeding frenzy.

Although it's tempting to write off the Wakwak story as nothing more than legend, sightings were being made as recently as 2023. The Island Garden City of Samal is divided into three districts, the northernmost of which is the Babak District. One night in January 2023, multiple eyewitnesses spotted a huge birdlike creature soaring through the sky above a residential neighborhood. According to a report made by the news website *Sunstar.com.ph* ("Wakwak spotted in Samal?"), local residents who saw it were "in a frenzy." One eyewitness noted that it made the sound "*wak wak wak*." Others found the story difficult to accept, dismissing it as a hoax or a case of mistaken identity — an ordinary bird, albeit a large one, being misidentified. There was no mention of the supposed Wakwak pouncing on any victims and ripping them to shreds. At the very least, the episode demonstrates that belief in the vampiric bird is still alive and widespread in the 21st century.[27]

Filipino culture certainly embraces its vampire lore. In addition to the Wakwak, there is the even more terrifying *Manananggal*. The two creatures bear striking simi-

The Manananggal of the Philippines looks like a bat-winged vampire and has the additional bizarre ability to separate its torso from the rest of its body.

larities; the Manananggal is also portrayed as a woman, usually an exceptionally beautiful one, but one that possesses a set of enormous bat wings. A key difference is that the Manananggal can literally separate itself into two halves, leaving its legs behind while the winged upper half takes flight.

Although the Manananggal is said to be perfectly willing to drink the blood of men, its target of choice is pregnant women — more specifically, their unborn babies. The creature has a long, hollow, prehensile tongue that extends from its mouth and snakes out in search of a female on whom to feed. Once it punctures the flesh of her abdomen, the Manananggal's tongue devours the fetus and then consumes her other organs for dessert — after liquefying them first, using a potent liquid pumped through the tongue.

It's a gruesome and graphic twist on the vampire lore, but there may be a very specific purpose that the Manananggal stories serve: whenever a woman lost a child during pregnancy, rather than deal with the awful fact that sometimes very bad things happen for no obvious reason, blaming the Manananggal for the cruel loss may have been easier to accept. The same train of thought has

"Aswang" is a catch-all term in the Philippines for ghouls, witches, vampires, and other human-like demons.

been applied to demons for centuries: they have been used as a catch-all umbrella to explain away tragedies and disasters both large and small. For the people of the Philippines, tales of the evil Manananggal may paradoxically bring comfort at a very stressful time of their lives. It is therefore not surprising that such creatures have a rich tradition in Filipino culture. Taken as a group, they are referred to as *Aswang*, basically a melting pot of vampires, werewolves, zombies, ghouls, shape-shifters, and other monsters, to form a potpourri of reasons to fear the darkness.

The year 2023 seems to have been a banner year for simmering Aswang fears to start boiling over in the Philippines. In February, one month after the Wakwak stories began circulating in Samal, sightings of a Manananggal took place in the city of Talisay. They were reported by the local media ("Manananggal in Talisay City? Public told to refrain from spreading unverified reports." — *Cebu Daily News*, February 10, 2023). In order to prevent panic, the police chief stepped in and reassured the residents of the city that there was nothing to be alarmed about.[28]

Police officers conducted an investigation to follow up on the reports but found nothing substantial to back them up. The scare originated with two girls who claimed they saw the winged monster perching on a rooftop next to their home. Detectives interviewed the owner of the home, who insisted that he neither saw nor heard anything out of the ordinary . . . apart from two nearly hysterical girls, that is.

Although it seems reasonable to assume that stories of Aswang, Manananggal, and other creatures of the night are harmless, they can sometimes have unforeseen —

and very tragic — consequences. Such was the case in 2011, when 29-year-old construction worker Efren Matedios brutally murdered his 6-year-old niece in cold blood. Matedios lived in a village located in a rural area outside the city of Cebu.

The killing of a child is always a terrible thing, yet the murder of Lara Mae Concodes was exceptionally horrific. After removing all of her clothes, Matedios stabbed her repeatedly, slicing her body open while she was still alive, before carving out her internal organs . . . and eating them.

Those who knew Efren Matedios were horrified and completely blindsided, telling journalists that he was "a good man with no vices," according to a report by Jucell Marie P. Cuyos ("I was killing a manananggal" — *Inquirer.net,* May 25, 2011).[29] He presumably showed no signs of being the homicidal maniac that he ultimately turned out to have been; he was described as "a doting uncle" of Lara Mae. Police officers who went to Madedios's home found him to be completely naked and unrepentant.

Efren Matedios showed not even the slightest shred of remorse. In fact, when interviewed he told detectives he was acting for the greater good, believing that his niece was a Manananggal and must therefore be destroyed. To that end, he had salted the dead girl's organs as a measure of preventing the Manananggal from returning to life — though why he then opted to consume them is unclear.

The house in which the murder took place became known as a place to avoid. Further fueling the fears of supernatural involvement, rumors began to circulate that the formerly genteel Efren Matedios had been cursed by a witch a few weeks before the killing.

The house in which the murder took place became known as a place to avoid. Further fueling the fears of supernatural involvement, rumors began to circulate that the formerly genteel Efren Matedios had been cursed by a witch a few weeks before the killing.

After being charged with murder, Matedios stuck to his story. It seems clear that this was a case of a folklore-triggered child killing. If Efren Matedios was telling the truth, then a previously undiagnosed mental illness was combined with a belief in Manananggal, leading to a tragic and apparently unforeseeable outcome.[30]

Vampires in Africa

Evoking images of mobs with pitchforks and burning torches, gangs of wannabe vampire hunters dispatched patrols seeking the undead in the southeast African country of Malawi as recently as 2017. Rumors of vampire activity were rife in the region, leading the populace to take up weapons and attempt to fight back. When they captured a suspected vampire, the mobs wasted no time in carrying out an execution. The situation was considered to be so dire that the United Nations withdrew its relief support personnel for fear that they too might be targeted by these vampire hunters.

This was nothing new in the southern regions of Malawi, where vampires, witchcraft, and dark magic were considered realities of everyday life. An intense fear of vampires had instigated civil unrest in 2002, when at least one individual had been killed and several others wounded because they were believed to be vampires. Strangers were looked upon with intense suspicion, sometimes being beaten or chased out of town. One man was stoned to death.[31]

An intense fear of vampires had instigated civil unrest in 2002, when at least one individual had been killed and several others wounded because they were believed to be vampires. Strangers were looked upon with intense suspicion, sometimes being beaten or chased out of town. One man was stoned to death.

In an effort to restore order, the authorities imposed a 5 P.M. curfew, making sure that civilians were off the streets before sundown. Police officers made more than 140 arrests, in the process dispersing mobs who were setting up unlawful roadblocks in an attempt to catch the vampires. For some, the efforts to restore order came too late. Eight people were killed before the hysteria subsided and a sense of normalcy returned to the region.

Matters erupted again three years later, in 2020, when another spate of vigilante killings took place. Five more lives were lost. Law enforcement officers were forced to intervene aggressively when an angry crowd set upon a group of field researchers from the National Statistics Office. Obtaining blood samples from members of the public had been part of the governmental employees' remit. This led to the misperception that they were vampires, and it was only with the deployment of tear gas canisters that police officers were able to break up the mob that wanted to kill them. Thirty-seven people were arrested.[32]

A Welsh Tragedy

It would be a mistake to assume that pathologically strong belief in vampires exists only in developing countries. In 2001, a sadistic and brutal crime shocked the nation of Wales in the United Kingdom. Mabel Leyshon was 90 years old and was by all accounts a kind and gentle soul who did harm to nobody. Sometime around November 25, 2001, 17-year-old Mathew Hardman broke into the home where she lived alone and murdered her. Mabel was hard of hearing and almost certainly never heard the youth breaking the glass in the back door and forcing entry into her house. When she finally realized what was happening, there was no way the frail senior citizen would have been capable of defending herself from the frenzied attack to which the teenager subjected her.

Hardman, an art student, had developed an obsession with vampires that was taken to dangerous levels. Months before the murder, he had begged a 16-year-old exchange student from Germany to bite his throat in the belief that the student was a vampire and wanted her to turn him into one as well. Hardman made the same request of a police officer, who responded by arresting him for breaching the peace after he hit himself in the face with sufficient force to draw blood.

Mabel Leyshon's body was discovered when a volunteer for the Meals on Wheels service came to her home to deliver food. She had been stabbed 22 times. Two fireplace pokers were arranged in the shape of a cross at the dead woman's feet. Her heart had been cut out of her chest, encased in pages from a newspaper, and then put into a saucepan, which was placed on a silver platter alongside her body.

At his subsequent trial for murder, it was revealed that Mathew Hardman had consumed some of Mabel's blood from the same saucepan, in what was most likely an attempt to bestow vampiric powers upon himself. He wanted above all else to become a vampire, and he was willing to kill an innocent woman if that was what it took to attain his goal.

Police officers obtained a warrant to enter Hardman's home and search for evidence. They found a trove of vampire memorabilia, including many books and movies. The teenager's browser history was replete with visits to vampire-related websites.[33]

Mathew Hardman denied culpability for the murder, insisting that he had never once set foot inside Mabel Leyshon's house. The fact that traces of his DNA were found inside determined that to be a lie, as did the discovery of a knife that contained traces of Mabel's blood. The innocent woman had been an easy target for him. As her paper boy, Hardman had ample opportunity to scope out her house and to plan his crime in advance.

At the conclusion of his trial, the jury found Mathew Hardman's flimsy denial to be unconvincing and found him guilty of murder. He was sentenced to be jailed for a period of at least 12 years.

The duality of humanity's fascination with and fear of the vampire is unlikely to abate for the foreseeable future. While countless hours of entertainment and inspiration have been derived from our cultural love affair with these creatures of the night, so too have horrific crimes and acts of cruelty been committed on their behalf. The case of Mathew Hardman serves as a chilling reminder that great evil does not necessarily emerge from the darkness with gleaming fangs and supernatural powers.

Sometimes it wears an all-too-human face.

By their very definition, cryptids and monsters are strange and unusual creatures. Even when measured by these standards, however, few are stranger in appearance and overall gestalt than the very curious case of the Fresno Nightcrawlers.

In 2008, a bizarre piece of security camera footage caused a sensation across the internet. Grainy and low resolution, the film clip showed what looked a lot like a pair of skinny, disembodied legs or trousers walking across the camera's field of vision. There were no feet, no arms, no torso or head. No eyes or mouth. Just two ghostly white legs that appeared wispy and flowing, as though they were clad in a pair of oversized silk pantaloons. The first figure was soon followed by a second.

It didn't take long for the video to go viral, spreading from its filming location in Fresno, California, across the entire planet. Subsequent analysis of the video led to the estimation that the Nightcrawlers were about the same size as a smallish adult, approximately five feet tall. Originally filmed by a surveillance camera, the video clip that is still circulating on YouTube and other media sites today is challenging to access because it is actually a second-generation copy of the original video, recorded from a screen that was replaying the master footage.

Despite its relative recency, the full facts of the case are by no means clearly established. The most common version maintains that, around 12:45 a.m. on November 5, 2007, the owner of the footage, identified only as "Jose," awoke in the night to the sound of his dog barking at some kind of disturbance. Jose checked his security camera system and, lo and behold, a new cryptid was added to the pantheon.[34]

In the hope of finding answers regarding the identity of the outlandish sighting, Jose contacted paranormal investigator Victor Camacho and submitted his footage for analysis. Camacho put boots on the ground, checking out the scene itself and the CCTV camera system Jose had installed. He found no evidence to suggest that Jose was attempting to mislead him.

Predictably, opinion as to whether the video was genuine or not was strongly divided, with some calling it a deliberate hoax, accomplished using either practical puppetry or computer-generated imagery. Proponents of the hoax hypothesis pointed to the fact that the grainy and distorted nature of the film-of-a-film was of sufficiently low resolution to potentially hide a multitude of tricks. On the opposite side of the fence, supporters of Jose and his video claimed that it showed no obvious signs of fraud and seemed to defy all rational explanation.

One of the key points regarding the Fresno Nightcrawlers is their cartoonish appearance. The being, for lack of a better term, looks almost as if it was drawn by an artist — a cartoon character, rather than something solid and substantial. Its surreal way of moving has led some to conclude that there is an air of the otherworldly associated with the anomalous subject of the footage.

Had this been the only appearance of the Fresno Nightcrawlers, the story would have ended there, as little more than a footnote in the chronicles of the weird. In 2011, however, another pair of Nightcrawlers — or could it have been the same ones? — turned up in a video that was taken in California's Yosemite National Park, located about 60 miles north of Fresno. Crucially, it's claimed that the owner of the camera in this case was not a member of the public; it was park security personnel. The footage was captured on security cameras and depicts two white figures that look and act very similarly to those recorded in Fresno four years prior.

Reviewing the footage today, it is clear that the second of the two figures is either significantly smaller than the

An artist's concept of a Nightcrawler in pursuit.

first, farther away, or both. There is a definite "person walking carefully on stilts" vibe, which is indeed one of the potential explanations that has been proposed for the video: human beings wearing white sheets, picking their way deliberately from left to right with exaggerated strides.

Videos of a similar nature began popping up on You-Tube. In stark contrast to the originals, the newer crop was often so clear, they were almost too good to be true — which may well have been the case.

There is no question that some or all of the Fresno Nightcrawler videos that proliferated after the original footage went viral in 2008 could have been faked. No longer were the Nightcrawlers restricted to California; videos have since come in from across the United States and a number of overseas countries. The lion's share has been definitively exposed as hoaxes; indeed, some were created with the express purpose of demonstrating that the Nightcrawler effect *could* be hoaxed with relative ease. However, that does not necessarily mean that *all* of the footage is fraudulent. The Fresno and Yosemite films are still analyzed and debated to this day.

In spite of their somewhat ephemeral appearance and behavior, Fresno Nightcrawlers are among the few cryptids out there that do not tend to evoke a sense of fear. On the contrary, they have a significant fan base that supports a cottage industry of creative merchandise ranging from plushies to clothing and everything between. The various artistic interpretations of the Nightcrawlers lean strongly on the cuteness factor, which goes some way toward explaining their popularity.

"They're coming to get you, Barbra!"

It's a line we all know from a movie that's iconic: the 1968 ultra-low-budget *Night of the Living Dead*. Directed by the then up-and-comer George A. Romero, the film put zombies on the map in a major way, not just spawning a cavalcade of sequels and spin-offs over the years but inspiring countless imitators, homages, remakes, and even outright rip-offs.

Made for just $114,000, smaller than the catering budget for some movies today, *Night of the Living Dead* was shot in black and white, which only adds to the film's ever-present sense of eeriness and dread.

Scenes of the living dead shambling through graveyards and across the grounds of the central location, an isolated farmhouse, have since become iconic. Audiences were shocked to see them ripping into the flesh of living victims, and although the movie's monochrome appearance reduced the gore factor slightly, subsequent zombie movies would feature gallons of blood spurting and jetting across the screen in glorious Technicolor.

In the decades that followed, the zombie has lumbered its way into the pop culture mainstream and taken root there. Other *Dead* movies and their ilk did well, yet today there is nothing comparable to the entertainment juggernaut that is *The Walking Dead*. Based on a series of comic books by Robert Kirkman, *The Walking Dead* has now expanded into a bona fide universe all of its own, with hundreds of TV episodes spread across multiple

George A. Romero's 1968 movie, Night of the Living Dead, *remains a low-budget classic to this day.*

different series that are almost impossible to keep up with.

Clearly, the zombies are here to stay, but why are we so fascinated by them?

First, the shambling, flesh-hungry living dead hold up a mirror and invite us to consider our own mortality. The majority of people have not seen a dead body in real life. The closest most people get to that experience is seeing photographs of corpses and cadavers on the internet. Outside of the funerary and medical professions, there is a pervasive sense that dead bodies should remain behind closed doors. This stands in stark contrast to the days in which wakes were held in homes, with family members gathering around the open casket of the deceased, socializing and sharing stories about the dead person before the funeral took place. We as a society have grown increasingly uncomfortable with death and the dead . . . yet the flip side of that coin is a fascination with the subject, which is in some ways healthy and in others somewhat macabre.

Into this milieu of curiosity staggers the zombie, depicted with artistic proficiency that only a multimillion-dollar TV and movie budget can provide. Resurrected dead bodies pursue the protagonists with grasping claws and snapping jaws, snarling and biting in their insatiable quest to consume the flesh of the living — who, in turn, are usually heavily armed with bullets, blades, and other weapons, hacking, slashing, and shooting their way through the undead horde in a miasma of blood, gore, and exposed vital organs. When the living, ostensibly the good guys, survive to fight another day, we are not just watching a battle between "good" and "evil" play out on our screens. We are watching the survivors literally triumph over death, albeit only temporarily. It is a reassuring and cathartic experience.

We live in times that seem increasingly dystopian, and a part of the appeal of zombie apocalypse shows is in imagining how we might personally cope with the end of the world. The possibility of environmental catastrophe leading to societal collapse is all too real, and far more terrifying than anything George A. Romero could ever dream up. Fighting across the ruins of a zombie-infested America, on the other hand, is just ridiculous enough that we know it is impossible, yet simultaneously credible enough that most of us can suspend our disbelief long enough to enjoy the ride. It's a paradox, but a fulfilling one. If the dead truly did begin clawing their way out of the grave, how would we personally measure up? Where is the first place we would go? For many British people, the resounding answer, as given in *Shaun of the Dead* (2004), the comedy pastiche of Romero's classic, was unequivocal: the pub. Locking oneself in the local watering hole and enjoying a few beers until "this all blows over" is a zombie survival strategy that resonates with those who live in the land of warm ale and fish and chips.

Human beings are, by our very nature, inherently capable of violence. We're reminded of this fact every time a road rage incident takes place, in which a seemingly mild-mannered individual gets cut off in traffic and suddenly snaps, provoked by a usually minor incident that becomes the proverbial straw that broke the camel's back. That violence lies within all of us. It is buried a little deeper in some than in others, but it is always there, lurking, ready to surface when conditions are right.

In a civilized society, one governed by a code of laws, there are consequences attached to violent behavior. Few of us want to spend time in prison, so when we're provoked, we tend to swallow the perceived insult, grit our teeth, and walk away. But who among us hasn't fantasized at least once about getting our own back? The primal urge to lash out at those who we believe have mistreated us is never entirely absent, no matter how calm and rational we might be. Obviously, we cannot (and should not) go about our lives reacting violently to slights and mistreatment. We all know that it is wrong, not least because human lives have value.

Not so the lives of zombies. When the flesh-eating terrors stagger in search of living humans to terrorize, it's open season on the living dead. Audiences cheer every time a zombie is decapitated, has its brains blown out, or "dies" a second time at the hands of an intended victim. The more creative the kill, the louder the audience cheers. It is a form of acceptable violence, based on the premise that the laws that govern human-on-human assault no longer apply where zombies are concerned.

These movies also represent a safe avenue for us to experience fear, similar to the way riding a fast-moving roller coaster allows the participant to experience an adrenaline-fueled thrill ride, safe in the knowledge that the danger is an illusion. It can be cathartic. No matter how much CGI blood splashes across the screen, no matter how many latex prosthetic limbs and organs are torn from the actors' bodies, deep down we know that it's a performance, not reality. The very idea of a reanimated corpse seeking the flesh of the living is patently unbelievable, for a multitude of reasons: rotted flesh and atrophied muscles; a shriveled, dead brain without the slightest hint of electrical activity, with no means of sending signals through what remains of the central nervous system; long-dead cells that are incapable of either generating or using energy. And even if the zombie somehow *could* gets its clawed hands on some living meat, it would have no way of consuming and processing any food.

One might ponder the appeal of zombies in movies and TV shows, but it can be viewed as a cathartic portrayal of guilt-free violence. It is permissible to kill zombies because they are already dead—and they are dangerous—so playing out one's violent tendencies on them is socially acceptable.

To make a long story short, once you're dead . . . you're dead for good. In the physical sense of the term, at least.

An artificially created virus seems like a more credible origin story for zombies, but is there anything akin to the zombies — of either the fast or the slow varieties — to be found in the real world?

Let's start with the term itself. There's some discussion over the origination of the word "zombie," but many researchers relate it to both the African word *nzambi*, which is synonymous with the souls or spirits of the dead, and the Haitian Creole word *zonbi*. The words "zombi" and "zombie" have been used interchangeably, though the former seems to predate the latter by many years. Zombis appear in nineteenth-century North American literature and became better known in the 1920s and 1930s when they started popping up in movies such as the Béla Lugosi–starring *White Zombie* (1932). The schlock horror film is set on a Haitian plantation and features the creation of zombies by using a special potion.

A drawing of a zombie in a sugar cane field in Haiti.

The zombie (we'll maintain that spelling going forward, for the sake of consistency) had long been an established part of Haitian cultural belief when the U.S. Marines splashed ashore on the island in 1915. The U.S. military went on to occupy Haiti for the next 19 years. Service personnel stationed there heard stories of zombies, and when they returned home, they took those scary tales along with them. In 1929 the author W. B. Seabrook's nonfiction Haiti travel memoir *The Magic Island* was published in the United States; it served to further stoke interest in all things zombie-related because of passages that referred to zombies being created and exploited for purposes of manual labor in the fields. Among other things, the book served as a source of inspiration for *White Zombie,* which was released three years later.

A practitioner of the magical arts in Haiti is known as a *bokor* or *caplata,* depending on their gender. Both are believed to be capable of performing acts of good and evil magic, and thus are held in high regard and, sometimes, no small degree of fear. They are able to zombify a living human being using a process that combines magical ritual with exotic pharmacology. Being forced to become a zombie is a terrifying prospect to many Haitians, a dreaded form of living death that is spent in servitude to the bokor or caplata responsible for creating them — in effect, a prison sentence from which the only escape is actual death.

There are said to be several ways of making a zombie. One method involves selecting a target and creating a special concoction of chemicals that is ground down with a pestle and mortar into a fine powder. This can then be slipped into the victim's food or drink without their knowledge or consent.

What happens next is horrifying. The victim's vital signs enter a state of rapid decline, with the heart rate, blood pressure, and other signs of life diminishing to undetectable levels. To all intents and purposes, they appear to be dead and may be pronounced dead by medical professionals. Yet the soon-to-be-zombie is still alive, but paralyzed. Behind their closed eyelids and lifeless face, the bokor's victim is cognizant of everything that is going on around them. They are able to think and, more unnerving still, actually feel. It is said to be akin to a state of suspended animation or hibernation, albeit with the individual being somewhat aware and semi-conscious throughout.

It's hard to imagine a more terrifying experience, yet Western medicine has its parallels. The medications rocuronium and succinylcholine are neuromuscular blockers that are used to paralyze patients quickly and effectively. One use for them is when an airway needs to be quickly and aggressively managed, and the patient is both conscious and struggling. Administering a bolus of rocuronium or succinylcholine through an IV renders the patient limp and unable to move, but crucially, they are not sedated — they retain awareness and can feel everything that's going on, not just around them but also what is happening to them.

Having a breathing tube inserted into one's throat is an extremely distressing and traumatizing experience, which is why any doctor, nurse, or paramedic worth their salt will administer a sedative alongside the neuromuscular blocker. If you're being intubated, you want the lights to go out before the tube enters your mouth. To make matters worse, there's no way of warning the medical team that you're conscious. There's nothing to do but lie there, unmoving, unblinking, not even breathing . . . and simply suffer.

Something similar is said to be happening during the

process of making a zombie. The hapless victim appears to be dead. Clearly, they cannot actually be dead. Even in a low metabolic state, the body requires a certain amount of oxygen and nutrients in order to survive, and if the cells receive them, the victim enters a hibernation-like state. At this point, according to many accounts, the zombie is buried — alive. The bokor or caplata waits patiently for the grieving mourners to depart, and then goes to the cemetery, usually in the dead of night, to dig up and take possession of the zombie.

The magical component involves ritual practices intended to bind the zombie's spirit or soul to the bokor's will. This can take several days and often incorporates special potions that have been prepared in advance. Controlling the zombie involves a combination of psychological pressure and the administration of potent drugs that render the patient borderline catatonic and extremely zombielike. They are still capable of carrying out assigned tasks such as picking fruits and vegetables for hours on end under the hot sun, without complaint or resistance. (This is not to say that the zombie possesses machine-like strength or stamina; they must still eat, drink, and sleep, just as any other human being has to.) There's a major component of conviction driving the zombies of Haiti, a tenet of the vodou (a.k.a. voodoo) belief system in which most Haitians are raised. Vodou is more than a religion to them; it is an entire way of life, influencing and shaping the way in which they conduct practically every aspect of their lives.

Voodoo rituals cover a wide variety of practices that are often misunderstood by those outside the practice. For the most part, the rituals are intended to restore healthy balances between the earthly and spiritual worlds and to strengthen community bonds.

These zombies are not the ravening flesh-eaters of the silver screen. On the contrary, they are pathetic, pitiable figures who eke out an existence shackled by enslavement. Haitians are not afraid of zombies, which they see as being outcasts and somewhat less than human. Their great fear is that they might potentially be tricked or forced into becoming a zombie themselves if they step out of line or incur the wrath of a bokor.

A Haitian houngan (vodoun priest) performs a ritual on a believer.

Among students of Haitian zombie lore, the classic example is the 1962 case of Clairvius Narcisse. In April 1962, this 40-year-old man was admitted into hospital with what sounded like symptoms of advanced tuberculosis: hemoptysis (coughing up blood), fever, chills, and generalized weakness. Despite the best efforts of the medical staff to diagnose and cure him, he died three days later.[35]

After less than a day spent in temporary storage, his body was released for burial. There was a funeral, attended by his friends and family. The story should have ended there, but 18 years later, a man claiming to be Clairvius Narcisse walked up to the dead man's sister and introduced himself. Initially skeptical, after speaking with him for a while Angelina Narcisse became convinced that the stranger was indeed her long-dead brother. He knew things that only Clairvius could have known, and once his identity was established, the dead man walking had quite a story to tell.

Clairvius Narcisse claimed to remember the late stages of his illness, including the subsequent "death" and burial in the cemetery. He did not see it, for he had been paralyzed and unable to open his eyes, but he had heard everything that happened. Clairvius recalled statements that had been made by the physicians at his bedside in the hospital, and also the anguished grief of the mourners who were present at his funeral service. For what must have seemed like countless interminable hours, he lay motionless in his grave, until finally the silence was broken by the sound of shovels removing dirt from above him.

This was no rescue, however. In fact, his ordeal was only just beginning. Resurrected as a zombie, he was taken to a sugar plantation, where he was forced to work the crops along with others who were similarly zombified. When the mood took him, the vodou priest who was responsible for the zombies' plight had them whipped or beaten.

It may have been the case that, when compared with other zombie victims, Clairvius Narcisse was one of the lucky ones. After returning to his family in 1980, following the death of the priest who had enslaved him, he lived for 14 more years, dying in 1994 at the age of 72. Not every zombie survived the experience. It has been speculated that, because of the unpredictability of the concoction used as part of the "death and reanimation" process, some unfortunate victims may have died of suffocation in their coffins before the vodou priests and their associates returned to dig them up. One can only imagine the sheer terror that must result from the feeling of slowly asphyxiating while being utterly incapable of doing anything whatsoever to stop it.

Canadian anthropologist and ethnobiologist Wade Davis is best known for his 1985 book about Haitian zombies, The Serpent and the Rainbow. *He is currently an anthropology professor at the University of British Columbia.*

Harvard University dispatched an ethnobotanist named Wade Davis to Haiti to investigate the mystery surrounding the zombie phenomenon. Initially skeptical regarding the existence of zombies, the 28-year-old scientist nonetheless set about his task with gusto. Davis immersed himself in the local culture, seeking out those who claimed to have knowledge and experience of vodou in general and zombies in particular. Much of his journey is charted in

Wade Davis theorized that vodoun practitioners could be using tetrodotoxin extracted from puffer fish—like the one pictured here—to create their potions. Side effects from the toxin, Davis felt, are similar to those described in "zombies."

his autobiographical book *The Serpent and the Rainbow* (1985), which is as much a study of the Haitian people and their beliefs as it is a quest to obtain and identify the potion and process through which zombies were created.

The possibility that there might be a pharmacological explanation was a tantalizing one, with considerable and wide-ranging potential benefits to the field of medicine — if it turned out to be genuine.

Speaking to Gino del Guercio of *Harvard Magazine* in 1986, Davis recalled his time in Haiti searching for the "zombie drug." After arriving on the island and spending time observing and participating in the Haitian way of life, Davis sought out a bokor and set about obtaining a sample of the potion that was used for the creation of zombies. After paying the man a small fortune in cash, the ethnobotanist was permitted to observe the bokor making the preparation, which included a visit to a graveyard to dig up a dead body. Human bone was one of the key ingredients.[36]

Highly educated in the science of pharmacology, Wade Davis could tell from the outset that he was being subjected to a scam. The bokor was conning him, gambling that the Canadian visitor would be taken in by the blend of voodoo ritual and obscure ingredients. In exchange for his money, all Davis got was wasted time.

Undeterred, he confronted the bokor and demanded that he supply the genuine article. This time, Davis later claimed, the potion was genuine: a powerful poison that, when administered in the correct amount, had the same effects as those experienced by Clairvius Narcisse.

It was certainly toxic and had the capacity of killing its target if the dose was excessive or if the person had an adverse reaction to it. A healthy 20-year-old would be able to tolerate it far better than a 60-year-old with heart disease or diabetes, for example.

Davis identified tetrodotoxin as a likely candidate. Found in puffer fish, the chemical is a strong poison that can be lethal if ingested. Writing in *Harper's Magazine* in April 1984 ("The Pharmacology of Zombification"), he stated:

> Case histories from the Japanese literature about fugu [puffer fish] poisoning read like accounts of zombification. A man who had died after eating fugu regained consciousness seven days later in a morgue. He claimed that he recalled the entire incident and said he feared he would be buried alive. Another case involved a man who walked away from a cart that was carrying him to a crematorium. Last summer, a Japanese man poisoned by fugu revived after he was nailed into a coffin.

All three examples cited by Davis sound like nightmarish experiences, and the parallels between puffer fish toxicity and the initial stage of the zombie experience are clear. As such, the ethnobotanist was offering an answer to the question of how zombified victims seemed to die, when they were actually entering a nonlethal state close to death. Those who survived administration of the poison were candidates for being unearthed later and enslaved by the bokor or caplata.

Yet, despite his best efforts, nothing in Davis's investigation could explain how such unfortunates *stayed* in that condition for long periods of time — sometimes decades. He hypothesized that other drugs might be involved, drugs that would have to be re-dosed on a consistent basis in order to maintain the zombielike state for so long. Davis posited that these secondary drugs, coupled with the great power exerted by a belief in vodou, may explain the long-term cases of people such as Clairvius Narcisse . . . cases that date back many years.

It should be noted that the scientific community does not necessarily agree with Wade Davis's conclusions. Writing in the May/June 2008 issue of Skeptical Inquirer *("Zombies and Tetrodotoxin"), Professor Terence Hines describes Davis and his book as being "an excellent example of a credulous foreigner taken advantage of by local tricksters and is full of scientific absurdities."*

It should be noted that the scientific community does not necessarily agree with Wade Davis's conclusions. Writing in the May/June 2008 issue of *Skeptical Inquirer* ("Zombies and Tetrodotoxin"), Professor Terence Hines describes Davis and his book as being "an excellent example of a credulous foreigner taken advantage of by local tricksters and is full of scientific absurdities." Clearly, Hines is pulling no punches. He also points out that by assisting the bokor in digging up the grave of a child in order to obtain the flesh and bone samples necessary for the potion, he was complicit in the acts of grave robbery and defiling human remains — unsavory at best, and potentially illegal.[37]

Hines also challenges Davis's assertion that the symptoms of puffer fish poisoning mimic those of zombification and adds that of the samples provided by the ethnobotanist for chemical analysis, no significant quantity of tetrodotoxin was to be found. Although popular at the time *The Serpent and the Rainbow* was published, Wade Davis's hypothesis has been largely dismissed by his peers.

Davis's book was adapted for the big screen by the director of *A Nightmare on Elm Street,* Wes Craven. It follows some of the broader brushstrokes of the book but sensationalizes Davis's experiences in Haiti and injects a great deal of supernatural drama into the mix. Shot partly on location on the island, it remains worth watching, if only for the colorful window on Haitian society that it offers.

Sadly, despite the best efforts of Wade Davis, there was no great medical advancement to be gleaned from the zombie potion. For the people of Haiti, the belief in vodou remains strong — as does the fear of being turned into a zombie.

The notion of slow-moving, lethargic zombies is scary enough. How much worse would it be if they were able to run?

Zombies have traditionally shambled and staggered rather than sprinted, which fits with their withered and desiccated physiques. It was only when writer Alex Garland and director Danny Boyle created *28 Days Later* in 2002 that screen zombies became more threatening: they went from being slow zombies to fast ones, running full tilt after their intended prey like tigers or wolves.

Rear Admiral Ali Kahn (pictured), who was the director of the Office of Public Health Preparedness and Response at the Centers for Disease Control and Prevention at the time, wrote in the 2011 CDC publication "Preparedness 101: Zombie Apocalypse" that if citizens prepared for hurricanes and other national disasters like they would from an impending zombie attack, they would be ready for anything.

The cause of Boyle and Garland's zombie apocalypse was a deliberately engineered bioweapon nicknamed Rage. Highly infectious, the virus instantly turned an ordinary human being into a ravenous beast completely devoid of all higher brain functions and personality. The Rage-fueled zombies are hunger and savagery personified, but they aren't the reanimated dead. The arrival of fast zombies heralded a new era in zombie mythology, one that appears to be here to stay.

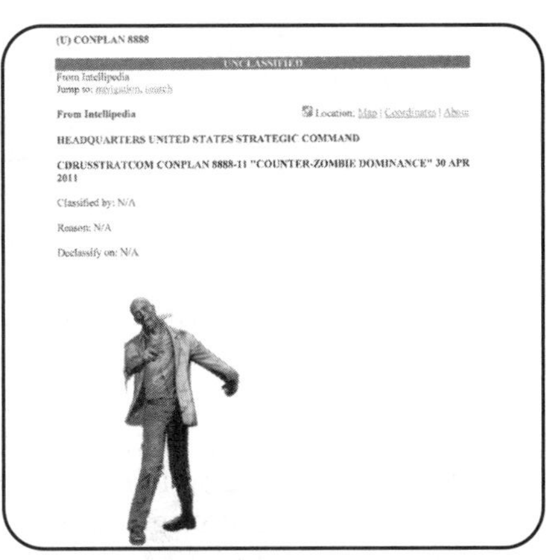

A screenshot of the homepage for CONPLAN 8888, which was basically a fictional training scenario developed by the U.S. Department of Defense Strategic Command that used a zombie attack to prepare junior officers for national emergencies.

Zombies have other uses than entertainment value. In 2011, the U.S. Centers for Disease Control (CDC) launched a campaign designed to educate the public on the issue of disaster preparedness. The milieu chosen by the CDC to engage public interest was a familiar one: surviving a zombie apocalypse. *Don't be a zombie,* the tagline ran. *Get a kit. Make a plan. Be prepared.*[38]

A poster campaign was accompanied by a graphic novella that highlighted issues of survival, preparedness, and protection, focusing on the adventures of two humans and their dog, Max, as they navigated the murky waters of a zombie outbreak. As reported by Melissa Bell of the *Washington Post* on May 20, 2011 ("Zombie apocalypse a coup for CDC emergency team"), the campaign was so popular that it crashed the CDC website. These particular zombies were soon getting millions of views and trending on social media.

Not one to be left out of the undead action, the U.S. military developed its own plan for responding to a zombie uprising. The document, named CONPLAN 8888: Counter-Zombie Dominance, was formulated by junior army officers between 2009 and 2010. Not that the military ever took the idea of a zombie apocalypse seriously. CONPLAN 8888 was an absolute hypothetical . . . one that conferred a number of advantages. For example, in the past, speculative war-fighting plans had been based on real nations. There were sometimes unintended consequences to this, as when ill-informed individuals mistook what was essentially the basis for a tabletop war game and assumed that it was an *actual* plan for invading another sovereign country. Great offense could be taken at what were perceived as imperialistic, warmongering activities by the defense establishment. As there were no actual zombies to be offended, and the notional battleground was the United States itself, such issues were neatly sidestepped. Finally, the scenario used baddies that everybody can agree on: zombies.

The purpose of CONPLAN 8888 (also known as CONOP 8888) was to train students in the art of military planning and coordination. The choice of zombies as the opposing force had an unintended but very welcome side effect: the fresh, out-of-left-field approach enhanced student engagement. In other words, they were both fascinated with and entertained by figuring out how the U.S. war machine would respond in such an off-the-wall scenario. At the conclusion of the training exercise, the plan was made available to the public so that a broader audience could appreciate it too.

The aims of the plan are divided into three different objectives. First, to "establish and maintain a vigilant defensive condition aimed at protecting humankind from zombies." Second, "if necessary, conduct operations that will, if directed, eradicate zombie threats to human safety." Last but by no means least, CONPLAN 8888 specified methods by which the military could "aid civil authorities in maintaining law and order and restoring basic services during and after a zombie attack."

As the plan unfolds, it becomes increasingly obvious how much forethought the students put into its design. They let their imaginations run wild, classifying the different types of flesh eaters as pathogenic zombies, radiation zombies, evil magic zombies (created by "some form of occult experimentation"), space zombies, weaponized zombies — think of the runners from *28 Days Later* — and symbiont-induced zombies. There are even entries for vegetarian zombies and chicken zombies, though how much of a threat the former would be to humanity is difficult to conceive.

If the idea of chicken zombies seems ridiculous, think

again. They're the only type of zombies on the list with a factual basis. In 2006, the news media began reporting on so-called "zombie chickens" surfacing throughout the state of California.

According to a December 5, 2006, article in the Associated Press ("Zombie Chickens Causing Debate Over Fate of Older Chickens in California"), the problem lay with chickens that had grown too old to lay eggs and had therefore outlived their usefulness. Farmers euthanized them via asphyxiation with carbon dioxide before turning their remains into fertilizer. Leaving aside for a moment the ethical concerns surrounding this practice, enclosing the chickens in airtight cases was not always effective. When the cases were opened, the chickens appeared to be dead and were disposed of in a compost heap. Some of them rose up, Lazarus-like, and tottered shakily from amongst the bodies of their dead peers . . . and so the phrase "zombie chicken" entered the lexicon.

It's good to know that the U.S. Army has given some thought on how best to kill them again.

Written in the style of a genuine military document, the methods for waging war against the undead are taken, if you'll excuse the pun, deadly seriously. The clinical manner in which the combat measures are described actually borders on the chilling.

The operational details of the counter-zombie dominance planning is where things really get interesting. Written in the style of a genuine military document, the methods for waging war against the undead are taken, if you'll excuse the pun, deadly seriously. The clinical manner in which the combat measures are described actually borders on the chilling.

"Issue orders for defensive forces to kill all non-human life on sight," is one such instruction. Some might take exception to the word "kill" in this particular context, but the meaning is clear: annihilate the zombies wherever they are found.

As the war continues, U.S. forces will "initiate bomber and missile strikes against targeted sources of zombie infection" and "target all main body and holdout vectors of zombie influence contagion using all available military capabilities." In other words, wipe out the zombies and the source of their infection using massive, overwhelming firepower.

Once the last zombie has fallen and been mopped up, how to stop the hungry undead from once more rising to stalk the living? According to the plan: "Ensure all zombie corpses are immolated." In other words, burn them all with fire.

With the big picture taken care of, what advice does CONPLAN 8888 have to offer? "There is no medical cure for a zombie pathogen. At this time, it can be assumed that once a human turns, they cannot be cured or reverted to human status." Therefore, "the only assumed way to effectively cause casualties to the zombie ranks by tactical force is the concentration of all firepower to the head, specifically the brain. The human brain will still be functioning in the zombie state, but it is universally agreed that the only part actually active will be the brain stem."

In other words . . . double tap to the head.

Most zombie movies depict the collapse of civilization, or the post-apocalyptic aftermath, as increasingly small pockets of human survivors banding together and desperately trying to hold out against the undead hordes. The U.S. military offers a more reasoned and optimistic vision of the final outcome between a living human-zombie clash on a national scale: all we have to do is wait them out. "Even if infected by a zombie contaminant or pathogen," the plan notes, "human biology requires a regular intake of food and water. Absent proper hydration to offset the effects of progressing zombie-ism, zombie-infected humans will experience organ failure that will immobilize or kill the host within 30–40 days."

Lest we get overly confident, however, the authors also point out that pre-positioned food stocks may not last that long.

Who would win — the living or the dead? Hopefully we'll never have to find out the hard way.

Until fairly recently, searching for monsters or cryptids was something of a fringe activity. Those who showed an active interest in the subject — setting down the books, getting out of their armchairs, and heading out into the wild places of the world in an effort to explore the matter at first hand — were relatively few and far between. Many considered this activity to be the province of cranks, people who had become disconnected with reality and went out chasing fairy tales.

The times have begun to change. In the late 1970s and early 1980s, one of the few television shows to cover the subject with any degree of seriousness was *In Search of . . .* Hosted by *Star Trek*'s Leonard Nimoy, the show was an outlier on the fringes of network television, delivering viewers regular boluses of ghosts, UFOs, strange phenomena . . . and mysterious creatures. Fifty years later, cryptids are fighting for our attention on TV screens everywhere, with shows such as *MonsterQuest, Expedition X, Finding Bigfoot, Mountain Monsters,* and a host of others, all competing for monster ratings from viewers.

As has proven true with many a cottage industry, once the amount of interest reaches a certain level, a degree of tourism starts to occur. The town of Point Pleasant, West Virginia, attracts hundreds of thousands of visitors, almost all of whom come to the small settlement for a single reason: Mothman. It is impossible to walk the streets of Point Pleasant without seeing images of the iconic, red-eyed entity looking back at you from storefronts. Mothman is emblazoned on countless T-shirts, baseball caps, and bumper stickers. A 12-foot-high stainless-steel statue in the center of town, located next to the world-famous Mothman Museum, tends to be the focal point for those who come to Point Pleasant, and has become the subject of a bizarre tradition: it is the done thing to be photographed pretending to insert a coin into Mothman's butt crack. Quite how this ritual got started is anybody's guess. Perhaps it began during the annual Mothman Festival, which draws crowds of around 15,000 people to Point Pleasant.

Cryptids have become big business, and Point Pleasant is hardly unique. According to the British Office for National Statistics, in 2019 an estimated 313,000 visitors came to Loch Ness and nearby Inverness, spending approximately 903,000 British pounds along the way. Nessie is indisputably one of the biggest tourism draws in the region, if not *the* biggest.

Cryptids have become big business, and Point Pleasant is hardly unique. According to the British Office for National Statistics, in 2019 an estimated 313,000 visitors came to Loch Ness and nearby Inverness, spending approximately 903,000 British pounds along the way.

For the would-be monster hunter who might be about to set out on an expedition to find one of these elusive cryptids, the best place to start seems obvious. You go where the concentration of monster sightings is the highest and the most recent.

In the continental United States, the state with the most per capita cryptid encounters and the richest monster lore is probably West Virginia (and the rest of the Appalachian region), although Texas and Florida can each make a strong case too. The small towns and rural areas of West Virginia have given rise to a host of weird creature stories — enough to satisfy even the most inquisitive of monster hunters.

Take the Grafton Monster, for example. On the night of June 16, 1964, a 17-year-old part-time local newspaper journalist named Robert Cockrell had just finished up his working day and was on the way home when he spotted something extraordinary through the windshield of his car: a large humanoid creature, which he

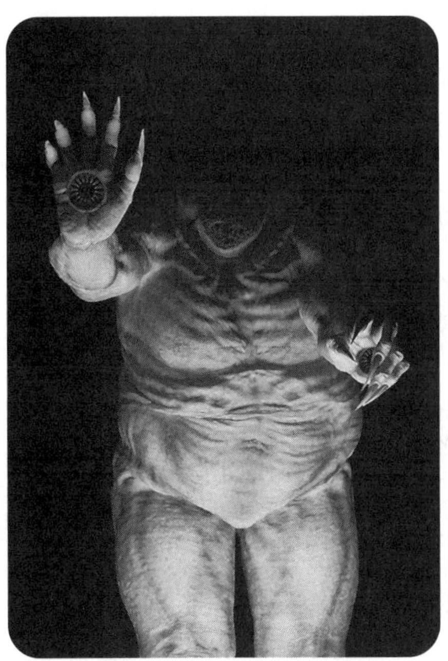

The hulking monster Cockrell reported seeing had no head and was white in color.

later estimated to be somewhere between 7 feet and 9 feet tall, in a clearing at the side of the road.

The thing was generally humanoid, Cockrell recalled, albeit hulking in form and lacking a head. Unless Cockrell's eyes deceived him, it was simply standing there, stock still, apparently minding its own business among the trees, bushes, and tall grass. It was completely white in color.

The sighting took place late in the evening, at around 11 o'clock. There was a first-quarter moon in the sky that night, meaning that roughly half the moon's surface was visible to reflect light back to Earth. There was little in the way of cloud cover to darken the night, so visual conditions were adequate, rather than optimal — or so we might think. Decades later, in a 2014 letter to Grafton's local newspaper, the *Mountain Statesman,* Robert Cockrell would refer to the 16th as a "dark night." The relevance of this observation will soon become apparent.

Robert Cockrell didn't stop to investigate further. Hitting the gas pedal, he drove home and called the cavalry, only returning to the scene later with two friends to act as backup. All signs of the monster were gone. Apart from some crushed vegetation, it had left no trace of its presence . . . if it had even existed at all. The only other anomaly was a low whistling that neither Cockrell nor his friends could either locate or identify.

That ought to have been the end of the matter, and if Cockrell hadn't been a journalist, it may well have been. Instead, he did what a reporter is supposed to do: he reported. The paper for which he worked ran the story, albeit not in the way Cockrell probably intended.

Once the article hit newsstands, monster hunting suddenly became Grafton's newest and most popular pastime. Mobs of local people formed and, grabbing bats, tools, and other implements, piled into their cars and drove out into the night looking for Cockrell's monster. Although eyewitness reports continued to come in and the *Grafton Sentinel* kept covering the story, it would later be revealed that the newspaper's editor actually placed little belief in its authenticity.

Although no concrete evidence of the creature's existence was ever found, there were numerous sightings of what soon came to be called the Grafton Monster. (Cockrell himself referred to it as "the Thing," and claimed to have found his brief glimpse of it to be terrifying.)

Nonetheless, a monster legend was born. As word spread, teenagers and adults alike continued to go out *en masse* looking for the creature. The hunting expeditions included officially sanctioned searches by law enforcement officers and presumably more rambunctious efforts by amateur monster hunters. Although no concrete evidence of the creature's existence was ever found, there were numerous sightings of what soon came to be called the Grafton Monster. (Cockrell himself referred to it as "the Thing," and claimed to have found his brief glimpse of it to be terrifying.)

After submitting the report to his editor, Robert Cockrell also documented his bizarre encounter in a detailed letter to author Gray Barker, which was written the following month. Barker was and remains a complex and controversial figure, one who would become embroiled in the cultural phenomenon surrounding Mothman.

In addition to self-publishing his UFO-related writings, Barker was a prankster. He was not just a harmless prankster; he was an outright hoaxer. His involvement with any seemingly genuine fantastical claim should be reason enough to cast doubt upon its authenticity. Barker was not beyond exaggeration or outright fraud when either suited his purposes. Barker, sometimes alone and at other times aided by fellow hoaxers, would write let-

One artist's concept of the Grafton Monster—in this case, unlike Robert Cockrell's account, it has a head—a hulking, tall, humanoid creature.

ters to well-known figures in the UFO field such as the self-styled "contactee" George Adamski. Whether the intent was to directly manipulate, to sow discord and confusion, or simply to amuse Barker is open to interpretation. John Keel, author of *The Mothman Prophecies* — of which, more later — was another target of Barker's hoaxing.

Author Gabriel McKee's biography of Barker, *The Saucerian: UFOs, Men in Black, and the Unbelievable Life of Gray Barker* (2025), paints a picture of a complex man who, when it came to the subject of UFOs and monsters, was probably not one whose word should be taken at face value.

Author Daniel A. Reed agrees. Writing for the magazine *Skeptical Inquirer* on August 8, 2024, Reed obtained access to Barker's annotated version of the Grafton Monster story, which was stored in the archives at the Clarksburg-Harrison public library — home to a treasure trove of Barker's correspondence and documentation. Barker's explanation for the monster was, at least, an original one: he likened it to a laboratory testing animal, perhaps dropped off on our planet by a visiting extraterrestrial species, presumably as part of an experiment or on a reconnaissance mission. Barker's hypothesis is as intriguing as it is unconventional, and his information-gathering visit to Grafton seemed to turn up little new information. For decades, the story of the Grafton Monster lay dormant, little more than an interesting footnote in the history of the town.[39]

To his credit, Reed retraced the footsteps of both Barker and Cockrell, not only pulling the primary source material from the library's Gray Barker Collection but also tracking down the scene of the 1964 encounter and sizing it up in person. This was probably the most diligent research conducted into this particular monster story in 60 years. Robert Cockrell died in 2022, but Reed uncovered a letter he'd written to the *Mountain Statesman* newspaper on April 23, 2014, which basically disavowed the encounter entirely.

The so-called monster was, he opined, actually a Grafton resident named Tommy Peters, who was a familiar sight in town and memorable for stacking boxes on his bicycle as he rode from point A to point B. Peters could be seen at any time of day or night. In the dark, Cockrell supposed, he might have been mistaken for a headless monster. Cockrell had told the friends who accompanied him back to the scene about the creature, and they in turn had told their friends . . . and so on, until everybody in town knew about the Grafton Monster — and wanted a piece of it for themselves.

Cockrell made the observation that "the monster will not die. Every so many years someone digs the story back up, adds non-existent details, and sends it back out the door." Storyteller after storyteller has repeated the tale in print (surprisingly, Gray Barker was not one of them), on television, and on the internet. The facts were finally so distorted as to have become almost unrecognizable.

"The fact is there is no Grafton Monster and there never was a Grafton Monster," Cockrell concluded. If anyone ought to know, it would be Cockrell. With Cockrell's retraction serving as a smoking gun, Reed makes an extremely strong and compelling case for viewing this particular monster story with skepticism.

And yet ... to play devil's advocate, what if Robert Cockrell was *not* mistaken? Seventeen-year-old eyes are usually pretty sharp. It was a relatively clear night, albeit quite dark. He seemed convinced enough at the time to enlist the help of two friends to head back to the scene that same night.

A simple case of a contemporary folk tale based on a trick of the light, one that grew and grew with each successive retelling — or a genuine monster, glimpsed briefly in the darkness from a speeding car?

In June 2024, Grafton held its first annual monster festival. It was popular enough that a second event took place in June 2025, celebrating the town's now-famous creature of the night.

The legend of the monster lives on.

"It Came from Outer Space!" screamed the poster for the movie of the same name. Emblazoned with a giant eye and four adults staring in terror at who knows what, the byline promised *"Amazing! Exciting! Spectacular!"*

Released in 1953 and conceived by renowned writer Ray Bradbury, the movie was one of a crop of similarly themed science fiction-ish/monster movie potboilers released during the early 1950s. Also gracing the silver screen in 1953 were the classics *The War of the Worlds* and *The Beast from 20,000 Fathoms*.

Two years earlier, in 1951, audiences thrilled to *The Day the Earth Stood Still* and *The Thing from Another World*, which would later be remade to terrifying effect by John Carpenter as *The Thing*.

Sandwiched in between those two banner years for space-themed creature features was a real-world incident that unfolded like the plot for one of those movies. The story goes like this:

On the evening of Friday, September 12, 1952, something strange fell from the darkening skies over Flatwoods, a small township with around 250 residents, located in rural Braxton County, West Virginia. At approximately 7:15 P.M., half an hour before sunset, a bright light streaked overhead, arcing on a downward trajectory before crashing into the ground at great speed.

The point of impact was on land owned by a farmer named G. Bailey Fisher. A group of local boys, two of whom were brothers, watched in awe as the light came down hard just a short distance away. Their confidence was bolstered by the idea that there would be safety in numbers, and the gaggle of boys set out to discover exactly what it was that had just made earthfall in their small, out-of-the-way town. Showing a keen instinct for self-preservation, they stopped off at the home of the brothers, Freddie and Edward May, to inform Mrs. May of what had happened.

After listening to their story, Kathleen May enlisted the help of a family friend, Eugene Lemon, who served in the National Guard and could therefore prove useful in case of emergency. Once they were assembled—the boys, Mrs. May, Eugene Lemon, and Mr. Lemon's dog—the group headed for the crash site on the nearby farm.

What they encountered there stunned them all.

The scene was reminiscent of something from a creature feature. Mist hung eerily, lit only by a bizarre red light that pulsed strangely. From within it emerged a figure with distinctly unearthly characteristics.

Near the Flatwoods town hall is a chair shaped like the monster that provides tourists with a photo opportunity.

The thing that confronted the group was between 7 and 10 feet tall and defied the laws of gravity by floating above the ground without any apparent effort. Its eyes glowed eerily in the gloom, fixing the seven incredulous locals with an unblinking gaze. Behind its circular head, red in color, was a tall collar that was shaped like a spade. Rather than legs, there was what appeared to be a skirt. The intruder did have arms; instead of hands, they terminated in what looked like a pair of claws.

The soon-to-be-titled Flatwoods Monster (sometimes known as the Green Monster for the color of its attire) hissed and advanced on them in what the group took to be a threatening manner. Understandably, they ran for their lives. On reaching home, they called the police. There was no sign of the creature when locals and law enforcement officers arrived in response to their plea for help. The Flatwoods Monster was gone, leaving a mystery behind.

Nine days after the strange encounter, stories of the monster were still spreading. Writing in a column titled "Bug Dust" in *The Raleigh Register* on September 21, journalist Thomas F. Stafford noted:

> 'tis said that the Flatwoods Monster has moved on to Raleigh County — to the vicinity of the Greenbriar Dairy, at that.
>
> Mrs. Earl Hutchinson of Skelton called to inform Bug Dust that she had seen a "shiny something" hovering in the sky some distance from her home.
>
> At first, she thought it was a man in a parachute, but when it kept swinging back and forth, and jumping up and down, she figured the Flatwoods Monster was on the way to Beckley [the seat of Raleigh County] — for a rendezvous with other monsters, no doubt.

Skelton and Flatwoods lie 80 miles apart as the crow flies. Despite the tongue-in-cheek tone of the article, one wonders what exactly it was that Mrs. Hutchinson saw in the skies. Was the thing that emerged from the darkness that September night in Flatwoods a monster? an extraterrestrial entity? or something else entirely?

Writing for *Skeptical Inquirer* in 2000, researcher and author Joe Nickell dismissed the UFO as having been nothing more than a meteor — one that was observed by eyewitnesses in no less than three neighboring states. As for the monster, the skeptic concluded that the most likely candidate for it was nothing more than a common barn owl.[40]

While this is conceivable, the explanation relies on the group of seven eyewitnesses vastly overestimating the size of the bird; no flying bird grows to such a massive size. There were a number of psychological factors in play, including the general zeitgeist in which UFOs and flying saucers had gained widespread national attention since pilot Kenneth Arnold's sighting near Mount Rainier, Washington, just five years before, in the summer of 1947.

Add to this the popularity of the aforementioned science fiction movies and it becomes easy to understand how a meteor blazing across the evening sky could be mistaken for an alien spacecraft, but how is a perfectly natural terrestrial animal — even if it *is* an unusually large one — misperceived as its unearthly pilot?

There's also another damning strike against the authenticity of the Flatwoods Monster: the case was investigated and then written up for publication by none other than Gray Barker, whom we also have to thank for publicizing the Grafton Monster. A questionable source, to say the least.

The Flatwoods monster was described as a tall, human-like creature with glowing eyes and a kind of spade-shaped collar. It either had no legs or they were concealed behind what looked like a skirt.

Much like its more famous neighbor, Mothman, the Flatwoods Monster has secured itself a place in popular culture. Those who play the video game *Fallout 76* may encounter the creature wandering about the post-apocalyptic digital landscape.

The game's creators, Bethesda Game Studios, have removed any ambiguity about its nature. Their version of the Flatwoods Monster is most definitely that: a monster.

Go to Braxton County nowadays and you can make up your own mind. Although the actual site of the encounter is on private property and access is forbidden to the public, you can visit the museum that is dedicated to telling the story of the strange encounter with its "Green Monster."

Perhaps best to keep your eyes on the sky at dusk . . . just in case.

Of the many cryptids and bizarre creatures that call West Virginia home, one stands head, shoulders, and wings above them all in terms of its popularity and the fascination it inspires in so many people. That entity is, of course, Mothman.

A great deal has been said about what is arguably the world's most famous cryptid. Some of it has been written by the Fortean researcher Tobias Wayland and me in our book *Mothman: Sightings and Investigations of the Iconic Flying Cryptid* (Llewellyn Books, 2025). Part of the research for that project involved putting boots on the ground in West Virginia and other states, visiting the locations in which the Mothman story played out. (Some investigators are convinced that it is *still* playing itself out to this day.)

Prior to the events in November 1966, Point Pleasant was notable primarily for being the site of a battle that took place on October 10, 1774. Named after the settlement, the Battle of Point Pleasant was fought between a force of Virginia militia and Native American warriors. Both sides bore firearms, although the rifles employed by the militia were superior to the flintlocks used by their enemies. As the battle ebbed and flowed, close-range hand-to-hand combat also took place, with bayonets and sword blades clashing against tomahawk heads.

The men on both sides fought bravely, and the battle raged on throughout the day. Ultimately, by nightfall, the militia were victorious. Its ranks paid a heavy toll for the victory, with 75 men killed — including one of their commanders, Colonel Charles Lewis — and twice that number seriously wounded. The number of casualties suffered by the defeated Native Americans, led by the Shawnee warrior Keigh-tugh-qua, otherwise known as Chief Cornstalk, remains unknown; in light of the fact that they were outnumbered by the militia, the butcher's bill must have been comparable, if not more severe.

Some historians have made the case that the Battle of Point Pleasant should be counted as having been the first true engagement of the American Revolution.

Chief Cornstalk lived to fight another day and reluctantly consented to a peace agreement. His story did not end happily. Three years after the battle, he was imprisoned by the whites at Fort Randolph while acting as a peaceful emissary bearing a grievance against increased white settlement along the Ohio River, which was in violation of the peace agreement to which he had been a

Before the Shawnee chief was killed by white men seeking revenge for the Battle of Point Pleasant, Chief Cornstalk cursed the land where he was murdered.

party. He was murdered in cold blood by a mob that was out for revenge after one of their comrades was killed by Native Americans. Cornstalk was shot dead without offering provocation and without having the means to defend himself.

Today, Chief Cornstalk's remains can be found in Tu-Endie-Wei Park in Point Pleasant, which directly abuts the Ohio River. The colonial militiamen against whom he fought are also buried there. The tragic end that befell the Shawnee leader was the catalyst for one of the great rumors to blanket Point Pleasant, one that some local people believe may explain the many strange occurrences that have surrounded the town throughout its history — including the arrival of the mysterious Mothman.

According to the legend, as Chief Cornstalk lay dying from multiple gunshot wounds, he used his last breath to gasp out a curse. The land upon which he had been murdered and its surroundings were to be forever plagued with misfortune and death. He then died. The supposed curse lives on and has been blamed for plane and train crashes, car wrecks, fire, flood, mining disasters, and illness over the centuries.

In December 1967, the curse would again be blamed for a disaster in Point Pleasant. Before we get to that, however, we fast-forward to a night in November 1966, when two couples — the Scarberrys and the Mallettes — got the shock of their lives one night when they set out exploring an isolated rural area and got more than they bargained for.

During World War II, an area to the north of Point Pleasant was used for munitions work — the manufacture and storage of high explosives, which explains the name it still informally bears today: the TNT area. The TNT would eventually fill artillery shells and bombs dropped on the cities of Hitler's Third Reich and Imperial Japan.

High explosives have to be stored under controlled conditions, preferably in a cool, dark place, and one that is easily secured. To that end, dozens of concrete bunkers were constructed, connected to each other by a network of roads for easy access. Should there be an uncontrolled detonation, the bunker walls were thick enough to contain the blast to the individual unit, preventing a catastrophic chain reaction from going off. Because of their rounded shapes, local people took to calling the bunkers "igloos."

After the war ended, there was no need for the system of bunkers anymore. The land on which they stood was put to other uses, but the bunker system was never torn down. It would have required too much effort for no appreciable gain. Teenagers and young adults from Point Pleasant frequented the area at night and on weekends. Some used it as the equivalent of a lovers' lane. Others simply appreciated the spooky atmosphere that the place had after dark. The night skies above were crystal clear, untainted by light pollution from major cities. To make matters even more interesting, a wave of UFO sightings took place in the Ohio River Valley at that time, and a number of strange lights were seen in the skies above the TNT area.

There wasn't a great deal for young people to do in Point Pleasant. For the Scarberrys and the Mallettes, driving around the deserted area outside town was a fun way to spend an evening. The night of November 15 found all four of them sharing a single car, just cruising around the TNT area, letting the vehicle's headlamps light the way. Although it wasn't unknown for people to drink and smoke marijuana out there, they vehemently denied using any alcohol or drugs that night. There's no reason to suspect they were not telling the truth.

Shortly before midnight, they encountered a seven-foot-tall, winged creature with glowing red eyes. The entity was human-shaped, having two sets of limbs just as we do. It froze in the glare, staring back at the astonished couples like a deer caught in the headlights . . . but this was no deer.

Shortly before midnight, they encountered a seven-foot-tall, winged creature with glowing red eyes. The entity was human-shaped, having two sets of limbs just as we do. It froze in the glare, staring back at the astonished couples like a deer caught in the headlights . . . but this was no deer.

Quoted in the newspaper article that introduced the entity

Mothman is generally described as a humanoid monster with wings and glowing red eyes.

to the world, Steve Mallette told a reporter from the *Point Pleasant Register* that the creature was "like a man with wings."[41] Could it have been exactly that? Highly doubtful, no matter how motivated a hoaxer might have been to spend his nights lurking in the countryside wearing a Mothman costume, waiting for some unsuspecting witnesses to happen along. According to the Mallettes and the Scarberrys, after that initial stare the thing took to the skies on wings that spanned around 10 feet across.

Terrified by whatever it was that confronted them, the couples fled. The creature soared through the air, keeping pace with their vehicle from above. The game of cat and mouse went on until Mothman finally disappeared into the darkness.

Spooked by the unnerving and bizarre experience, the Mallettes and the Scarberrys went to the sheriff's office and made out a report. Deputies dutifully went out to the TNT area to check out their story and found nothing of any consequence except for what one of them described as "a strange pile of dust."[42]

Some skeptics have dismissed this precipitating incident as having been nothing more than either an intentional hoax, cooked up by four bored people who had nothing better to do with their time, or as the honest misidentification of a perfectly natural creature such as a large bird. Indeed, in the days and weeks afterward, as sightings of the mysterious flying figure compounded, it was initially referred to as "the Bird," "the Big Black Bird," or some variation thereof. The sandhill crane and the South American vulture, two of the largest birds found in the United States, have been singled out as potential candidates for explaining away the Mothman phenomenon.

Upon closer inspection, it is not an explanation that holds a great deal of water. For one thing, it fails to account for the humanoid proportions and the glowing red eyes that are a commonly reported characteristic of many Mothman sightings. For another, while we might find it credible that somebody could misidentify a large bird at night, it is much less likely that this would happen during the daytime, with better lighting conditions.

As for the character of the original eyewitnesses, all four had solid reputations in the Point Pleasant community. None was perceived as being the kind of person who would make a story like this up for whatever reason, let alone make a false police report and waste the valuable time of law enforcement officers by sending them out on a late-night wild moth chase. When questioned by reporters, the couples stuck to their outlandish story.

Much like the case of the Grafton Monster, as word spread, hordes of wannabe monster hunters swarmed the TNT area in search of the mysterious beast.

Much like the case of the Grafton Monster, as word spread, hordes of wannabe monster hunters swarmed the TNT area in search of the mysterious beast. Some were armed (how does one hunt monsters without a weapon?); with hindsight, it's extremely fortunate that nobody was accidentally shot. Rather than being out for blood, however, the vibe was one of entertainment. Folks were out for a spooky, fun time, and it's doubtful that the majority of them truly believed they'd run into an actual creature. The road leading into the TNT area was jammed with parked cars each night, their occupants chatting and laughing as they watched the sky and looked for the telltale glowing red eyes among the trees.

At that same time, the TNT area was home to an abandoned power plant, which by 1966 was little more than a vacant shell of its former shelf. Because Mothman was sighted in close proximity to the building, some speculated that the creature was using it as a nesting site. If this was the case, no evidence was ever found to support that contention. The disused structure has long since been demolished.

As time went on, sightings continued to mount, not just in Point Pleasant but also in the surrounding Ohio River region. Contemporary newspaper reports continued to refer to it as a "bird" or "creature," though estimates of its height ranged between 6 and 10 feet tall. One eyewitness compared the creature's size to that of a light aircraft, such as a single-engine Cessna.

One of the most popular shows on television in 1966 was *Batman*, starring Adam West and Burt Ward as the titular Caped Crusader and his sidekick, Robin. Small wonder that journalists looking for punchy headlines should crib the name of West Virginia's weird flying creature from that of the well-known superhero. Indeed, Batman went up against a villain named Killer Moth in the comic books. Although the exact origin of the name remains subject to debate, Mothman has become so enshrined in popular culture that one would be hard-pressed to find somebody who hasn't heard of it.

Sometimes overlooked in the many retellings of the Mothman story are the mysterious lights and UFO sightings that accompanied the spate of appearances by the winged humanoid. A number of unexplained glowing anomalies haunted the night skies above that particular part of West Virginia, and many people have speculated that they tied in with the Mothman phenomenon somehow. The UFO reports extended throughout 1967, and while some were credibly debunked (such as the time when a crowd of eager Mothman hunters mistook an airliner for a flying saucer), not all of them were so easily explained away. They easily outpaced the number of Mothman sightings.

Tragedy came to Point Pleasant on the evening of December 15, 1967. It was the height of the holiday season, and with Christmas just 10 days away, the bridge that linked Point Pleasant with Gallipolis, Ohio, was packed with traffic. Many were out shopping for gifts. None had an inkling of the disaster that was about to befall them.

The Silver Bridge was a disaster waiting to happen. The construction process was completed in 1928, and for decades the bridge conveyed the people of Point Pleasant and Gallipolis back and forth across a 1,760-foot section of the Ohio River without a hitch. Yet unbeknownst to anybody, there was a tiny flaw buried within its structure.

The traffic load imposed on the Silver Bridge was distributed using eyebar chains. This specific type of bridge

A historical marker describes the tragedy of the Silver Bridge collapse that killed 46 people and injured nine others. It also led to better standards in national bridge inspections.

design was the first of its kind in the United States. Other bridges also employed eyebars, but crucially, their designs tended to use three eyebars for each link; the Silver Bridge only used two per link, which saved on money and weight, but the tradeoff was that if one eyebar failed, there was little in the way of redundancy. Never was the saying "A chain is only as strong as its weakest link" proven to be more accurate.

During the previous 39 years, having endured stress induced by the passage of hundreds of thousands of vehicles and the worst weather that Mother Nature could throw at it, one of the eyebars, #330, had developed a fault. Slowly, inexorably, it began to weaken.

At approximately 5 p.m. on that cold December night, it finally gave out. Witnesses would report hearing a loud crack — most likely the sound of the eyebar snapping and the supports giving way — before the Silver Bridge catastrophically failed, plunging all 32 vehicles that were making the crossing down into the icy depths of the Ohio River.

Forty-six human lives were lost in the collapse of the Silver Bridge. Only 44 bodies were recovered from the water. It was a tragedy that would forever scar the communities of Point Pleasant and Gallipolis. Although the construction of a replacement bridge was expedited, the site of the Silver Bridge, and the memorials that were subsequently placed there, serve as a perpetual reminder of the tragedy.

In the aftermath, there were those who claimed to have had nightmares in the days before the collapse. Ominously, they involved packages wrapped in Christmas paper floating down the river, bobbing and drifting in the current. With hindsight, it's easy to see how they came to be perceived as an eerie and prescient foreshadowing of the Silver Bridge disaster — in other words, precognition.

At that time, the people of Point Pleasant did not connect the Silver Bridge collapse with the Mothman sightings that had begun 13 months before, or with the UFO flap that had spread throughout the Ohio River Valley. That link was attributed to an author named John Keel.

John Keel's 1975 book, The Mothman Prophecies, *relates his investigations into sightings near and around Point Pleasant from 1966 to 1967.*

Keel wrote the immensely popular nonfiction book *The Mothman Prophecies* (1975), which would later be adapted for the big screen into a 2002 movie starring Richard Gere and Laura Linney. Keel was a researcher of Forteana, a type of weirdness that harkened back to the work of the late 19th-century investigator and writer Charles Fort. Forteana is a broad term that encompasses phenomena as diverse as lights in the sky, ghosts, lake monsters . . . and flying humanoids.

John Keel built a writing career focusing on the weird, the wonderful, and the Fortean. He researched the Mothman case extensively, and it's fair to say that without his input, Mothman would probably be little more than a footnote in the cryptid lore of West Virginia. It's highly unlikely that we would still be talking about the creature today. Keel was well versed in the realm of the bizarre. His book has surprisingly little actual Mothman content in it; the creature is a part of the larger tapestry of weirdness being painted by the author. Yet it was only after the book's release that Mothman came to be perceived as a herald of disaster. Despite there being not a shred of evidence to connect Mothman with the Silver Bridge, the tale grew in the telling.

There's a common misconception that Mothman was spotted either standing on or flying around the Silver Bridge prior to its collapse. Such claims tend to be based on "friend of a friend" accounts, with nothing substantial to back them up. Nonetheless, take a walk through the gift shops and look in the storefront windows of

Point Pleasant today, and it won't be long before the visitor finds artwork depicting the cryptid and the bridge tying together. It is the opinion of this author that this extremely tenuous connection does a disservice to the memory of the 46 souls that were lost during the 1967 disaster.

The appearance of Mothman, it came to be said, meant that very bad things were about to happen. In some stories, the flying creature is held responsible for whichever disaster it has become associated with. In others, its presence is thought to be a warning.

Legend has it that workers at the Chernobyl nuclear facility in Ukraine either dreamed of or actually saw a huge black bird prior to the catastrophic meltdown and explosion of the reactor on April 26, 1986. The parallels between what came to be called the Black Bird of Chernobyl and Mothman are both obvious and striking. Like the Silver Bridge, the reactor at Chernobyl contained a hidden design flaw that would prove to be catastrophic.

Stories of a winged black creature flying in the region were first widely reported by an Australian archeologist named Robert Maxwell, who spent time on the ground at Chernobyl and heard the accounts from locals. Unfortunately, Maxwell's research began in 2010, by which time many of the eyewitnesses had died. With few primary sources left to draw upon, the versions that Maxwell heard were retellings of the story, repetition of the tale that had been passed on from one person to the next. As has previously been mentioned, such tales grow in the telling much like a game of "telephone." Distortions, exaggerations, and sometimes outright fabrications are woven into the fabric of the narrative, until it is all but impossible to separate fact from fiction.

In a June 2019 article written by L.J. Charleston of the *New Zealand Herald,* Maxwell is quoted as having said that "there are a couple of different versions of the Black Bird story, and the earliest account seems to have come from 2005."[43]

Stories of Mothman from the United States might have entered the collective conscious of the world and inspired visions of black-winged creatures presaging disasters such as the nuclear plant disasters in Chernobyl and Fukushima.

Herein lies one of the problems with the Black Bird of Chernobyl narrative. The film adaptation of *The Mothman Prophecies* was released in 2002, three years prior to that. It may be that the story is genuine and simply flew under the radar until Robert Maxwell brought it to a wider audience. Alternatively, it may be that the movie inspired the folklore in Chernobyl, causing some of the people who saw it to create a Mothman legend of their own. At this point in time, so far removed from the nuclear disaster, the truth of the matter is impossible to determine for certain.

Mothman, or something very much like him, certainly seems to get around. Following the March 11, 2011, nuclear accident in Fukushima, Japan, sightings of a black-winged figure began to circulate online. The creature had the classic set of big black wings and glowing red eyes and was supposedly seen making flybys of the power plant by a western visitor named Marcus Pules and an unnamed companion.

The creature flew over the reactor multiple times, uttering a high-pitched shriek, Pules said; allegedly this encounter took place in February, several weeks prior to the reactor meltdown. This disaster, second only to Chernobyl in scale, was the result of a major earthquake, which in turn caused a tsunami that knocked out the power to the cooling systems at the facility when it smashed its way ashore. The physical description of the creature matches that of Mothman closely, and its proximity to a disaster scene in both location and time served to feed the narrative of Mothman as being a harbinger or a causal agent of destruction.

Although *The Mothman Prophecies* is by far the best-known book on the subject, forever cementing John Keel's literary reputation and simultaneously intertwining him with the Mothman phenomenon, he is far from the only author to write a book about the strange goings-on in West Virginia during the late 1960s. Indeed, he wasn't even the first. The now-familiar Gray Barker takes that distinction. His own book, *The Silver Bridge*, beat Keel to the punch, appearing as it did in 1970 — a full five years earlier. Upon opening the book, the reader is faced with a dedication that is both simple and exceptionally telling: "To the Bird Creature."

Barker had already introduced readers to the concept of the Men in Black in the pages of a 1956 book (*They Knew Too Much About Flying Saucers*). Residing in Clarksburg, about 120 miles northeast of Point Pleasant, he was closer in proximity to the Mothman episodes, and the plethora of high strangeness that accompanied them, than Keel was . . . which can only have made it all the more galling when Keel's book took off, where-

Best known for his book They Knew Too Much about Flying Saucers *(1956), author Gray Barker also penned a work about Mothman called* The Silver Bridge *in 1970.*

Newell Partridge reported seeing glowing red eyes that looked like the eyes of no animal he had ever seen before in his life.

as Barker's basically sank without a trace. Yet the two books are quite different, and so were their authors. Keel was more strait-laced and traditional a writer and researcher, contrasting with Barker's flamboyance and flair for the dramatic.

Barker's version of events opens with him investigating the disappearance of a German Shepherd dog named Bandit, which was, its owner believed, taken away in the night by Mothman. The night in question was November 15, the same night that the Scarberry-Mallette encounter had taken place. The Partridge family lived in Salem, almost 100 miles away from Point Pleasant. Sometime around 10:30 that night, their television set began acting up, hissing static as though some unseen energy source was interfering with it. This was accompanied by an unusual whine. Newell Partridge had never heard anything like it before.

The television wasn't the only thing whining. So was Bandit. Newell went outside to see what was distressing his dog. Some distance away in the shadowy barn, he saw a pair of glowing red circles that he took to be eyes. Considering himself to be good at judging distances, even at night, Newell Partridge told Barker that the pair of red disks had to be larger than the eyes of any ordinary animal.

Suddenly, Bandit tore off in the direction of the barn, heading straight for the eyes. When Barker interviewed him later, Newell Partridge would allude to what has become a common characteristic of Mothman encounters: feeling a sense of deep unease, sometimes even abject fear and terror, for no discernible reason. Whatever the red-eyed thing was that now lurked in his barn, Newell Partridge refused to go down and chase it out of there, even with the added security of a firearm in his hands. Instead, he went back to bed, sleeping with the gun alongside him for the remainder of the night.

Although he didn't know it at the time, Mr. Partridge would later learn that the Scarberrys and the Mallettes would see the corpse of a dog lying in the road as they were being pursued by Mothman just a short while after Bandit vanished. The two couples would testify that the dead dog, which they all claimed to have sighted, somehow disappeared. It could not later be found when police officers searched the area. It is entirely possible that this was the last ever sighting of the unfortunate Bandit.

Gray Barker notes in *The Silver Bridge* that when Newell finally plucked up the courage to go down to the barn in broad daylight, he found that Bandit's paw-print tracks simply stopped, as though the dog had disappeared into thin air — at the same place where he had seen the red eyes. No other animal tracks than Bandit's were evident. After interviewing Newell Partridge, the author wrote on page 28 that the dog weighed around 110 pounds. This is a reasonable size for a fully grown German Shepherd, and if the glowing red eyes were indeed connected to the hapless animal's disappearance, then the "Mothman is really a sandhill crane" hypothesis is effectively blown out of the water. Sandhill cranes can reach heights of around 4 feet, with wingspans stretching out to between 6 and 7 feet. As big as this may seem, it is inconceivable that even the largest and strongest such bird would be capable of carrying away a 110-pound dog, let alone fly it a hundred miles across country before dropping it off in the TNT area, only to then scoop it back up again and make off with it once more.

Mothman, on the other hand, would be a different story.

Whatever it was that snatched Bandit, it was certainly no bird. There is also no explanation at all for the disappearing dog that the two couples encountered while fleeing the TNT area.

Only one thing is for certain: much to the heartbreak of his family, Bandit was never seen alive again.

Despite its title, *The Silver Bridge* contains just a handful of pages pertaining to the bridge collapse, and while it stops short of either pinning the blame for the disaster on Mothman or even explicitly drawing a line between the two concepts, it also takes the liberty of fictionalizing the horrific events for dramatic effect.

Gray Barker put effort into tracking down and interviewing not just Mothman experiences but also those who claimed to have encountered other bizarre phenomena in the region. This included a case that still today provokes comparable controversy to the Mothman sightings; the claim made by a salesman named Woodrow "Woody" Derenberger that he had repeat meetings with a humanoid alien named Indrid Cold, beginning in November 1966. Cold beetled around in a strange flying machine, which was apparently invisible to most passers-by, but which Derenberger could see with ease.

According to Derenberger's account, Cold hailed from a world named Lanulos, and while some earthly concepts were familiar to him, others seemed entirely alien and had to be explained (such as the notion of a "city"). Cold, who looked and for the most part acted entirely like a regular human being, supposedly drifted in and out of Derenberger's life, sometimes meeting his family, sometimes bringing friends of his own to the salesman's house. It was not unknown for Derenberger to disappear for prolonged periods of time. When he returned, he told his wife that he had accompanied his strange friend to Lanulos.

Although the mysterious Indrid Cold has no apparent connection with Mothman . . ., his inclusion in Mothman literature has served to link the two beings together irrevocably.

Although the mysterious Indrid Cold has no apparent connection with Mothman, other than the fact that the timing of his first appearance was within weeks of the initial encounters with the red-eyed entity, his inclusion in Mothman literature has served to link the two beings together irrevocably. On November 4, 1966, the *Raleigh Register* ran an article titled "Parkersburg Salesman Speaks with Spaceman," in which Woodrow Derenberger recounted his story to a journalist.

Questions have been raised about the veracity of the salesman's account, as have concerns about Woodrow Derenberger's mental health. Although he wrote about his experiences in book form (*Visitors from Lanulos*, published in 1971) and his daughter Taunia authored her own version of the story in 2016 (*Beyond Lanulos: Our Fifty+ Years with Indrid Cold*), Woodrow profited little from his experience — no matter what actually happened — and led something of a troubled life after gaining minor celebrity status due to his connection with Indrid Cold.

This, coupled with the UFO flap and the soon-to-be-headline-grabbing Mothman reports, tells us that *something* truly strange was taking place that winter of 1966. The question is — what exactly was it?

Of the two primary written accounts, Keel's is the more straightforward. Barker's book contains flashes of imagination and scenes that are better described as fiction than as fact. One could quite easily treat *The Silver Bridge* as a novel rather than a straight-arrow documentation of the facts exactly as they occurred. Some of its material is 100% made up. Yet there is also no denying that both authors put boots on the ground, not only in and around Point Pleasant, but also roaming further afield in their respective quests to get to the heart of the Mothman phenomenon. Copious phone calls were also made to interview witnesses.

The problem with Barker's book lies in not knowing exactly where he draws the line between fact and fiction. His love for pranking and hoaxing also serves to make him a distinctly questionable source. Barker was rarely above dramatizing and fictionalizing events if they made for what would be, in his opinion, a better story.

Mothman sightings continued to come in long after the cryptid's final reported appearance in Point Pleasant

The annual Mothman Festival in Point Pleasant has been ongoing since 2002, allowing the town to make some tidy cash off of the cryptid beast.

just prior to the collapse of the Silver Bridge. Inevitably, following the terror attack on the World Trade Center that took place on September 11, 2001, there were claims that Mothman was seen in the vicinity of the Twin Towers — claims that remain completely unsubstantiated. The release of *The Mothman Prophecies* in movie theaters the following year only served to push the entity further into the public consciousness.

Mothman's banner year was in 2002. It saw the first of many Mothman Festivals to be held in Point Pleasant. The festival is now an annual gathering that draws over 10,000 visitors to town, all of them eager to steep in Mothman lore and to walk the grounds of the TNT area for themselves.

No disaster, no matter how large or small, is ever immune from being connected with the Mothman. Since the arrival of Photoshop, it has become child's play for pranksters to insert flying humanoid silhouettes into pictures taken at the scene of a tragedy or an accident. At 1:30 a.m. on March 26, 2024, the 984-foot-long cargo ship MV *Dali* struck the Francis Scott Key Bridge in Baltimore, Maryland. The ship experienced a power blackout while navigating the Patapsco River, veering off course and slamming into a support pier that helped hold up the bridge. The bridge span came down onto the stricken vessel in a tangle of twisted metal.

Although nobody on the ship was killed, a construction crew was working on the bridge when the collision took place. They fell into the river when it collapsed beneath them. Six of them died; only one survived to be rescued.

Predictably, it didn't take long for the ugly side of social media to rear its head. A photograph quickly began to circulate online purporting to be the Mothman clinging to the side of the Francis Scott Key Bridge, providing more fuel for the "Mothman as herald of disaster" fire.

Just one day after the accident, on March 27, a post made on Facebook read:

> Somebody shared this photo of a black figure on the bridge before it collapsed and I thought who knows photoshop [sic] maybe but then I saw a video made 3 weeks ago where a woman had visions of bridges collapsing in the near future. The even crazier part is she mentioned a dark figure as well in the video I will share it below.

Except it wasn't true. Leaving aside the poster's inept punctuation and grammar, the structure in the photograph was clearly not the Francis Scott Key Bridge, as the website *Politifact* pointed out. They determined that the photograph in fact dated back to at least 2008.[44]

Sightings of Mothman and similar winged humanoids continue to occur not just across the United States but in other countries, right up to this day. Blurry photographs and out-of-focus video footage are the closest we have to objective evidence in support of the claims. The biggest challenge for Mothman researchers of the 21st century is to carefully sift through these claims, doing their best to separate fact from fraud in a good-faith effort to get to the truth.

We can be sure of one thing. There is no single, one-size-fits-all explanation for the Mothman phenomenon. Undeniably there were elements of misinterpretation, emotional grandstanding, exaggeration, and outright fraud involved; yet once all the extraneous fluff is removed, most credible researchers agree that there is a root cause that defies easy identification. On this, everybody can agree: the final chapter in the Mothman saga has yet to be written.

Speak of the (Jersey) Devil

If ever a place looked like it ought to be the home turf for monsters, it would be the New Jersey Pine Barrens. Even the name has an air of the mysterious about it; "Pine Barrens" is a description derived from the ecological field and can apply to any area in which the inhospitable terrain is, according to the Pinelands Preservation Alliance, "sandy nutrient poor soils, acidic water and soil and fire adapted plan communities."[45]

If this sounds rather hellish, it should be borne in mind that the New Jersey Pine Barrens form a complex ecosystem that is home to numerous species of plant and animal life. The landscape is picturesque, particularly in the fall when green and orange compete for dominance. Despite their name, the Barrens are anything but barren. It is a popular place for hikers to explore, and the waterways are frequented by canoeists. The 1,700-square-mile (more than a million acres) New Jersey Pine Barrens are a peaceful place in which families can spend a day outdoors, enjoying the fresh air.

That isn't to say that the Pine Barrens are all sweetness and light. The region was used by the Mob for many years as a convenient place for them to dump the bodies of those they had killed. Penetrate deeply enough into the depths of the Pinelands and a corpse might not be found for years — if ever. So well-known is this area for the illicit disposal of murder victims that when the remains of Emanuel Gambino, part of the Gambino organized crime family, were discovered in a shallow grave just outside the area in February 1973, a police officer sardonically observed: "They must have gotten lost. They stopped too soon."[46]

The New Jersey Pinelands were protected in 1978 by an act of Congress that created a reserve spreading over 1.1 million acres (445,000 hectares) of land. The United Nations also has classified it as an International Biosphere Reserve. But the Jersey Devil simply calls it home.

The practice of dumping bodies in the New Jersey Pinelands was immortalized on the popular HBO TV series *The Sopranos*. In addition to the numerous victims of Mob hits that have been found there (and doubtless many more that have yet to be discovered), if the legends are to be believed, something monstrous lurks amidst the trees and the shadows of the Pinelands . . . a creature named the Jersey Devil.

It is not unusual for the origin stories of the Jersey Devil to grow in the telling — such is the way of folklore, particularly that of the oral tradition — and the tale of what was originally referred to as "the Leeds Devil" is no exception. There are variations aplenty, both major and minor, in the way the details differ.

Folklorists agree that the story begins in 1735, in the small township of Leeds Point. It was there that a woman named Mother Leeds became pregnant with what would be her thirteenth child. Although we tend to think of the number 13 as being unlucky today, there's no historical consensus as to when that particular number was first painted black. However, according to one of the more prominent variants of the Jersey Devil legend, a curse was placed on the unborn thirteenth child

Born of a liaison between a woman and Satan, the Jersey Devil was born with a horse's head, wings, a tail, and hooves.

of Mother Leeds because of its perceived misfortune — rather a raw deal for both mother and child, who had done nothing wrong.

In another version, the child is the result of an unholy but entirely willing sexual union between Mother Leeds and the devil himself.

No matter how its conception and gestation were described in any given retelling, most iterations of the story maintain that the baby, when it was finally born, turned out to be no baby at all; it was a horse-headed, winged creature with hooves or pigs' trotters and a tail. To add a further splash of horror to the story, the unholy birthing took place on the stereotypical dark and stormy night, with thunder booming and lighting flashing within the clouds.

Free of the womb, the malformed abomination then made its way into the wilds of the Pine Barrens, where it would be labeled the Jersey Devil and set about terrifying all who saw it for the next 290 years — and counting.

Life was hard in 18th-century North America, particularly in rural areas such as the Pine Barrens. People were religious, possessing deep faith, and equally superstitious. Many lived in fear of witchcraft and black magic, ghosts, demons, and other supernatural terrors. The Salem Witch Trials had taken place only 40 years before the Jersey Devil story came to life. Spectral evidence was accepted in the courtroom. The notion of Satan and his minions literally walking the Earth among everyday humans, meddling in their affairs and tempting them onto the dark path toward hell, was accepted as the gospel truth.

Tales such as that of the Jersey Devil were all too easy for them to believe.

As times changed and British rule became increasingly unpopular, the legend of the Jersey Devil mutated in order to keep up with the times; when the story was told around campfires and in front of tavern fireplaces, the storytellers said that the child's father was a British soldier, and the pregnancy was cursed from the moment of conception because of Mother Leeds having consorted with a Redcoat.

The Leeds House (shown here in 1937) is located on Moss Mill Road, Leeds Point, New Jersey.

Leeds Point is a real place. The Leeds family were real people who lived in the area that bore their name, although the vaguely named "Mother Leeds" has never been identified conclusively — if, that is, she ever existed at all. As the publisher of an almanac, one Daniel Leeds of Burlington (1651–1720) had earned himself something of a reputation for dabbling in the realm of the mystical. A Quaker by belief, Leeds drew fire from other members of his faith for publishing the *The American Almanack* and other writings that, to their disapproving minds, smacked of astrology and the occult.

As something of a mystic, Daniel Leeds inevitably found himself at odds with the more traditionalist adherents of the Quaker faith. He ultimately became an outcast from their ranks, severing ties and pursuing his own spiritual path . . . a path of which they most definitely did not approve. By 1700, Leeds had become such a pariah that some Quakers branded him as being in league with the devil. These were strong words for that particular climate, and an accusation that had the potential to do significant harm to Leeds's reputation.

The Leeds-Quaker falling-out ushers the beginning of the relationship between the names "Leeds" and "Devil." One can see the monster story beginning to take shape, particularly when we take into account the fact that the Leeds family crest contains a wyvern — a mythical dragon-like creature that looks a great deal like the Jersey Devil would later be described. The crest would take pride of place on issues of the *Almanack*, which may have been a red rag to a bull where the Quakers were concerned.

Daniel Leeds underwent a transformation from devoted Quaker to one of the Quakers' most outspoken critics, primarily using the medium of print to get his message across. The ire he received from the Quaker community did not prevent him from continuing to write and publish his almanac. If anything, it only made him more resolute.

The elder Leeds continued to distribute his work until 1716, four years before his death, when he handed the reins over to his son, Titan, who kept the family business going. *The American Almanack* didn't have the forecasting market cornered, however; none other than Benjamin Franklin, the founding father himself, was putting out a rival publication named *Poor Richard's Almanack*. In the battle of the almanacs, Titan Leeds came off worse. *The American Almanack* lost out to *Poor Richard's Almanack*, which enjoyed greater popularity and wider distribution.

Authors Bryan Regal and Frank J. Esposito have done sterling work in painstakingly tracing the evolution of the Jersey Devil legend through its various incarnations in their book *The Secret History of the Jersey Devil: How Quakers, Hucksters, and Benjamin Franklin Created a Monster* (2018). Future scholars of the Jersey Devil owe them a debt of gratitude. Following the tangled threads as the popularity of the story waxed and waned cannot have been easy work. Throughout much of the nineteenth century, it was relegated to the status of a local folk tale, barely known outside of the Delaware Valley region.

On February 2, 1893, the *Butte Weekly Miner*, a Montana-based newspaper, ran an article headlined "New Jersey Devil." The story alludes to the "Leeds Devil" being seen again and quotes a railroad engineer who claimed to have encountered the creature himself one October a few years prior while crewing a train that passed through South Jersey. An ear-piercing shriek presaged the arrival of the creature, which stuck its head through the cab window.

"It was the ugliest and most terrifying-looking head and face that a person could conjure up in his wildest dreams," the engineer recalled. "The head was much like that of an owl, although larger than that of the biggest owl I had ever seen. The face was that of an ape or monkey."

"It was the ugliest and most terrifying-looking head and face that a person could conjure up in his wildest dreams," the engineer recalled. "The head was much like that of an owl, although larger than that of the biggest owl I had ever seen. The face was that of an ape or monkey. The cheeks were sunken and almost white, and above them glared a pair of fiery and protruding eyes, with a black streak over each eye, extending diagonally up toward the erect and pointing ears. This hideous creature had a feathered or perhaps

The Jersey Devil has been described in various ways. Sometimes its head is horselike; other times it is more like a monkey's head. But it is always ugly in appearance.

hairy body and a pair of huge wings, which worked as noiselessly as shadows and kept the demon-like bird in the air abreast of the engine without any apparent effort."[47]

The description of an ape- or monkey-like face is at odds with traditional descriptions of the Jersey Devil, most of which portray the creature as having a long head akin to that of a horse. (Some versions have the creature as being kangaroo-like in appearance.) So shocking was the monster's appearance, the engineer claimed, that his fireman, who was responsible for shoveling coal into the engine's boiler, dropped into a dead faint at his feet. In an effort to defend himself, the engineer smashed the Devil in the face with a nearby poker. The creature simply shrugged it off and kept pace with the speeding locomotive, refusing to be dislodged. It finally left of its own accord, vanishing into the woods as abruptly as it had arrived.

After recounting the experience to a local resident of some advanced years, the railroad engineer's assumption that he had encountered some kind of giant owl creature was corrected: *"That ain't no owl; that's the Leeds Devil back ag'in sure as you're livin'!"*

The old man went on to say that, although he had never seen the creature himself, he remembered the days when hunting parties went out looking for it. Either the monster was bulletproof or they were terrible shots (however, they were said to be "some of the best marksmen there was in all o' South Jersey") because despite their best efforts, the Leeds Devil "couldn't be killed."

Of particular note is the year of publication: 1893. The senior resident said: "But it's more than 50 years since it was seen or heard of in these parts, and everybody thought long ago that it must have come to an end on earth somehow or other."

The legend of the Leeds Devil was a generational one, passed on from generation to generation, while doubtless receiving embellishments along the way. The article also offers yet another alternative origin story for the creature. In this version, blame falls yet again on Mrs. Leeds, who "had a good-sized temper of her own, too, and when she found that she was goin' to be a mother, the story is that she became regular wicked in her complainins' and goins' on to her husband, and she actually cursed the day she got married."

On the evening before she was due to give birth, Mrs. Leeds was allegedly in rare form, throwing her hands into the air and shouting: "I hope it'll be a devil! I hope it'll be a horrible devil!"

In a clear case of "be careful what you wish for," Mrs. Leeds's hopes came true the next day. What should have been a cause for joy and celebration instead proved to be a horrifying happenstance, according to the nurse who was in attendance at the birth: "The Leeds baby is born! But it was a monstrous thing, all deformed and devilish, and it flew up the chimney and away, shriekin' and yellin'."

One of the more macabre variants has the Devil turning first on its own mother, savaging her to death, before killing everybody else in the room and making its escape. This brings up the obvious question: if that were true, who was left to tell the story?

Initially, the people of Pine Barrens found the story of the Leeds Devil hard to believe. Their skepticism was challenged when a hunter claimed to have encountered the creature in the region's woods. The hunter's description matched that of the nurse. More sightings followed, until finally men set out to hunt the creature down. All attempts to kill it met with failure, even those that used silver bullets, the time-honored method of dealing with vampires and other supposedly evil creatures.

According to the storyteller quoted in the *Butte*, the tale of the unholy birth was told to him by the great-granddaughter of the nurse, who still lived in the locality and said that the story had been told for generations in her family. The article closes with the railroad engineer's remark that while some attributed the strange encounters to nothing more than a large owl, others were convinced that the Leeds Devil had returned after an absence of half a century.

No less a luminary than Stephen Decatur, a U.S. Navy Commissioner and *bona fide* war hero, is also associated with the Jersey Devil. On February 16, 1804, as a young naval lieutenant in the First Barbary War, Decatur led a daring mission in Tripoli Harbor in which he and his sailors set fire to the USS *Philadelphia*, a frigate that had been captured by the Tripolitans. It had been determined that the U.S. warship could not be retrieved and equally could not be left in the hands of the enemy. Decatur crammed 75 men into a captured ship built to hold less than half that many, a ship he appropriately dubbed the *Intrepid*. After disguising the ship as a merchant vessel, Decatur boldly sailed straight for the captured *Philadelphia* and led a boarding party. He and his men moved quickly, setting fires throughout the frigate's hull and deck and escaped before the Tripolitans had time to react.

An officer in the U.S. Navy (Continental Navy) from the Revolution through the War of 1812 and Barbary Wars, Commodore Stephen Decatur certainly makes a reliable witness to the Jersey Devil—if the story is indeed true.

Decatur's brave leadership was lauded back

in the United States. His commanding officer recommended him for a captaincy, which was duly granted. At the age of just 25 years old, Stephen Decatur became the youngest captain ever to serve in the U.S. Navy. As of 2025, he still holds that distinction.

It is fair to say that Decatur was, and remains, a legend in the annals of U.S. naval history. How did somebody of that ilk become embroiled with the Jersey Devil? In reality, he almost certainly never did, but the story is simply too colorful to ignore. According to a legend that is completely unsubstantiated by documentation, in 1804, Decatur was fulfilling one of the less glamorous but essential responsibilities of a naval officer — visiting the Hanover Iron Works in order to inspect cannonballs and other ordnances that were being manufactured there for future use by the navy.

The ironworks facility was located in the Pine Barrens, part of the Jersey Devil's hunting ground. The stage was set for a showdown between a war hero and a spawn of Satan. Spying the monstrous creature flying through the air, Decatur wasted no time in loading a cannon and training it on the sky. When he judged the moment right, the dashing mariner lit the fuse and fired off a shot. Naval gunnery has come a long way in the last 220 years. Decatur's twenty-first century successors have sophisticated computer-based targeting systems to aid their marksmanship. In the age of sail, gunners had to rely on a knowledge of mathematics and the time-honored art of dead reckoning to successfully put iron on target.

It could be challenging enough to accurately slam a cannonball into the hull of an enemy warship when it was bobbing up and down on the high seas, rolling and pitching, or making headway with the wind. The chances of hitting a target that was *flying* were an order of magnitude worse. It should therefore come as no surprise that Decatur's shot missed. Rather than attack the gallant captain or perhaps frightened off by the roar of the cannon, the Jersey Devil apparently decided that discretion was the better part of valor and flew away.[48]

As good as the story is, it is almost certainly nothing more than a particularly colorful bit of folklore — a tale told around fires at inns over a mug (or six) of beer. So too are tales that tie the Jersey Devil in with the English privateer Captain William Kidd. There are stories that have the Devil seen in the company of the ghost of one of his crew, which has the makings of the greatest episode of *Scooby Doo* ever. Although Kidd was hanged in 1701 in London, there were whispers of the sea captain having left buried treasure thousands of miles away in the New World — a small fortune that was concealed somewhere in, you guessed it, New Jersey. It is a treasure cache that has not been found to this day.

This isn't as far-fetched as it may seem at first. The waters off the coast of New Jersey were a favored haunt not only of pirates but also of pirate hunters in the seventeenth century, as was much of the Eastern Seaboard. Kidd started out as a privateer, granted a letter of marque by the king of England that bestowed on him the right to hunt down pirates in the name of the Crown. When this proved to be a less-than-lucrative field of endeavor, Kidd became a pirate himself, which soon put him on the opposite side of the law and ultimately led to his capture and execution.

Privateer (and then pirate) Captain William Kidd was famous for his exploits in the West Indies and up and down the Atlantic Coast during the seventeenth century. There is also a ghost story related to his crew and the Jersey Devil.

The most frequent Jersey Devil story tied in with Kidd involves the apparition of one of the captain's crewmen haunting Barnegat Bay. According to the legend, it is here that Kidd buried his now long-lost treasure, and the phantom seaman keeps an eternal watch over the horde of riches. In some retellings, the sailor's ghost is headless, intentionally decapitated by his ruthless captain in order to provide a guard for his secret stash of spoils. Although history tells us that William Kidd was known to have a temper, there's no evidence to suggest that he ever cut off anybody's head, let alone that of one of his own men. One also can't help wondering just how good a lookout and guard a headless pirate could possibly be.

Still, local lore has it that the headless pirate and the Jersey Devil met one dark night and, after getting off to a bit of a shaky start, soon became firm friends. Perhaps they're still out there, keeping one another company away from the prying eyes of 21st-century humanity.

The Jersey Devil's brushes with historical celebrities don't end with Stephen Decatur and William Kidd. Following his string of defeats at the hands of the Duke of Wellington during the Napoleonic Wars, Joseph Bonaparte, the brother of Napoleon and erstwhile king of Spain, relocated to the United States in 1815, after his brother was roundly defeated at the Battle of Waterloo. Bonaparte made landfall in New York and kept a relatively low profile while visiting some of the major population centers on the East Coast such as Philadelphia and Washington, D.C.

The exiled Bonaparte led a mostly quiet life, enjoying books and outdoor pursuits as he explored and grew acquainted with his new country of residence. He made his home in a manor house named Point Breeze, located in Bordentown, New Jersey. Situated between New York City and Philadelphia, the estate gave Joseph ample opportunity to ride, to fish, and to hunt whenever he felt so inclined. It was on one such hunting excursion that the emperor's brother suppos-

Yet another notable figure in history to be connected to the Jersey Devil was Joseph Bonaparte, the brother of Napoleon and former king of Naples and Spain.

edly encountered the Jersey Devil, according to S. E. Schlosser, author of *Spooky New Jersey: Tales of Hauntings, Strange Happenings, and Other Local Lore* (2017).

Catching sight of some unusual tracks that did not appear to be those of any creature with which he was familiar — the closest approximation was a donkey — Joseph set off to run the unidentified animal down. This was a bold move on his part, as he was hunting alone, without any backup to pull his iron out of the fire if matters should get out of hand. Following the tracks as far as he could, Joseph must have been puzzled when he discovered that they had stopped suddenly. The reason was simple: the prey he was pursuing was now airborne, and to make matters more dangerous, it was now stalking *him*. The hunter had now become the hunted.

Faced with the screeching, shrieking Jersey Devil, flapping its wings and hovering in the air above him, Joseph Bonaparte had only one recourse: his hunting rifle. But before he could take aim and squeeze off a shot, the monster had flown away, in keeping with its pattern of fleeing from confrontation rather than staying to duke it out.

Unfortunately, this appears to be yet another great story that has nothing to back it up apart from the classic "it is said" that thoroughly permeates folklore. As for Joseph Bonaparte, he did not stay in the United States for the remainder of his life, but he seems to have left at least some of his heart there. His ghost is reputed to haunt Point Breeze to this day, perhaps an echo in time of New Jersey's wayward former king.

After a fraudulent sideshow-style exhibition of an animal (most likely a kangaroo) mocked up as the Jersey Devil, January 1909 saw a spate of public sightings and beyond, not just in the Pine Barrens but also throughout New Jersey and Pennsylvania. The flap caused no small degree of fear and public unrest, particularly when word began to circulate that pets and farm animals were at risk of being snatched and eaten by the winged

This drawing of the Jersey Devil was published in a 1909 issue of the Philadelphia Bulletin.

monstrosity. People responded to the mass panic in the time-honored way: arming themselves and setting out to hunt the monster down. Unsurprisingly, the roving parties of hunters were unsuccessful in locating and tracking the Devil, let alone putting an end to it.

In the more than hundred years since then, both residents of and visitors to the Pine Barrens have continued to encounter the Jersey Devil — or at least, to claim that they have. Doubtless some cases can be attributed to simple misidentification; others are tall tales and outright hoaxes, created for reasons best known to the hoaxers themselves. After looking closely at the Mothman phenomenon and the associated flying humanoid cases that accompany it, one is forced to wonder whether this particular aerial creature bears any relation. If there is any legitimacy to the claims, could the Jersey Devil simply be another manifestation of the ultraterrestrial hypothesis espoused by author John Keel — a phenomenon that involves the deliberate fooling and skewing of human perception by immensely powerful inter-dimensional beings?

The mind boggles.

Another similarity to Mothman is the contention that the Jersey Devil is said to make an appearance before great disasters and tragedies strike. In his article in the February 10, 1957, issue of the *Newark Star-Ledger* titled "Poor Jersey Devil hasn't got a ghost of a chance today," Joseph R. Coyne observed: "The appearance of the Jersey Devil was supposed to mean war. It was reportedly seen before the Civil War, just before World War I, and again in 1935 before Italy squared off against Ethiopia."[49] On the other hand, where was the creature in December 1941 prior to the Japanese attack on the U.S. Pacific Fleet at Pearl Harbor? Or the March 20, 2003, U.S. invasion of Iraq? Or during any of a thousand other wars around the world that did not seem to merit an appearance by Mother Leeds's little darling?

Sightings of the Jersey Devil do still happen to this day. As with other cryptids and avatars of high strangeness, this once again brings up the question: in an age when each of us has a high-definition camera in our pocket, where are the compelling photographs, or even better, the 4K video footage showing us the creature in flight?

In 2015, that question was answered by David Black, who was returning home at the end of the working day when he claimed to have had his own encounter with the Jersey Devil. According to his interview with ABC News, Black's sighting occurred at approximately 6:00 in the evening.[50]

"It was like seeing a minion from another realm," Black told reporters. "This thing sprouted wings . . . then it was gone."

Gone — but not before Black was able to take a picture. The photograph in question shows a black shape in midair that does indeed bear more than a passing resemblance to the Jersey Devil. He added that his grandfather had also seen the creature back in the 1950s.

To add fuel to the fire, video footage surfaced shortly afterward, also purporting to show the Devil flying through the air. It was taken in Leeds Point, some nine miles away from the site of David Black's photograph. Apparently shot at twilight, based on the lighting conditions, the subject of the 32-second video clip looks like the silhouette of a stuffed toy with flapping wings either mounted on or perhaps digitally overlaid across it. The head, torso, and legs of the "creature" barely move, giving it a suspiciously lifeless appearance.[51]

Despite criticism from internet commenters, Black stuck to his story and insisted that his photograph was

Garden City, New Jersey, resident David Black claimed to have taken a video of a flying Jersey Devil in 2015 (pictured is an illustration that is not from the film, which can be viewed here: https://abcnews.go.com/US/man-claims-photographed-mythical-jersey-devil-legend-dating/story?id=34442356.)

not faked. The video, submitted to the news media by a teacher named Emily Martin, is hard to take seriously, and it should be borne in mind that both Martin and Black's "evidence" was put into circulation in mid-October, in the run-up to Halloween, when the print and television media are actively looking for spooky stories.

In spite of its fearsome reputation, the Jersey Devil has long since transformed from a source of fear to one of fondness and affection for the people of New Jersey. A common misconception holds that it was legally declared to be "the official demon of New Jersey," although there's no documentation to support this claim . . . nor, despite its name and appearance, does the Jersey Devil fit the criteria for being a demon.

The skies above the Garden State are protected by the 177th Fighter Wing of the New Jersey Air National Guard, operating F-16 Fighting Falcon jets out of Atlantic City International Airport in Egg Harbor Township. The fighter wing's unit patch is a distinctive one: the glowering face of New Jersey's most notorious monster.

Not every monstrous creature has a sports team named after it, but some do. The city of Round Rock, Texas, has a minor league baseball team named the Chupacabras. Seattle's ice hockey team is named after the legendary Kraken.

Last but by no means least are the New Jersey Devils. I have it on good authority that "the Leeds Devils" just didn't have quite the same ring to it.

The Goat Sucker – El Chupacabra

The island of Puerto Rico, spring and summer of 1995. Something wild was on the loose. Something that preyed on livestock that were penned in or tied up, helpless to flee or defend themselves. No chicken, goat, or domesticated family pet was safe if left outdoors overnight. A steadily increasing number of defenseless animals was found dead by their owners, apparently completely drained of blood. Puncture wounds in the necks of the carcasses implied that something vampiric was at large.

The creature that stalked and then savagely killed the animals was glimpsed in flashes at first. Then there were longer sightings. Eyewitnesses described the predator as being akin to a large dog, yet completely hairless with gray, leathery skin.

As losses mounted, the people of Puerto Rico gave the creature a name: *el Chupacabra,* the Goat Sucker.

Neither was the creature confined to Puerto Rico. Reports came in from across South America. 1996 saw Chupacabra sightings start popping up in the southern United States and Mexico. As stories of the Goat Sucker spread, a wave of fear bordering on mass hysteria accompanied them. In the Rio Grande Valley of Texas, many unexplained animal deaths were blamed on the Chupacabra. In May 1996 19-year-old Texan Sylvia Ybarra told reporter Fernando Del Valle of the *Austin American-Statesman*: "I think it's watching over us. It might happen again. We never know when it's going to come back."[52]

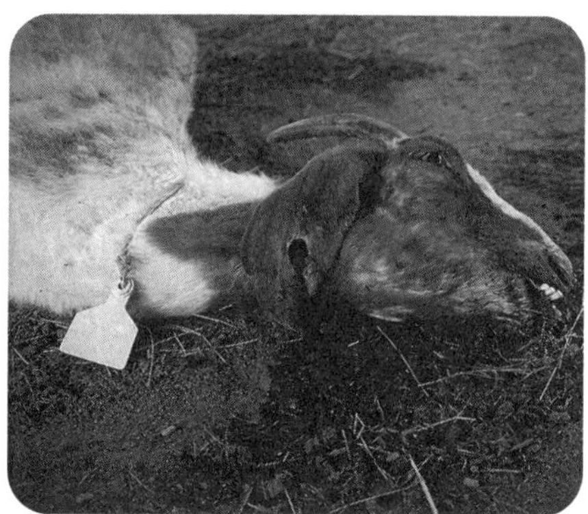

The Chupacabra's name (the Goat Sucker) comes from the fact that it sucks the blood out of goats and other livestock. At first, ranchers thought the deaths might be the result of UFO activity, but by the 1990s they were blaming the Chupacabra.

When Ybarra's goat was killed, fingers were immediately pointed at the Chupacabra, stories of which had already begun to circulate within the region. Despite the clinical judgment of a veterinarian that the killer had most likely been a dog, belief in the vampiric beast was already firmly entrenched in the minds of the public. Each successive animal death represented another notch on the fear scale.

This was not the first time that death by exsanguination had plagued the region. The generation prior, in the 1970s, had dealt with a series of animal mutilation deaths in which all the blood seemed to be drained from the victims either during or after the assault. Such deaths were widespread throughout the United States, with thousands of cases occurring in Texas, New Mexico, Colorado, and Arizona. The list of potential suspects was long, including the U.S. government conducting secret experiments, extraterrestrials traveling in by night via flying saucers, Satanic cults, covens of witches, and condors, coyotes, and other natural predators, to name just a few.

Conspiracy theories flew thick and fast with stories of UFOs and unmarked black helicopters, Men in Black (MIBs), and more. It was only during the mid-1990s, with the questionable benefit of rather skewed hindsight, that the Chupacabra entered the equation. Alarm among ranchers reached such heights that the Federal Bureau of Investigation was requested to formally investigate the matter. At first, the FBI declined to do so, citing a lack of jurisdiction — for them to become involved, the Bureau said without even a trace of apparent irony, the dead livestock would have to have been transported across state lines.

The FBI only changed its tune when mutilations began taking place on Native American land.[53] In 1979, New Mexico's assistant attorney general, Philip B. Heymann, wrote to the director of the FBI and suggested that there may be a cult or ritualistic element to the livestock deaths.[54] If this was true, Bureau leadership reasoned, then a crime had been committed, and Native American land fell under the purview of the federal government rather than that of the state. FBI agents were duly dispatched to look into the matter. Despite writing a comprehensive report on the matter, the investigators were unable to determine who or what was to blame for the deaths and mutilations.

Some historians and researchers have dismissed the cattle mutilations as having been nothing more than hysteria, groupthink, or economically motivated complaining by farmers and ranchers. Whatever one may think, such incidents do still occur today. As recently as 2023, three southeast Texas counties experienced mysterious death of cows, which, the Madison County Sheriff's Office spokesperson announced, included "the tongue [being] completely removed from the body with no blood spill. It was noted there were no signs of struggle and the grass around the cow was undisturbed. No footprints or tire tracks were noted in the area."[55]

The lack of any kind of marking around the bloodless animals' bodies means that the Chupacabra cannot be blamed for their deaths — unless, that is, one gives credence to the scarcer subset of stories that claim that the creature is sometimes seen to sport a set of bat wings, gliding through the air and swooping down on its terrified victims from above. Even many of those who find the Chupacabra stories to have some credibility often consider this to be a bridge too far.

The injury patterns evidenced in many of the animal mutilation cases did not fit with the mechanism of an animal attack, be it by Chupacabra or something more conventional. In the case of the Chupacabra, it is often claimed that the creature sucks blood from twin puncture

In the case of the Chupacabra, it is often claimed that the creature sucks blood from twin puncture sites in the neck of its larger victims, raising inevitable comparisons to the bite of a vampire.

The fame of the Chupacabra has reached all the way to Russia, as evidenced by this display at the St. Petersburg Bestiary Museum.

sites in the neck of its larger victims, raising inevitable comparisons to the bite of a vampire. Although there may be a few minor scratches and claw marks, alleged Chupacabra attacks are said to be typically far more subtle than the brutal, frenzied killings performed by bears, mountain lions, coyotes, and other predators.

In the case of these animal mutilations, commonly targeted areas tend to be the tongue, anus, genitalia, eyes, and other soft tissue. Organs were sometimes removed with what appeared to be deft, clean cuts of almost surgical precision, rather than having been torn away leaving a rough and ragged wound behind. Skeptics attribute the apparently clinical characteristics of these wounds to the expansion of gases within the body of the deceased animal, which gradually bloats and swells until tearing of the soft tissue and skin occurs. Such tears can be remarkably straight and precise in appearance, in some cases looking as if they were performed by a surgeon with a scalpel rather than a natural biological process: decomposition.

Despite the lack of puncture marks, the common factor between the mysterious mutilation deaths and the Chupacabra cases is striking: both types of killing seem to be entirely bloodless in nature, with the carcasses being drained almost to the last drop, and there is no evidence of blood having dripped, spurted, or pooled on the ground around the remains.

Decades after the first cases of postmortem animal

mutilation entered the mainstream, debate still persists as to the reasons behind it.

No matter how far-fetched one might find these stories to be, it is an unassailable fact that belief in the vampiric creature is still widespread throughout Texas, New Mexico, Colorado, and northern Mexico. It has become an indelible part of regional culture.

Unlike with its peer cryptids in this book, such as Bigfoot, the Hodag, Nessie, and Mothman, we do have some physical evidence that can help us assess the validity of Chupacabra claims. Some of those claims likely have an entirely mundane explanation, in the form of a relatively common pathology that afflicts numerous animals each year. In a 2017 paper, academics John M. Tomeček, Scott Henke, and Terry Hensley attribute accounts of the Chupacabra to the disease named mange.[56]

Mange is an illness that primarily affects the skin of a wide variety of animals, ranging from dogs and cats to foxes, bears, wolves, deer, and coyotes. There is even a human version of the disease, in the form of scabies. Mange manifests in the form of microscopic mites, which burrow under the skin of the infected animal. In the process, the parasitic mites inflame and irritate the flesh. Shortly after their arrival, the parasites lay eggs within the soft tissue, which typically leads to widespread hair loss in the host animal, giving the hapless creature a balding, sickly appearance. The term "mangy" is often used to describe a scrawny, hairless animal, whether the poor creature is actually infected by mange or not.

A red fox suffering from mange resembles the descriptions of the Chupacabra remarkably well. Could this be what people are seeing when they report experiences with the beast?

One of the noteworthy characteristics of the disease is its contagiousness. Mange spreads from one animal to the next with relative ease. Once a coyote is infected and the disease begins to progress, its hair quickly falls out, exposing a doglike creature with leathery grey skin and a monstrous appearance. This tracks closely with many descriptions of the Chupacabra.

In addition to its depilatory effects on the coyote's integumentary system, the progression of mange also causes a generally degenerative effect on the animal's overall health. It becomes sickly and weak, incapable of running down its typical prey of rabbits, squirrels, and other relatively fast and nimble rodents. The coyote is therefore forced to seek out food sources that are incapable of fleeing. Notes Tomecek et al.:

> In stories and folktales, the Chupacabra preys on goats and other small livestock. It is possible that this stems from animal behavior caused by mange. Any predatory animal that is debilitated must seek out easier prey because wilder prey is typically agile and wary. In most cases, the losses livestock raisers report as Chupacabra predation are animals confined in pens and corrals. This is consistent with predation by a sick animal, such as a coyote with mange.[57]

Although Chupacabra encounters reportedly take place after dark, a number of sightings do occur during daylight hours. A fascinating example of this took place on August 6, 2017, on a golf course in Santee, South Carolina. Golfer Doug Stewart had teed off and was making his way across the green when he spotted an ugly, hairless four-legged creature that he photographed and then published on social media with the hashtag of *#ThatAintNoDog*.

Speculation was rife as to the identity of the creature, which met the description of a Chupacabra to a T. Many went online and left comments to that effect. The local news channel got involved.

Although Jay Butfiloski, a coyote expert employed by the South Carolina Department of Natural Resources, agreed with Stewart that it certainly "ain't no dog," he also offered the same explanation as the researchers from Texas A&M. "It's a canine with mange, it's not a Chupacabra."[58]

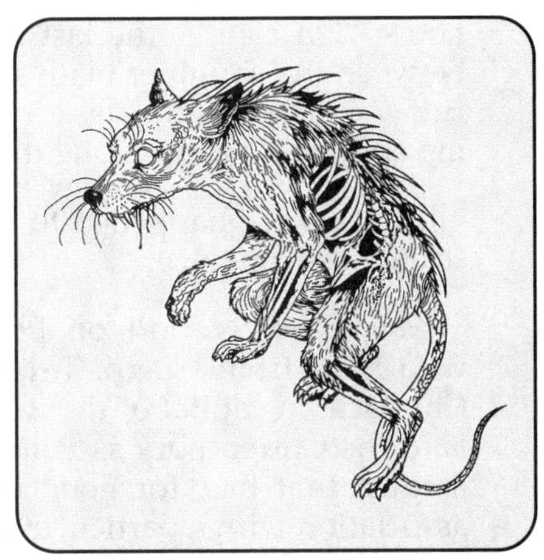

In some reports, the Chupacabra is described as being bipedal, either all the time or alternating between walking on its hind legs and walking on all fours.

Although Butfiloski couldn't say for sure whether the emaciated creature was a coyote or a fox, there was no doubt in his mind that this was no goat sucker. Because of how scrawny it appeared to be, the wildlife expert judged the case of mange to be so severe that the animal would most likely soon be dead of starvation.

It would be easy to simply lump all Chupacabra sighting reports into the category of "canid with mange" and leave it at that, yet to do so would be a disservice to the bigger picture. For one thing, some descriptions of the Chupacabra have the creature walking on its hind legs rather than on all fours; others have it transitioning back and forth between a two-legged and four-legged gait, sometimes interspersed with hopping and leaping kangaroo-style, depending on the circumstances. Many variants have the Chupacabra possessing some combination of glowing eyes, powerful jaws with razor-sharp fangs, and daggerlike claws capable of slashing its victims open.

A subset of eyewitness accounts maintain that the creature has a series of long, sharp protuberances projecting up from the curvature of its spine like spikes, a physical feature that can still reasonably be explained by the "coyote with mange" hypothesis. Dr. John Tomeček notes: "On canids, the last place they lose fur is right between the shoulder blades in an area that we call the ruff . . . . This fits the descriptions of Chupacabras having spikes or a ridge along their backs."[59]

If only there happened to be a Chupacabra body for scientists to analyze.

Well, there is. Sort of. Phylis Canion is a rancher who hails from Cuero, Texas, known to some as the Chupacabra capital of the world. In some ways, Cuero is to the Chupacabra as Point Pleasant is to Mothman: a town that has, for good or for ill, forged a strong association with a particular cryptid.

In 2007, Canion had the questionable fortune of happening across the dead body of what seemed to be a Chupacabra lying in the road outside her ranch. Speaking to reporter Kristen Cabrera of the *Texas Standard,* Canion recalled: "I drug it out of the road because I didn't want anybody driving over it and I laid it on the feed sack and took a picture. And as they said, it went viral."[60]

It's easy to see why. At first glance, the creature, which Canion took to a taxidermist and then mounted in her living room, certainly looks like a Chupacabra — complete with an arching spine and an open maw that could just as easily be panting as growling, depending on the angle from which it is photographed. The beast is hairless, with the characteristically tough gray skin of Chupacabra legend, and a pair of pointed, backswept ears. Notably absent, however, are the spikes that are supposed to protrude along the crest of the creature's spine.

Kudos to Phylis Canion for not simply leaving the stuffed creature as a talking piece in her home without probing further into the mystery. In search of answers, she extracted several DNA samples from the animal for laboratory testing. The result: it has the genetic structure of a coyote-wolf hybrid, also known as a coywolf or an eastern coyote. Scientists cannot agree on whether coywolves constitute a completely separate species or are merely a subspecies of coyote, but they are entirely real. Their existence is well documented.

The coywolf is a coyote-wolf hybrid that does occur in nature. They are sometimes called eastern coyotes because of their prevalence in the eastern United States.

Coywolves are not usually hairless, just as coyotes and wolves are not. It is here that the subject of mange arises once more as a sensible and compelling explanation for the monstrous appearance of Phylis Canion's uninvited property guest.

That isn't to say that there may not be Chupacabra out there, stalking the wilds around Cuero. After all, sightings of similarly strange-looking creatures continue to be reported in the vicinity, including one that was captured on video by police deputies on patrol, running away from their cruiser.[61] The fleeing creature looked a great deal like the creature that now stands guard over Phylis Canion's ranch.

Chupacabra, coywolf, or something else entirely?

The jury is still out.

Human beings, it has to be said, love their monsters; and there can be no more recognizable monster than Bigfoot, a.k.a. the Sasquatch. For any reader who might be wondering what the difference is, the two terms are basically interchangeable. Different names for the same thing — a large, hairy, elusive humanoid creature that ought to be crowned the king of hide-and-seek if such a title were a real thing.

To keep our terminology straight, Bigfoot/Sasquatch is not the same thing as the Yeti/Abominable Snowman. Although they are described as being very similar in appearance and behavior, the former names refer to the North American variants of the creature, whereas the latter relate strictly to its Asian counterpart.

Sightings of Bigfoot pour in from numerous different parts of North America each year, although the lion's share of them seems to originate in the heavily forested Pacific Northwest. As a general rule, wherever there are vast, isolated areas of woodland, one tends to find stories of these mysterious humanoids — from coast to coast, and north of the border.

More Americans than ever believe in the creature's existence, and that belief seems to be growing. According to Noah Brode, writing for the website civicscience.com, belief in Bigfoot has risen from 11% of the U.S. populace in 2020 to 13% in 2022.[62]

Now, more than ever, it appears that we *want* to believe, though the reasons why are open to interpretation.

One possibility is that a belief in things that were previously considered to be "fringe" or paranormal is on the rise. A 2024 research poll revealed that 56.9% believed in the reality of aliens/UFOs/extraterrestrial life; 61.4% believe in ghosts, and by implication the survival of human consciousness after death in some form; and 70% believed in the literal existence of the devil, and therefore demons and demonic possession. An overwhelming 83% believed in the reality of miracles.[63/64]

More and more, Americans are coming to believe that there are indeed Sasquatch living in North America and perhaps elsewhere in the world.

When seen in light of those statistics, our belief in Bigfoot is lagging significantly behind our belief in ghosts, spirits, aliens, and Lucifer. However, 13 out of every 100 people is not an insignificant number. With regard to such nontraditional subjects, we truly do live in unprecedented times. No less an authority than the U.S. Navy has released footage of Unidentified Aerial Phenomena (UAPs) and has made the extraordinary admission that the U.S. military does not know what those flying objects are—objects that can run rings around some of the finest fighter aircraft in the arsenal of the U.S. Navy and Air Force. Congressional hearings gave the spotlight to whistleblowers who spoke with apparent candor about the reality of extraterrestrial life, the recovery and storage of alien bodies, and a myriad of related topics that for decades have been the subject of governmental denial and outright ridicule.

Taken by comparison to such remarkable revelations, which many American citizens seem to have accepted at face value, the notion of an as-yet-unproven species of hairy humanoid roaming the woods and forests of North America doesn't exactly require great suspension of disbelief.

Although he made a living writing for a local newspaper, Andrew Genzoli (1914–1984) was as knowledgeable about history and the events of the past as he was of current affairs. No professional historian, he was nonetheless well read and passionate about his subject. The journalist was a U.S. Army veteran, having served in the Pacific Campaign of World War II, and after returning to civilian life he built an impressive career filled with many accomplishments. Today he is best remembered for having popularized the term "Bigfoot" in 1958.

Genzoli wrote local interest stories for the *Humboldt Times*, focusing primarily on his own patch of Northern California. This part of the state is well known for its forests and was used as a filming location for the forest moon of Endor in *Star Wars Episode VI: Return of the Jedi* (1983). The giant, towering redwood trees and lush green canopy make Humboldt County perfect Sasquatch country.

In September 1958, a letter from a reader caught his attention. It had been penned by Mrs. Jess Bemis, who stated that her husband worked in the deep woods and had seen a set of unusually large humanoid footprints.

The densely forested terrain of Northern California is prime Bigfoot territory—and also makes a good setting for Ewoks in a Star Wars *film.*

> On their way to the job, tracks were seen going down the road. The tracks measured 14 to 16 inches in length. The toes were very short but were five to each foot. The ground was soft, and the prints were clear. In soft places the prints were deep, suggesting great weight. The tracks were wide as well as long. Things, such as fruit, have been missed by those camping on the job.[65]

That same summer, Gerry Crew (some sources spell it Jerry) was employed as a heavy equipment driver/operator by a logging company. He and his fellow workers were constructing a road through some arduous terrain, which first had to be cleared. Crew operated a Caterpillar tractor, and it was around this machine that Jerry found a series of strange footprints at the start of one workday. The footprints, circling all the way around the machine he was supposed to drive, seemed humanlike but were much bigger than those of even the tallest, beefiest man — some 16 inches long and 7 inches wide. Based on the separation distance between footprints, it was apparent that whoever or whatever had made the tracks must have had an enormous stride.

Nor was this the only work site at which the bizarre footprints had appeared. Upon hearing about the weird occurrence, Andrew Genzoli wrote it up for the *Humboldt Times* in Eureka, California, and created a minor sensation. A plaster cast of one of the prints was taken, with a stern-faced Crew posing alongside it, and the photograph was printed in the newspaper on October 6 — along with Genzoli's chosen descriptor, Bigfoot.

Armchair quarterbacks deluged the newspapers with pet theories to explain the footprints, such as a human being suffering from what was then called elephantitis, a condition we now term elephantiasis. Usually the result of a parasitic infestation, this illness involves swelling of parts of the body, particularly the feet and legs, because of blockages in the lymph nodes that cause fluid to become trapped. As the feet enlarge, the skin thickens, becoming tougher and less elastic.

This is a plaster cast of a footprint found in Elkins Creek, Georgia. It's similar to the one reported by Andrew Genzoli for the Humboldt Times *in Eureka, California.*

Looking at photographs of feet that have undergone elephantiasis-induced swelling, it is easy to see why they might be advanced as candidates to explain Bigfoot tracks. There's one significant drawback to this hypothesis, however. Elephantiasis is a painful condition, and one that reduces the mobility of the sufferer as it progresses. The likelihood of somebody who is suffering from its symptoms to be wandering around in the woods at night, taking a keen interest in mechanical equipment, is exceptionally low.

It didn't take long for the controversy to start, and almost 70 years later that controversy is still going strong. On one side of the fence were those who claimed to have spotted a large, shadowy figure watching them from the depths of the forests or while moving from tree to tree. Tools and gear at worksites and camps had been moved, as though picked up and scrutinized by a curious observer before being discarded in favor of something else. Opposing this were those who said that the whole thing was a hoax, a prank played by bored outdoorsmen on one another to help pass the time.

On October 14, 1958, the *Eureka Humboldt Standard* published an article titled "Promised Hoax Expose of Mysterious Footprints Fails to Materialize." The story alluded to claims that the tracks found by Crew were made by an unidentified hoaxer, somebody whose name was known and documented on an affidavit. Particularly noteworthy was this statement: "Last night, it was learned that the sheriff's office had sent word to Raymond Wallace, owner of the Wallace Logging Company in Willow Creek, to come in and explain the 'joke.'"

For his part, Wallace not only refused to cooperate but said that he would have no hesitation in suing the sheriff for slander if the issue was pressed any further. Accusatory fingers were pointing in his direction, and Wallace vehemently denied any responsibility for having made what everybody had now taken to calling Bigfoot tracks.

More people came forward to report their own experiences, primarily workers who had spotted similarly weird footprints. These weren't limited to the vicinity of Crew's worksite. Bigfoot, it seemed, liked to travel; either that, or there was more than one creature roaming the woods, which made more sense. There were no paranormal hypotheses making the rounds in 1958, so

While walking in the woods, Crew and his companions would get the strange feeling that they were being watched….

many of those who found the "creature explanation" to be credible were open to the possibility that whatever Bigfoot was, it was probably something that ate, slept, and bred in ways not dissimilar to those of human beings.

There were no paranormal hypotheses making the rounds in 1958, so many of those who found the "creature explanation" to be credible were open to the possibility that whatever Bigfoot was, it was probably something that ate, slept, and bred in ways not dissimilar to those of human beings.

Crew and his colleagues reported the eerie sensation of being watched by unseen eyes while they were at work in the wooded country. While it's possible that this was indeed the case, it should also be borne in mind that environments such as the deep woods and even open areas of rural wilderness can be spooky places, where it is easy for one's imagination to run wild. Forestry workers were also fond of telling one another spooky stories around the campfire at night, stories that often involved ghosts and monsters. They sometimes competed to one-up each other. It's believed by folklorists that this is how stories of such mythical creatures as Colorado's Slide Rock Bolter, a huge wormlike creature said to cling to the tops of mountain peaks and to feast on unwary travelers, came into being.

As more and more Bigfoot stories came to light, so too did attention begin to focus on Raymond Wallace. A taxidermist named Robert Titmus scrutinized the cast that Crew had made of the track and declared that not only were the tracks human, but in his view there was "no doubt about it."[66] Local law enforcement got involved, attempting to determine whether the whole thing was genuine or nothing more than a prank that had gotten out of hand.

Certainly, people were seeing *something*. Two construction workers told a reporter that when they were going back to their camp on Bluff Creek Road in the early morning hours of October 12, they both saw a figure that was "tall, hairy, walking stooped over, with long, dangling arms, four feet across the shoulders."[67] The creature was on all fours, drinking water out of Bluff Creek when the two men claimed to have encountered it. All three of them were equally surprised. Rather than spark a confrontation, Bigfoot turned and ran away, quickly disappearing into the darkness of the undergrowth.

In 2002, Ray Wallace died at the age of 84. Although he refused to admit that he had hoaxed the Bigfoot tracks of 1958 and the subsequent plethora of other alleged sightings and encounters he claimed to have undergone, his children had no qualms about doing so. His son, Michael, revealed that Wallace delighted in playing pranks on others, and had carved a foot from wood in order to get one over on Gerry Crew. No malice was intended, and it seems likely that Raymond Wallace never expected the matter to explode in the public consciousness the way it ultimately did. At that point, with even the police asking pointed questions, he had the proverbial tiger by the tail; letting it go would have meant a shameful confession and a huge hit to his reputation. Instead, Wallace went all in, doubling down on the Bigfoot angle and helping cement the cryptid's place in popular culture for all time. Without him and his pranksterism, we would not be seeing Bigfoot's instantly recognizable silhouette on T-shirts, bumper stickers, and baseball caps today.

The entire Wallace family knew that their father had perpetrated, and perpetuated, the hoax, Michael told Scott Martelle of the *Los Angeles Times* shortly after Raymond's death. "He's up in Heaven laughing."[68]

The Bigfoot Field Researchers Organization (BFRO) contends that, while he did fake some photographic evidence and regularly attempted to pass off manufactured Bigfoot casts as being genuine to customers at a store he owned, Wallace was never able to successfully pull off a significant Bigfoot hoax on any kind of scale.

Not everybody believes that Raymond Wallace faked the tracks, however. The Bigfoot Field Researchers Organization (BFRO) contends that, while he did fake some photographic evidence and regularly attempted to pass off manufactured Bigfoot casts as being genuine to customers at a store he owned, Wallace was never able to successfully pull off a significant Bigfoot hoax on any kind of scale. The organization adds that the feet on the wooden

Without Raymond Wallace, Bigfoot might not have become the pop culture figure of today, a fun mystery that graces everything from T-shirts to chotchke-filled souvenir shops.

"track stompers" produced by his family after Wallace's death differ from the actual footprints that were found by Crew in 1958. Even if this is correct, then it still would not prove definitively that either Raymond Wallace or an entirely different prankster wasn't responsible for those tracks. BFRO also points out that the Wallace family only came forward with their story after the death of Raymond in 2002, when he could not make a rebuttal. Whether this was done to spare him from any discomfort the claim would cause or for some other reason is something on which this author will not speculate.

Just because Ray Wallace may well have hoaxed the Crew Bigfoot tracks, and most likely others as well, that does not mean that there was no genuine Sasquatch activity taking place in that part of the country. Satisfactorily explaining a handful of incidents still leaves a vast global array of sightings unaccounted for.

Nine years later, in 1967, Bluff Creek was once again the center of Bigfoot-related controversy. This time the subject of contention was more than just a few tracks in the ground; it was a full-color motion picture capture of what was purported to be the elusive creature. Because of the area's reputation as a hot spot for Bigfoot sightings, it was at Bluff Creek that Bob Gimlin and Roger Patterson set out to track it down and capture indisputable evidence of its existence once and for all.

On the afternoon of October 20, 1967, they may have been successful. The two men were riding through the forest on horseback that day, keeping a watchful eye out for signs of Bigfoot, when they happened upon one of the creatures just sitting at the creek-side, minding its own business. Initially startled, they recovered quickly and had the presence of mind to start rolling 16mm film through the camera they had rented. The three of them made eye contact, before the Bigfoot, which appeared to be a female, loped away, turning to look back at them over its shoulder along the way.

What would later become known as the Patterson-Gimlin film ultimately ran to just under a minute in duration and has taken its place among the most analyzed and hotly debated segments of film footage in all of history.

This still from the Patterson-Gimlin film has astonished many who believe it is the most convincing evidence that Bigfoot exists.

The footage is certainly iconic, having been screened as part of countless documentaries. The image of the creature itself graces T-shirts and posters and can be seen in numerous books and magazines on cryptozoology. From the moment it was made public, the film was divisive. Some viewers were impressed with what they found to be a highly realistic and lifelike creature, which moved in a natural yet non-humanlike way. Others scoffed at what they thought was simply a man in a fur-covered suit and mask, in what was plainly a hoax being perpetrated either for profit or for fun.

Viewing the film today, one is struck by how surprisingly well it holds up. There's a degree of frustration to the "shaky cam" style of filming, which can be explained by the two men's story about the encounter being a surprise, and their having to hastily grab the camera and start filming as quickly as possible. On the other hand, skeptics point out that the story could have been contrived in order to justify the lack of stability depicted in the film.

At about the 26-second mark, the footage reaches its point of greatest clarity. It is here that we have the opportunity to closely study the gait of its subject. The creature strides quickly, swinging its thick arms, turning toward the camera for an instant and then back again before wandering off out of frame with an air of what almost seems like nonchalance. There is no suggestion that the Bigfoot has been spooked or frightened, or that it may feel threatened by the presence of the two cameramen. It simply turns and leaves, heading from the middle distance into the trees in the far distance.

When assessing claims of the mysterious or the paranormal, it is wise to ask the question: Who benefits? In other words, when extraordinary claims are being made, are the person or people making them likely to gain from those claims being true, either financially or in terms of fame or notoriety? If the answer is yes, then there is increased reason to regard those claims with a healthy degree of suspicion.

There is no denying that Patterson and Gimlin made money from their Bigfoot film, including a documentary film that was screened in movie theaters. Patterson made significantly more money than his partner. Bob Gimlin sold his share of the film rights for just $10, practically throwing away a cash cow with both hands. A natural showman, a reason for which many proponents of the hoax theory hold him in disfavor, Patterson exploited the footage to the hilt, both in terms of fame and of financial gain.

Roger Patterson died in 1972, five years after the encounter, at the age of 38. Bob Gimlin has never quite separated himself from his Bigfoot association. The notoriety that accompanied these gains proved, in some ways, to be detrimental to his personal life. In 2016, he told reporter Matthew Dunn that he wished he had never been a part of the media circus that arose from the film that bore his name.

Roger Patterson died in 1972, five years after the encounter, at the age of 38. Bob Gimlin has never quite separated himself from his Bigfoot association. The notoriety that accompanied these gains proved, in some ways, to be detrimental to his personal life.

"It ruined me," Gimlin said. "My wife was a teller at a savings and loan institution. Of course, she was sitting right there, and the public would come in and make smart remarks . . . This went on and on until she came home crying. She'd say 'I'm not tough enough.' A couple times we were going to split up over this."[69]

Criticism and ridicule of Patterson and Gimlin's film, and by extension of Bob Gimlin himself, were widespread. Some went so far as to publicly call him a fraud and a faker. Through all of the hoopla, he stuck to his guns, steadfastly maintaining that he had never and would never have been party to a hoax. Assuming that he was telling the truth, this still leaves open the possibility that Roger Patterson organized a hoax behind Gimlin's back. In his 2004 book, *The Making of Bigfoot: The Inside Story*, author and researcher Greg Long posited that Roger Patterson was the mastermind behind a scam that encompassed not only the Patterson-Gimlin film but also a much broader con game. According to Long, the "Bigfoot" in question was actually a man named Bob Hieronymus wearing a fur suit. Hundreds of thousands of words have been written both in support of and defending against Long's attempted dissec-

The Bigfoot walking pose that is commonly used in all kinds of art regarding Sasquatch is clearly influenced by the famous film from Patterson and Gimlin that shows the cryptid's distinctive stride.

tion of Patterson and his film.

Critics also highlight the sheer good fortune of Patterson and Gimlin's Bigfoot encounter. The two men rode out into the woods in search of one of the most hard-to-find creatures on the planet, their logic goes, and lo and behold, after hardly any time had passed, they found it. What are the odds? While this point has merit, the flip side of the coin might be to consider the case of a ghost hunter who travels to a haunted house in search of paranormal activity. It seems reasonable that if the ghost hunter chose a location that was heavily reputed to be haunted, then the likelihood of their experiencing something potentially paranormal would be greater than average — if one believes in ghosts in the first place, that is. By the same token, Patterson and Gimlin chose a part of rural California that was already renowned for Sasquatch sightings, and they presumably chose it for that very reason.

Right up to his death from cancer, Patterson denied faking anything. There was no deathbed confession. Bob Gimlin, who is alive at the time of writing, has not wavered from his story over the decades. He has appeared at events on the increasingly popular Bigfoot circuit, where many of those who know him tend to judge him as being honest and forthright of character. Inevitably, there are also those who insist that he was a willing part of a hoax.

The one thing that the Patterson-Gimlin skeptics and believers have in common is the sheer strength of conviction each holds, not just in their insistence that the film shows a genuine Bigfoot or does not, but also that the other side must be wrong. It is an emotionally heated subject, within a field that is known for its extremely vocal contention. More than half a century later, the truth about that maddeningly fascinating 59.5 seconds of film footage remains as uncertain, and as hotly debated, as it was back then. Unless an actual suit turns up in a dusty attic or storage unit somewhere as the proverbial smoking gun (assuming its authenticity could be verified), the debate is unlikely to ever be settled to everybody's satisfaction. The authenticity or lack thereof of the Patterson-Gimlin film will remain a matter of individual belief forever.

It is important to bear in mind that, whether the film shows a genuine Sasquatch or a man in a suit, it is a single data point in the midst of a dataset that spans generations and thousands, if not tens of thousands, of other purported encounters with mysterious giant creatures. It is fair to say that many of them are fictitious, fraudulent, or the result of well-intentioned, honest misinterpretation — but even if this applies to the majority of such cases, there still remains a core number of sightings that defy easy dismissal. Perhaps the biggest challenge for the aspiring cryptozoologist is to sift through the vast morass of hoaxes and mistakes in order to reach those relatively rare nuggets that may be the genuine article.

It is important to bear in mind that, whether the film shows a genuine Sasquatch or a man in a suit, it is a single data point in the midst of a dataset that spans generations and thousands, if not tens of thousands, of other purported encounters with mysterious giant creatures.

The Crew-Wallace and Patterson-Gimlin cases are milestones in Bigfoot/Sasquatch lore, considered the gold standard in compelling proof by some, and laughable hoaxes by others. Each has gotten vast amounts of attention over the years, particularly from the media. Each case has a number of deeply concerning credibility issues associated with it, most notably in the "colorful" characters of Raymond Wallace and Roger Patterson, yet despite this, both cases have attained the same status as Kenneth Arnold's famed sighting of flying saucers around Mount Rainier, or Tim Dinsdale's Loch Ness Monster photography. It is next to impossible to talk about Bigfoot without addressing them both.

There are many photographs and sections of video footage purporting to show Bigfoot. With the widespread usage of camera phones, the days of grainy 16mm film captures are long gone. In October 2023, the creature made national news again after a sighting made from a moving train in Durango, Colorado. A couple named Shannon and Stetson Parker visited the region from their home in Wyoming, riding the rails and checking out the sights of the beautiful southwestern Colorado countryside. The two visitors were celebrating their tenth wedding anniversary in style, on the lookout for elk and taking in the scenery. What they found instead was something entirely different.

In an interview, Shannon Parker told *New York Post* reporter Alex Mitchell, "It was at least six, seven feet or taller. It matched the sage in the mountains so much that he's like camouflaged when crouching down. . . . If you asked before our trip we would have said maybe [Bigfoot] could be real, but now we're convinced."[70]

The video footage was posted to Facebook and shared widely across not only that platform but other social media applications as well. It became an overnight sensation. The video looks like a modern-day equivalent to the Patterson-Gimlin film, showing a sandy-colored, shaggy-haired creature stomping across the mountainside with long-legged strides. The thing abruptly pivots and squats, as though suddenly becoming aware of the train's presence. What the viewer makes of this footage is really going to depend on their personal beliefs and biases with regard to the Sasquatch phenomenon. If you find the Patterson-Gimlin footage compelling, the Parker film makes an equally convincing companion piece. If you take the opposite view, then it's just as easy to see this as being nothing more than a prankster in a Sasquatch suit aping it up in the Colorado countryside, either for their own amusement or as a publicity stunt.

The *Post* consulted with the Bigfoot Discovery Museum's curator, Michael Rugg, who came down on the side of the footage being a hoax. "I have to say, I looked at the video and [the creature] had the strong possibility of being a guy in a suit," Rugg told journalist Megan Palin. "It didn't look right to me. It's not muscular enough. There's not enough detail to be able to judge it,

The Bigfoot Discovery Museum in Felton, California, was run by Michael Rugg until 2021.

but it wouldn't surprise me if somebody from [another Bigfoot] museum was out to build up publicity."[71]

Most media coverage tended to agree with Rugg, declaring that the sighting was probably a hoax. Although it seems like a stretch to ascribe such a specific motive to the perpetrator — *if*, that is, it really was a hoax or prank — Rugg does make a valid point. On the other hand, it fails to account for one key factor, as do many "Bigfoot is just a person in a suit" claims. Each year, there are approximately 1,000 hunting-related accidents in the United States. Of those, around 100 result in a death. It is not unusual for a hunter to mistake another human being for a deer. When viewed in that light, anybody wandering around the wilderness in an animal costume runs the risk of being shot dead by a hunter in a case of mistaken identity . . . especially if the hunter believes they have just been presented with an opportunity to bag the elusive Bigfoot.

In a country that prides itself on having the right to

bear arms, putting on a Sasquatch suit could prove to be an extremely dangerous undertaking.

This danger doesn't stop with hunters armed with bows and guns. In 2012, 44-year-old Randy Lee Tenley was hit by two cars on a busy highway in Montana. Tenley was wearing a full-body ghillie suit at the time. Often worn by military snipers and hunters, ghillie suits are a specific type of camouflage that offers the means of blending in with the background outdoors. Made of netlike material entwined with cloth strips, they are meant to provide concealment. In Tenley's case, the suit had a different purpose: he was pretending to be Bigfoot.

According to an officer of the Montana State Patrol, this wasn't the first time Tenley had attempted a Bigfoot hoax, but it *was* the first time he had done so while standing in the middle of the highway. Tragically, it was also the last. It was 10:30 at night, making it easy for drivers to not see him in the darkness. Designed to conceal, the ghillie suit did its job all too well. The first car knocked Tenley off his feet. The second drove over him. He was killed at the scene of the incident. Officers said that, in terms of the cause of an accident, they had never experienced anything quite like it before.

Six years later, still in Montana, a 27-year-old man went shooting and got more than he bargained for when bullets started coming his way, forcing him to take cover in the trees. His attacker told him later: "I thought you were Bigfoot. I don't target practice — but if I see something that looks like Bigfoot, I just shoot at it."[72]

Fortunately, tragedy was avoided, albeit narrowly, but these cases do serve to illustrate the dangers of perpetrating a costumed Bigfoot hoax. Equally remarkable is the fact that, given the willingness of some hunters to shoot at something in the woods they think *might* be a Sasquatch, why has there never been a carcass found and submitted for forensic examination?

Skeptics quite rightly ask why, given the sheer volume of Sasquatch sightings that are made each year, medical science has yet to have had the chance to examine a single corpse. Supporters of the Bigfoot cause posit that when such creatures die, they may do so in remote places, meaning that their remains are picked apart, eaten, and dispersed by other critters before they are discovered — if they are even discovered at all. Although claims have been made to the contrary, no reports of supposed Bigfoot remains have ever been proven to hold water. The same is true of DNA testing, which at best may turn up "unidentified" genetic material. To the skeptic and the believer alike, this proves nothing.

Researching sightings of strange, unidentified humanoids is a fascinating field of endeavor. Many cryptozoology enthusiasts devote countless hours and considerable amounts of money in pursuit of what they are convinced is a real phenomenon.

I'm about to fill my rucksack, lace up my hiking boots, and go out into the wilds to join them.

When it comes to the domain of Bigfoot/Sasquatch, equally as fascinating as the creatures themselves are those men and women who spend their time in pursuit of them. Such people come from all walks of life and range from the casual enthusiast, who likes to head out into the woods occasionally to see what they can see, up to the serious devotee who invests great sums of money and years of their life to the search.

Some of them are trying to get rich, hoping to hit it big by capturing and capitalizing on proof of the existence of Bigfoot — a description that also applies to some of the hoaxers who plague the field of endeavor. Others seek fame over fortune, seeking to make a name for themselves or to score a job in television. Not that there's anything wrong with such motives, as long as they are pursued honestly and with integrity.

Others develop a passion for the chase itself, sometimes to the point of obsessiveness. For a certain type of individual, hunting down Bigfoot can be an all-consuming endeavor that ends up taking over their lives.

Bigfoot remains the muse for a number of creative individuals, artists who document their quest on film or in print. Wanting to gain a greater understanding of the mindset of the Bigfoot field researcher, I invited seasoned veterans Alan Megargle and Jesse Morgan to share their personal experiences with me.

Jesse Morgan took his first steps on the Bigfoot trail in 2009, when he and his best friend since boyhood,

The Sasquatch statue in Whitehall, New York, stands 11 feet tall and weighs half a ton. It is a centerpiece for the town when it holds its annual festival.

Alan, visited Whitehall in upstate New York. In the same way that Point Pleasant embraced its Mothman legacy, the town of Whitehall went all in on Sasquatch. The town is home to an 11-foot-tall, 1,000-pound steel statue of the creature, which stands by the side of Route 4. Both residents of the town and visitors alike have reported numerous sightings of Bigfoot over the years. Another parallel with Point Pleasant is the annual Sasquatch festival that Whitehall hosts, attracting tourists with a fascination for the humanoid ape creature.

The people of Whitehall are fond of their resident monster, as reflected in the fact that they have declared it an endangered creature and made it illegal to hunt or kill a Sasquatch either in or around the town — quite the legal feat, considering that the creature may or may not actually exist. That would make for quite the court case if things ever got that far. It currently remains a hypothetical situation and is likely to remain so for the foreseeable future.

Sasquatch is the official animal of Whitehall, and it is difficult to go anywhere in town without seeing some reminder of this fact. Everything from giant statues to merchandise in shop windows attests to the creature's popularity, making Whitehall a logical place for Jesse and Alan to begin their quest.

Visiting Whitehall caused the two men to be bitten by the Bigfoot bug. Their next stop was the Ohio Bigfoot Conference. By the time *that* was over, their fascination with the Bigfoot phenomenon was cemented. The pair never looked back.

"Bigfoot is highly unlikely to be a danger to human beings," Jesse observes. "In all of the credible witness interviews we've done, most of the encounters have been brief sightings. In some cases, we hear about rocks being thrown, wood knocks, logs being dropped onto the ground; but 99.9% of the stories do not contain any form of aggression or negativity on the part of the Sasquatch."

It might seem like a foregone conclusion, but does Jesse believe in the objective existence of Bigfoot? "I need tangible proof. It would have to run up to me and literally slap me and be like *I'm real!* — and then run away. I've heard a lot of things while investigating, but I need to see something."

Hypothetically speaking, if Jesse were to actually find what he's looking for, how would he react? "Bigfoot is not aggressive. Think of it as being curious, like a cat. The thing to do is go out there and spend time in the woods, without being scared. The evidence suggests that it isn't a violent creature by nature."

Whitehall residents are so fond of their local Bigfoot population that they have declared it an endangered species and made a law imposing penalties for killing a Bigfoot.

Jesse's research partner, Alan, concurs with that statement and adopts a similar philosophy. Alan's fascination with all things cryptid-related stems from his childhood, when he was weaned on a steady diet of paranormal-themed TV shows such as *In Search of . . .* and *Sightings*. He grew up to make documentary films that tread on similarly themed ground. Alan tells me that he was also a field investigator for the Bigfoot Field Researchers Organization (BFRO) and has ultimately come to the conclusion that, while there is definitely a physical element to the Bigfoot phenomenon, there is also most likely a paraphysical aspect as well.

"The possibility that Bigfoot may be inter-dimensional makes a lot of sense," he opines, "and I've had direct experiences that don't fit with an ape running around out here in the woods."

On more than one occasion, Alan and his Squatching companions seemed to have been pursued by one of the creatures.

"I believe that there's an intelligence level at work that we don't quite understand, but one that's possibly really high, or at least equal to our own. One night, the Bigfoot that was following us doubled back across our trail, crossing from our rear left and ending up in front of us on the right-hand side. It slipped on some mud and fell into the water with a loud splash. It seemed to have an almost military-like instinct, tracking and flanking us."

Either that, I think, or there was more than one of them.

"There's something else that people don't think about," Alan tells me. "I learned this while watching them through a thermal camera. The Bigfoot was lying on the ground. We think of Bigfoot walking like we do, but they can crawl, they can run on all fours, there are a lot of different ways they can maneuver." He recounts a time during his tenure as an investigator in Ohio when a farmer called to report what he had initially believed was a bear walking across his field one night — until it abruptly stood up and revealed itself as an approximately eight-foot-tall humanoid, and ambled off into the woods.

I'm interested in hearing about Alan's most compelling Bigfoot encounter from all his years of field investigation. It took place in rural Oregon, in a stretch of woodland behind a private residence. The property owner and a few of his colleagues believed that the woods may have contained a portal of some kind, which immediately earned Alan's interest. The owner

According to Alan Megargle, Bigfoot are not actually dangerous and will most likely leave you alone if you do not provoke them.

set up a bench in the woods for the express intention of observing potential phenomena among the trees. He ended up getting more than he bargained for one night, when something very large approached him from behind under cover of darkness and placed a huge hand on his shoulder.

Taking a somewhat unconventional approach, Alan enlisted the help of a psychic medium to investigate the location along with him. Alan and the medium sat side by side on the bench late one night. They closed their eyes, and the medium attempted to put out "psychic feelers." Both of them heard distinct movement coming from behind and above them, at the top of a steep hill. The medium claimed that she could sense the presence of a Sasquatch up there, looking down and watching them both.

"They know why we're here, and they want to participate," the psychic medium said.

Alan could hear the sound of footsteps slowly and gingerly picking their way toward him from his right, moving with great deliberation. They stopped approximately 6 feet away. Alan anticipated being touched in a similar way to which the property owner had been, but instead, the center of his chest suddenly began to feel extremely warm. Something hot felt like it was swirling around in the vicinity of his heart.

"The only way I can describe it was like being hugged from the inside," Alan says, searching for the proper words. "There was a feeling of intense love. It turned out to be a really pleasant experience. Then it kind of . . . faded. I opened my eyes and the first thing I noticed was that I could see in the dark, as if I was looking through night vision. I turned around quickly to look at the place where the footsteps had stopped, and there was nothing there. Whatever had been there was gone before I could see it."

Alan's experience leans heavily toward the spiritual and the metaphysical, and contrasts sharply with Jesse's more biologically based mindset toward Bigfoot. That's not to say that either or both views lack validity. They simply seem like two sides of the same coin.

"This is not a monster in the woods to be feared," Alan concludes, paraphrasing his investigative partner. "This is something that we don't understand, but I do think that it wants to help us in some way, either individually or globally. There's some purpose to it all.

"Don't try to define Sasquatch. Just let Sasquatch be whatever it is."

Many states seem to have their Bigfoot "hubs" or sighting hot spots, places where the creatures are reportedly seen more frequently than anywhere else. In Colorado, that place is Park County, located southwest of Denver. It's rural, mountainous country, and has no shortage of forest and woodland. Sitting at 7,740 feet above sea level, the town of Bailey is Park County's best-known community. It is also home to the Sasquatch Outpost, a store that is dedicated to all things Bigfoot. What started out as a grocery store is now a major draw for curious visitors and Sasquatch enthusiasts alike.

Clearly, when it comes to hunting for Bigfoot in Colorado, Park County is a great place to start . . . which is what brings me there on a hot summer afternoon. Along with friend and fellow author Erin Taylor, Alan, Jesse, and their camera operator, Anna, we all set out to go Squatching.

A hotspot in Colorado for Bigfoot hunting is Park County near Denver, a forested, mountainous area perfectly suited to the shy beast.

Squatching is the name given to any serious (or even semi-serious) attempt to locate the Sasquatch. There are many enthusiasts actively engaging in the activity throughout North America. For some people, it's little more than a lark, a way to get out into the woods and have a little fun in much the same way that ghost enthusiasts will attend events at haunted locations in the hope of having a brush with something otherworldly. For others, however, it can become an obsession, an all-consuming quest to be the first to find the Holy Grail of Squatching: undeniable proof that Bigfoot actually exists.

Squatching combines elements of hiking, camping, and hunting, and pairs them with the potential of encountering a creature that is either completely mythical or 100 percent real. It's not difficult to see the allure, and some Squatchers sink tens of thousands of dollars into the pursuit. In addition to travel costs, they purchase state-of-the-art camera equipment and audio recorders. The gear list for Squatching can be as expensive as it is extensive, as can be seen on popular television shows such as *Finding Bigfoot* and *Mountain Monsters*. *Finding Bigfoot* ran for 12 seasons over a span of almost 8 years and found little in the way of conclusive evidence for its trouble. In 2019, *Expedition Bigfoot* took up the Squatch-hunting mantle and ran with it. At the time of writing, there have been 6 seasons of the show, which has similarly attempted to find Bigfoot — and has yet to be successful.

That's not to tear down the popularity of these shows or the efforts of those who make them. Skeptics point to the lack of what they consider solid evidence and the lack of success to date as proof that that there is nothing to find — that Bigfoot is not real. Yet some proponents of Squatching like to counter with the argument that the elusive nature of the creature can be attributed to some sort of supernatural element, perhaps the ability of the Sasquatch to travel between dimensions in some manner that science cannot currently explain.

I'm determined to approach the subject with an open mind, which is no less than it deserves. Our hosts, Jesse and Alan, have laid out a fairly detailed plan for my first Squatching experience. We're all going to meet up an hour before sunset at a trailhead in Bailey, then begin our hike away from civilization. At an appropriate spot, we'll set up a gifting site, leaving some offerings as a token of respect — and perhaps some enticement — for any Sasquatches in the area.

"You leave gifts, shiny trinkets, or sweet food offerings," Jesse explains, "and in return, usually after some time, you'll come back and find that Bigfoot has taken the gifts and replaced them with other things, like a pile of pinecones." Some researchers have left out jars of peanut butter and returned to find only the lid. No signs of the jar or its contents is usually found. If a bear or other animal was responsible, some evidence of its having torn its way through the packaging ought to be evident. Unscrewing the lid of a jar would typically require prehensile fingers, although it should be noted that raccoons have an almost preternatural ability to manipulate objects in this way. I'm adding raccoons to my list of critters to watch out for on this Squatching foray.

Apparently, according to Alan and Jesse, if you leave gifts in the woods for Bigfoot, it will retrieve them and leave something in exchange, like a pile of pinecones.

Once the gifting site has been set up, we'll venture deeper into the woods and attempt to communicate with the creatures via the practice of wood knocking. This is exactly what it sounds like: hitting things loudly and repetitively, making enough noise to draw the Sasquatch out . . . or so we hope. In addition to the wood knocking, Jesse and Alan advocate making a series of howls and whoops as an alternative means of attracting their attention. They will both be carrying parabolic microphones to listen for possible responses.

By then, it should be dark. Although I've never been Squatching before, I have spent many years investigating claims of ghosts and hauntings. On reading the itinerary, I'm pleasantly surprised to learn that there's some overlap between the two activities . . . in terms of the equipment we'll be using, at least. This includes night vision and thermal camera gear, ideal for seeing in the dark, and also some of the more esoteric items from the ghost hunter's stock in trade, such as REM-Pods, EMF meters, and spirit boxes. I'm intrigued to see how our guides will be putting these devices to use when we're out Squatching.

It's one thing to investigate claims of ghosts and creatures such as Mothman, neither of which have a reputation for harming people . . . but what about Sasquatch? This is no armchair research case. I will be actively going out into the woods that form Colorado's most popular hot spot, intentionally trying to encounter one. Are there any risks?

Although dissenting opinions are out there, the consensus among members of the Bigfoot/Sasquatch community is that the creature seems to be little threat to human beings.

Personally, I'm more worried about stumbling upon one of the black bears that are known to be active in the Bailey area than I am about anything a Sasquatch might do to me. My reasoning goes that if I do come to a sudden and unexpected demise at the hands of such a creature, it will make for one heck of an ending to the book you're now reading.

Personally, I'm more worried about stumbling upon one of the black bears that are known to be active in the Bailey area than I am about anything a Sasquatch might do to me. My reasoning goes that if I do come to a sudden and unexpected demise at the hands of such a creature, it will make for one heck of an ending to the book you're now reading. (Spoiler: The fact that you *are* now

You're much more likely to run into a black bear in the forests of Colorado than a Sasquatch, and the black bear is going to be more dangerous unless you are familiar with ways to protect yourself from a confrontation.

reading it means that I did not in fact get eaten by Bigfoot.)

Like most Coloradoans, it's been drilled into me that if one should come face to face with a black bear, there is a specific way to behave in order to maximize one's chance of surviving the encounter. First, do not panic. That should go without saying, but it's easier said than done. Second, one should under no circumstances turn one's back on the bear or break into a run; this can make the bear perceive you as its next meal and react accordingly. Instead, you should back slowly away, being careful to make no sudden movements that might spook the animal and maintaining eye contact as you go. Climbing a tree in an attempt to escape is ill-advised, as many bears are almost certainly better tree climbers than most humans.

One possible bear avoidance strategy is trying to puff oneself up in an attempt to appear bigger than one actually is, which can involve raising the arms and letting the sides of a coat or jacket dangle down to add more apparent mass to one's frame. This may, it is hoped, make the bear perceive you as being bigger, tougher, and therefore less like a target of opportunity than you really are . . . particularly if the bear is hungry and on the lookout for food.

Yelling and hollering, one of the things my guides will be using as a tool to attract Bigfoot, can also be employed as a method of scaring the black bear away. Some Squatchers advocate using bright lights, the most powerful flashlights that can be carried, to scare the creatures away if they should become aggressive. For unknown reasons, the light is said to be a more effective deterrent than anything else, including the use of firearms or brandishing other weapons.

The possibility of a chance encounter with a mountain lion is something else that makes me break out in a cold sweat. There are an estimated 4,000 of them in Colorado, most often found in proximity to their natural source of prey — deer, of which there are plenty in the woods of Adams County. If I am unfortunate enough to cross paths with one, the de-escalation and retreat techniques used with black bears will also apply. Let's hope they won't be needed.

We've arranged to meet an hour before sunset at a trailhead in the woods. I get up to Adams County a couple of hours early, with the intent of visiting the Sasquatch Outpost in Bailey. Bailey's a relatively small community, with a population just shy of 10,000. Bigfoot tourism in general—and the Sasquatch Outpost in particular—are a big draw for the area, and it's sufficiently close to Denver that a steady stream of visitors comes to town, many of them curious to learn more about Bigfoot.

The owners of the Outpost, Jim and Daphne Myers, clearly aren't in this to make a quick buck. Spend even

The Sasquatch Outpost in Bailey, Colorado, is a gift store specializing in Bigfoot merchandise. You can also purchase camping gear and other supplies needed for Squatching.

a few minutes perusing their store and it becomes apparent that they have a passion for Sasquatch research and education. At the back of the store, there's a museum dedicated to all things Bigfoot. A timeline of Sasquatch lore and sightings throughout North America adorns one wall, stretching from 1870 to the present day. There are casts of purported Bigfoot tracks, including one made by Roger Patterson in 1964 — three years before his video went the 1960s equivalent of viral. Other tracks have been photographed, many of them from nearby, including small footprints in the snow said to be those of a toddler Sasquatch.

It is here at the museum that I learn about part of the phenomenon of which I was unaware: braiding. A tattered Stars and Stripes mounted in a display case has been torn longitudinally, the rips made deliberately in parallel with the red and white stripes of the flag. The frayed ends of the strips have been braided, in a similar manner to that in which long hair can be braided. U.S. flags seem to be a favorite target for Bigfoot braiding, as do the manes of horses; one can only imagine how the horses must feel about it as it's happening! The mysterious braiding takes place primarily at night, and there is rarely if ever any indication that the horses were harmed in any way. Could this be an attempt by the Sasquatch to communicate in some way, or is it simply a relaxing, therapeutic activity, in much the same way that some people knit or crochet recreationally? A series of braided manes are presented in a display case for the visitor's perusal. One comes from as far afield as Oregon, while its neighbor originated right here in Bailey.

A display on the Patterson-Gimlin film leaves me in no doubt as to where the curators of the museum stand: firmly in the camp of the believers, rather than with the skeptics.

Photographs of unusual wooden structures found in Coloradoan forests catch my eye next. Teepees made of tree limbs and "X" shapes made from crossed tree trunks are attributed to "raw physical power that defies belief," with each trunk estimated to weigh at least 1,000 pounds. If these ad hoc structures are in fact the work of hoaxers, then one is challenged to find a reason why they would invest so much time and effort

Branches in the shape of a teepee to form a crude shelter have been found in Colorado's forests. Is Bigfoot capable of basic building skills?

into an activity that barely makes a newspaper byline, let alone being front page news. Hoaxing Bigfoot tracks or putting a person in a fake suit is one thing; it's fairly simple to do, particularly when you can buy a Bigfoot costume on Amazon for under a hundred dollars. But cutting down and manipulating tree trunks is an order of magnitude more difficult, not to mention potentially dangerous, and with very little payoff to be had.

Assuming for a moment that these woodland creations are the work of Sasquatch, the next logical question is also: why? What purpose do they serve? It's a question with no clear and obvious answer. The same is true of tree arches, in which saplings are bent back on themselves at a near-180-degree angle, forming the equivalent of an archway. Once again, a significant amount of strength would be required to achieve this effect, bending the trunk almost to breaking point and then wedging its tip underneath an anchor point such as a hefty rock. The reason behind this, too, is unknown. Some examples of arching are probably due to entirely natural causes — weakened trees breaking and collapsing — but this explanation by no means applies to them all. Just like the tree structures, the creation of arched saplings seems to involve a great deal of effort for precious little gain — for a human prankster, at least. Perhaps they could be meaningful for Sasquatches.

In the final display section, visitors are invited to compare their own height with that of Bigfoot, a cardboard cutout some 8 feet high that dwarfs my puny 6′ 2″ frame. Life-sized mannequins of an adult Bigfoot and a Bigfoot child stand guard over the exit.

I appreciate the fact that the museum, while clearly owned and operated by people who believe in the reality of the Bigfoot phenomenon, stops short of telling its visitors exactly what they ought to believe. Some of the exhibit placards pose the question "Could this have been the work of Bigfoot?" That small degree of uncertainty, however slight, is definitely healthy. Considering the number of children who visit the museum — I see several walking around during my time there — encouraging them to ask questions and to think for themselves is a refreshing approach, and one that I applaud.

When I bought my ticket for the museum, I was handed a token by the gentleman who was staffing the front desk. Now, having pondered the exhibits and reached the exit, I am presented with the opportunity to cast that token into a container that signifies whether I believe in Bigfoot or not.

I barely hesitate. It goes in with those of the other believers.

On my way out, I can't pass up the chance to grab a pair of Bigfoot-themed socks and a couple of fridge magnets. Admittedly, the museum caters to tourists, but it also provides a great overview of the Bigfoot phenomenon as a whole and offers food for thought to anybody who's willing to ponder things. The sun is starting to sink toward the horizon as I leave the Sasquatch Outpost and head for my rendezvous with the Squatchers. This is my first foray into Bigfoot-related fieldwork, and I'm equal parts excited, fascinated, and apprehensive. I have no idea that something very bizarre is about to happen to us in the woods after nightfall.

Fellow author Erin Taylor and I meet up with the trio of filmmakers at the trailhead in the woods. Jesse, Alan, and Anna have come loaded for bear — or, more accurately, for Sasquatch, though they have brought bear repellant spray just in case.

As previously mentioned, they're seasoned Squatchers and we're comfortable putting ourselves in their capable hands. It feels like things are about as safe as it's possible to be, heading into the woods at night . . .

. . . until we were met by something rather disturbing at the trailhead. Hanging from a tree branch at waist height is the severed leg of what appears to be a deer. The upper parts of the leg, the femur, tibia, and fibula, have been stripped down to the bone, which gleams white without its muscle, tissue, and hair. The remainder of the leg has been snapped forcefully at the lowest joint, bent back on itself at a perverse angle. The hoof and the few inches of bone directly above it are still covered in fur. There's not a trace of blood, and no evidence of the rest of the deer's body is anywhere to be found.

It's a bizarre discovery and doesn't fit the behavior profile of either a mountain lion or a bear. It's possible that a hunter is responsible, perhaps hanging the deer up by its hind legs in order to skin it. Later, I do some research online and find potential explanations that range from hunters hanging deer legs in order to help train their hunting dogs to track more effectively to a Bigfoot perhaps marking its territory.

Our guides deploy a drone, making use of the final hour of sunlight to scan the woods for signs of movement. A howling sound in the distance seems more like that of a dog than a Sasquatch, but the night is young. After we record on-camera interviews for documentary purposes, it's time to go Squatching. The first order of business is to leave some gifts out for Bigfoot, an offering in the form of bottled honey, some strawberries, and a couple of bananas; hopefully these sweet treats will prove irresistible to the creatures. This is not bait, meant in the same way that a hunter would bait a trap. Rather, it's an attempt to build a rapport and establish a connection with them. We're told that it usually takes several repeat attempts to achieve this goal, but it's worth starting out as we mean to go on.

The first order of business is to leave some gifts out for Bigfoot, an offering in the form of bottled honey, some strawberries, and a couple of bananas; hopefully these sweet treats will prove irresistible to the creatures. This is not bait, meant in the same way that a hunter would bait a trap. Rather, it's an attempt to build a rapport and establish a connection with them.

Surrounded by dense woods, the hunters walked parallel to a shallow creek. Across the water, they heard a strange noise, possibly one coming from a Sasquatch.

The long track winds its way into the woods, and before long it's dark. Red flashlights help preserve our night vision. Once we're completely surrounded by the trees, Alan breaks out a night vision camera. We've been walking parallel to a shallow creek on our left-hand side. We hear movement coming from the undergrowth on the opposite side of the creek. Showing not a trace of fear, Jesse heads straight toward it, while Alan keeps a close watch. Alan suddenly catches sight of what he thinks is a human-shaped form moving quickly from left to right. The naked eye doesn't catch it, but the camera does. It barely registers for a second and then it's gone. Jesse searches the area thoroughly with his flashlight and finds nothing.

Either Alan's eyes and the low-light conditions are playing tricks on him — a distinct possibility — or we may have company out here in the woods.

About a mile deeper into the woods, our hosts produce a club and hand it to me. They're coaching me on the technique of knocking. Some believe that Bigfoot will knock on trees as a warning to humans not to venture any further into their territory, the equivalent of putting up a *Warning — Keep Out!* sign. Others say that knocking is a two-way process, a method by which human beings can call out to the Sasquatch and that can also serve as a crude method of communication. On YouTube, one can find a plethora of videos purporting to have captured this phenomenon.

Taking the club, I use it to rap smartly on the nearest tree trunk three times in a row. All five of us stand in silence, waiting for a response. There's none. I repeat the process three more times, with the same lack of result. If

Bigfoot is out there, they don't seem to be interested in knocking back.

"Knocking works maybe 15, 20 percent of the time," Alan says. "When it *does* work, the results may not be what you expect. You don't always get wood knocks back in return. Sometimes you'll hear a whoop or a howl. Other times, it'll be the sound of something large moving around out there."

On prior Squatching outings, Alan has attempted wood knocking without any apparent response, only to have an unseen something stealthily trail his group for the rest of the night.

"Sometimes, it would have been sitting up on a large tree branch, and we'd hear it thump [as it hit the ground] and start following us."

We go another half mile along the trail. A familiar sight awaits us. Another deer leg, similarly fractured and skinned, has been hung from a tree branch at about the same height as the first. Again we ask ourselves, Was this the work of hunters or was it Bigfoot — or something else? Occam's razor suggests the former, but it's impossible to say for sure.

Heading deeper still into the woods, we walk on until we find a suitable clearing. Our hosts set down a REM-pod, an electronic device that measures the ambient air temperature and also generates an electromagnetic field. When that field is disturbed, lights on the REM-pod flash and an alarm sounds. The device is used by many ghost hunters as a method of detecting or communicating with spirits, a purpose for which it has drawn a great deal of criticism from the skeptical community — and understandably so. Radio waves can set the device off; this includes transmissions from passing police cruisers and fire trucks, or any other vehicle-mounted radio unit. Walkie-talkies will also trigger the device. When I use a REM-pod as part of a paranormal investigation, I shield the device from stray radio signals by enclosing it in a Faraday cage, a simple device that shuts out those extraneous radio waves.

Out here in the middle of nowhere, there are no emergency vehicles nearby, or even roads for them to drive on. It's almost midnight, which makes it unlikely that somebody would be wandering around the woods speaking on a walkie-talkie. We're not using any radio transmitters. There should be nothing around that's capable of triggering the device.

The REM-pod is positioned within sight of the clearing, about a hundred feet along the track. We each take a seat on the hillside or along the bank of the creek, and I add another critter to my list of concerns for the night: ticks. We'll have to check ourselves over thoroughly at the end of the night.

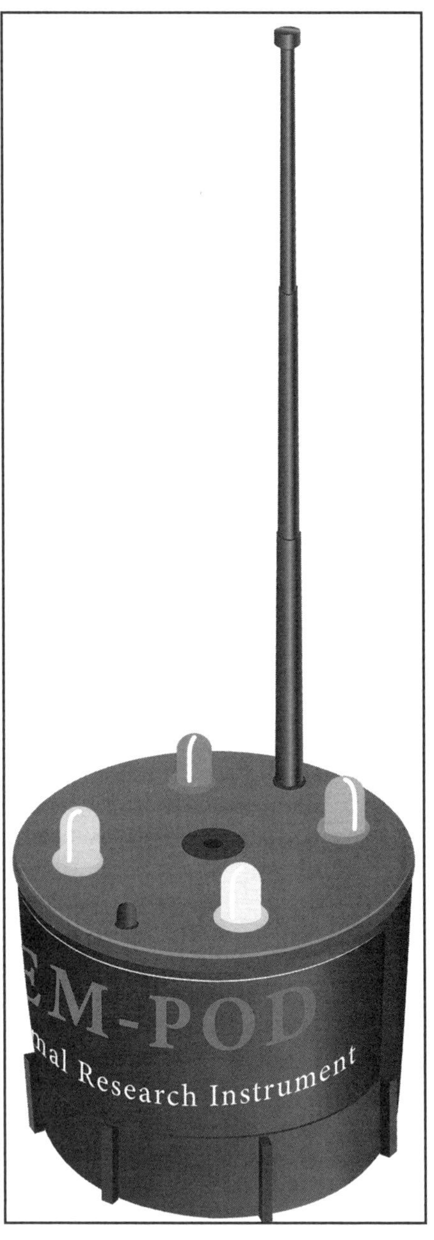

Investigators use REM-pods to detect changes in local electromagnetic fields and ambient temperatures, which is one way to find spirits and other supernatural entities.

The idea behind this particular experiment is to enter a semi-meditative state and open ourselves up spiritually to the possibility of connecting with Bigfoot. If you're thinking that this seems like a rather New Age approach to Squatching, you'd be right. Generally speaking, there are two schools of thought among those who believe in the reality of Bigfoot. One takes the biological view, positing that Bigfoot is a flesh-and-blood entity in the same way that humans, apes, bears, and other mammals are biological. In the opinion of researchers who adhere to this perspective, the creatures live, sleep, and hide out in the wild, and no supernatural explanation is necessary for humanity's failure to conclusively prove their existence.

At the forefront of this branch of research is Jeff Meldrum, Ph.D., a highly qualified anthropologist and zoologist. Meldrum's 2006 book *Sasquatch: Legend Meets Science* painstakingly dissects many of the physical characteristics associated with the phenomenon, including in-depth analysis of the subject's gait from the Patterson-Gimlin film, a plethora of ostensibly Sasquatch footprints and tracks, and even what is claimed to be the imprint of Bigfoot's buttocks. Meldrum is no crank. On the contrary, he is an academic of no small accomplishment. No less an authority than the renowned primatologist Dr. Jane Goodall, universally considered the world's foremost expert on chimpanzees, who made the monumental discovery in 1960 that chimps made and used tools, had this to say: "Jeff Meldrum's book . . . brings a much-needed level of scientific analysis to the Sasquatch — or Bigfoot — debate."

Meldrum's book deserves a place on the shelf of anybody who has even a passing fascination with Bigfoot. His conclusion:

> The pervasive sightings and notable correlations of consistent anatomy, behavior, and vocalization also point to a real animal — one that displays remarkable parallels to known great apes, while exhibiting unique characteristics appropriate to its particular ecology. The deeply rooted cultural and historical knowledge of a hairy wildman possessed by indigenous populations attests to a zoological entity. (p. 276)

Bigfoot researchers and enthusiasts refer to this as the "Aper" perspective.

At the opposite end of the spectrum are the researchers who associate Bigfoot with strange light anomalies, UFO activity, reputedly haunted places, other cryptids, and portals — hypothetical interdimensional doorways that are thought to allow transit between our own plane of reality and others. The portal hypothesis is much beloved of ghost hunters, providing a convenient explanation for how spirit entities may travel between realms. In the context of Sasquatch, such doorways offer a theory for why the creatures are often said to appear and disappear abruptly, seemingly out of thin air, and also might explain why they are so notoriously difficult to track down. If Bigfoot happens to spend most of its time on another plane of reality, only passing into our own periodically, the chances of encountering one are significantly reduced. This hypothesis also addresses the question of why biological remains such as bones are so uncommon.

Some theorize that not only Bigfoot but other cryptids and mysterious beings have access to our world through some kind of interdimensional doorway, perhaps one controlled by aliens.

When I began my career as a paranormal investigator in 1995, the field was siloed. There were folks like me, the so-called "ghost people"; we kept to ourselves. Then there were the "UFO people" and the "Bigfoot/monster people." Three distinct and separate interest groups, investigating what we thought were three separate types of phenomena. It was only when investigators started comparing notes and eyewitness accounts that they recognized the commonalities between them. Weird light phenomena, disembodied growls, and inexplicable battery drainage or equipment failures are mainstays of Squatching and ghost hunting.

Writing in *The Essential Guide to Bigfoot*, cryptozoology field researcher Ken Gerhard discusses an opposing viewpoint to that of the Aper, one that is commonly referred to as "the Woo." Encompassing the gamut of metaphysical explanations for Bigfoot, the Woo is defined by Gerhard as "essentially, the belief that these creatures are otherworldly beings with cosmic abilities and well-meaning intentions toward humans."

Elements of the Woo, according to Ken Gerhard, include that Bigfoot is inter-dimensional in nature, utilizing portals as a means of travel; can communicate with humans via telepathy or through some other form of mind-to-mind contact; and possesses a chameleon-like paranormal capacity to camouflage itself, only becoming visible to humans when it so chooses. He also points out that many of these ideas are not new, having been around for decades, but are now seeing a resurgence in popularity. To this I would add that all of these attributes have also been applied to extraterrestrial or extra-dimensional visitors in relation to the UFO phenomenon, particularly as it relates to the abduction of human beings from their homes and other places.

It's this "Woo" — paranormal, psychic, call it whatever you wish — hypothesis that we're testing now. Sitting in the darkness of the forest clearing, we invite Bigfoot to approach and make contact with us. All five of us attempt to clear our minds as much as possible, getting as close to a meditative state as we can. I personally have zero expectations, but no sooner have our guides extended this invitation than the REM-pod begins to alarm. There's no obvious reason for it to do so, unless there's some high-power radio transmitter in the vicinity that we're unaware of. A check of Google maps done later shows no obvious broadcast source for many miles around.

After a few seconds, the device goes quiet. Then it sets off alarms again . . . and again. Clearly, *something* is disturbing the electromagnetic field, but the question is, What? Certainly, there's nothing visible. Feeling quite self-conscious, I address whatever it is by the name "Bigfoot" just in case and tell it that I'm going to count to 50, during which time I am requesting that it stay away from our REM-pod.

I begin counting aloud in a slow, measured tone. "One

one thousand, two one thousand . . . " all the way up to "fifty one thousand," at which point I ask Bigfoot to approach the REM-pod again. The device instantly goes bananas, lighting up the darkness with multi-colored flashes and warbling loudly. The timing was so precise, so on the nose, that I have a hard time believing that this is simply random. Something managed to disturb the field at precisely the right time.

There's an almost indefinable sense of presence in the woods to that point. As someone who almost never feels such things, even I find the atmosphere to be a little odd — the equivalent of being watched by unseen eyes. Maybe we are. On the other hand, the power of suggestion can have an influence, especially as we're all discussing it and each of us feels something similar.

There's an almost indefinable sense of presence in the woods to that point. As someone who almost never feels such things, even I find the atmosphere to be a little odd....

It isn't long before the weird sensation dissipates. One moment it's there, the next it's gone, almost as if a switch has been turned off. This is something else reported by ghost enthusiasts, the feeling of sudden inertness that portends the onset of quietness and inactivity.

Jesse frankly admits to "struggling" with the metaphysical side of this, finding the paranormal hypotheses challenging to accept. "I think that the phenomenon of Bigfoot alone is enough," he says, implying that anything beyond the more commonly accepted Aper perspective is a bridge too far for him.

Although I'd love to think that the experience with the REM-pod connects to the Bigfoot phenomenon that we're out here in the woods to research (and it may), there are also other explanations to consider. A believer in the paranormal side of things might say that the woods were haunted and that this was a form of spirit communication — particularly as we found an ornate box containing human cremains close to the trailhead, inscribed with the decedent's name. Some would say this was an *elemental,* one of the nature spirits said to arise from and to guard the woods, streams, and rivers, a belief that has been around for centuries, if not millennia. On the other hand, a skeptic would point out that simply because no conventional explanation is readily apparent, that does not mean we should default to a paranormal one.

Ultimately, it all comes down to what the individual believes. It preoccupies my mind on the long hike back to the trailhead. When we reach the gifting site, I'm disappointed to find the fruit and honey has not been touched. Perhaps next time, I think as we shake hands and go our separate ways. Perhaps Bigfoot simply wasn't hungry; perhaps it wasn't in the area tonight; or perhaps it was never there at all.

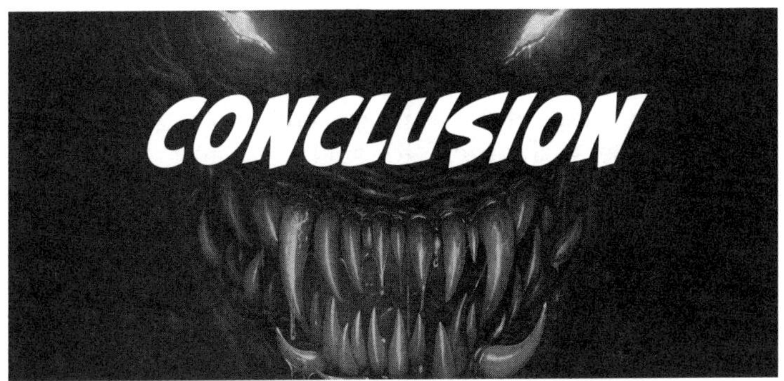

As all good things eventually must, our journey through the world of monsters, myths, and cryptids has come to an end. Our journey has taken us beneath and above the sea's surface, swimming with giant squid in the dark waters of the ocean, being careful not to awaken the many-tentacled behemoth Kraken as it slumbers away the years down in the bone-cold depths.

Morgawr swam across the waters of Falmouth Bay and along the Cornish coast, perhaps conjured to the surface by a psychic experiment carried out by a coven of witches . . . an experiment that also enfolded Morgawr's Scottish cousin, Nessie. The icy waters of Loch Ness are renowned for never giving up their dead, and the same may be true of the infamous lake monster, which has fascinated and sometimes infuriated generations of experiencers and would-be monster hunters.

Strange creatures stalked the woods, be it the Black-Eyed Kids and their neighbor, the werewolf of England's Cannock Chase, or the Jersey Devil, a folk tale that took on a life of its own and in the process became the mascot of an entire state — and an Air Force fighter squadron. In the forests of North America, Bigfoot played hide-and-seek between the trees, leaving tracks in the mud and photos to be pondered, yet always maddeningly one step ahead of its would-be trappers.

In the Land Down Under, Australia, Yowies play hide-and-seek with those who are brave enough to venture into the wilds. Bunyips lurk in the swamps, ready to pounce on the unwary, thereby proving that there's more to fear in the southern hemisphere than snakes and spiders.

Vampires stalked the silver screen, as generations of moviegoers shivered to such classics as *Dracula* and *Fright Night*. Stepping into the real world, we met those who believe they are truly vampires, feeding on the blood of willing donors as they live a lifestyle far beyond the mainstream. The vampire hysteria that gripped New England led to the desecration of innocent victims, such as Mercy Brown and her family, while in medieval England, the Alnwick Vampire held a reign of terror after the death of its human body.

As the full moon rose in the night sky, the howl of wolves split the air. From a Southend man who was said to be possessed by the spirit of a wolf demon to Norse warriors from ages long past who venerate the wolf and dressed in its fur to carry out blood-thirsty raids, we examined the history of the werewolf through the lenses of myth and medicine.

Werewolves are far from the only reason to fear the night. Wakwaks and Manananggals swooped down from the darkness on great leathery bat wings, pouncing on their victims from on high. The beating of those giant wings heralded the arrival of flying bloodsuckers, whereas in India, the Chedipe rode tigers into the hunt for the blood of sleeping men.

Equally bloodthirsty was the Chupacabra, the coyote-like spiky-backed creature that preyed on the blood of goats, chickens, and other livestock . . . leaving behind the remains of an animal that was completely devoid of blood, with the only sign of the beast's involvement being a set of twin puncture marks in the neck of the unfortunate prey.

Depending on the cinematic era, zombies either staggered or sprinted in search of living human flesh to feed their insatiable hunger. Some were the risen and reanimated dead, whereas others were living humans infected with a carefully engineered bioweapon virus. (Oh, and let's not forget the zombie chickens.) Fortunately, the U.S. military was on hand to save us, with a meticulously detailed warfighting plan to coordinate its all-out offensive to liberate the country from the rotten-fingered clutches of the living dead.

Two red eyes cut like laser beams through the darkness of the night sky as Mothman took to the skies above West Virginia — and possibly disaster sites around the world.

From swamps to seas, and from flatlands to forests, we have followed the thread of monsters, myths, and legends across the globe and over the span of centuries. It is a path that was well-trodden, although I have strived to offer fresh perspectives and insight within these pages. I would be remiss if I did not offer gratitude and respect to those authors who explored these murky waters long before I did. If you have enjoyed this book, I encourage you to seek out their works, which are listed in the Further Reading at the back of this book.

End Notes

1. Denny Sargent. "Becoming a Werewolf: Ancient Shamanic Dog Magic." Llewelyn.com. June 13, 2016. https://www.llewellyn.com/journal/article/2573
2. Clinical lycanthropy: https://pmc.ncbi.nlm.nih.gov/articles/PMC8542696/
3. https://medical.23andme.com/wp-content/uploads/2018/02/Unibrow.pdf
4. BEK: https://www.staffordshire-live.co.uk/news/local-news/couple-traumatised-after-terrifying-encounter-7770097
5. https://www.bbc.co.uk/stoke/content/articles/2009/09/29/werewolves_in_staffs_feature.shtml
6. https://www.stokesentinel.co.uk/news/stoke-on-trent-news/cannock-chase-horror-couple-spot-9608277
7. https://pubmed.ncbi.nlm.nih.gov/17256692/
8. https://pubmed.ncbi.nlm.nih.gov/25407032/
9. https://pubmed.ncbi.nlm.nih.gov/15166467/
10. "Brave Bishop Saves Snarling Werewolf" *The Sunday People,* July 30, 1989 by David Alford
11. https://boulderweekly.com/special-editions/krampus-you-better-watch-out/
12. Coast Guard Bermuda Triangle: https://www.history.uscg.mil/Frequently-Asked-Questions/
13. https://archive.org/details/naturalhistoryNc2Pont/page/214/mode/2up?view=theater
14. https://www.telegraph.co.uk/obituaries/2024/07/31/tony-shiels-artist-magician-st-ives-loch-ness/
15. https://www.bbc.com/news/uk-scotland-highlands-islands-49495145
16. https://nhm.org/press/plesiosaur
17. https://journalofscientificexploration.org/index.php/jse/article/download/2549/1637
18. https://www.newspapers.com/newspage/557492165/
19. https://www.newspapers.com/image/751651588/
20. https://www.newspapers.com/image/907165815/
21. https://www.newspapers.com/image/1113582513/
22. https://www.youtube.com/watch?v=C4M2R1voOcU
23. https://www.bbc.com/news/uk-scotland-highlands-islands-36024638
24. https://www.dailytelegraph.com.au/does-a-prehistoric-monster-haunt-the-hawkesbury-river/news-story/b77b47c46f6d225cb132f346c7f78f10
25. Hawkesbury River Monster: "Monsters in our Midst," *Sydney Morning Herald,* August 9, 1980, letter to the editor by Rex Gilroy, director of the Kedumba Nature Display
26. http://www.fordham.edu/halsall/basis/williamofnewburgh-five.asp

27. https://www.sunstar.com.ph/davao/local-news/wakwak-spotted-in-samal
28. https://cebudailynews.inquirer.net/488430/manananggal-in-talisay-city-public-told-to-refrain-from-spreading-unverified-reports
29. https://newsinfo.inquirer.net/9631/emotional-healing-for-mom-lola
30. http://news.bbc.co.uk/2/hi/africa/2602461.stm
31. https://www.voanews.com/a/africa_malawi-grapples-recurring-problem-mob-attacks-accused-vampires/6186768.html
32. https://www.bbc.com/news/uk-wales-66478360
33. https://www.youtube.com/watch?v=a_cjmy_ehiI
34. https://www.harvardmagazine.com/2017/10/are-zombies-real
35. https://harpers.org/archive/1984/04/the-pharmacology-of-zombies/
36. https://centerforinquiry.s3.amazonaws.com/wp-content/uploads/sites/29/2008/05/22164506/p60.pdf
37. https://stacks.cdc.gov/view/cdc/6023
38. https://skepticalinquirer.org/exclusive/the-curious-case-of-the-grafton-monster/
39. https://skepticalinquirer.org/2000/11/the-flatwoods-ufo-monster/
40. "Couples See Man-Sized Bird … Creature … Something!" *Point Pleasant Register*, November 16, 1966.
41. "Winged, Red-Eyed 'Thing' Chases Point Couples Across Countryside," *Athens Messenger*, Mary Hyre, November 1966.
42. https://www.nzherald.co.nz/world/the-frightening-supernatural-story-of-the-black-bird-of-chernobyl/KH2SKIIUGWLXPJPMIKI2LXG2PI/
43. https://www.politifact.com/factchecks/2024/mar/29/facebook-posts/no-this-isnt-a-photo-of-a-black-figure-on-baltimor/
44. https://pinelandsalliance.org/learn-about-the-pinelands/ecosystem/pine-barrens-vs-pinelands/
45. https://www.nytimes.com/1973/02/05/archives/mob-favors-pinelands-for-burials.html
46. https://www.newspapers.com/image/958193603/?
47. https://navyhistory.org/2021/10/seapower-satire-and-superstition-stephen-decatur-and-the-hunt-for-the-jersey-devil/
48. https://www.njstatelib.org/is-the-jersey-devil-the-official-state-demon/
49. https://abcnews.go.com/US/man-claims-photographed-mythical-jersey-devil-legend-dating/story?id=34442356
50. https://www.youtube.com/watch?v=6UP0hbWN_WI
51. "Folk Monster Stirs Anxiety in South Texas," *Austin American-Statesman,* May 9, 1996.
52. https://vault.fbi.gov/Animal%20Mutilation
53. https://www.riograndesun.com/news/rio-arribas-x-files-reopened/article_dffe7345-1282-55a6-9935-2902edce6377.html
54. "The Unsolved Riddle of the Texas Cow Mutilations," Gerrard Kaonga, *Newsweek*, April 28, 2023.
55. *El Chupacabra! The Science Behind a Latin American Mystery.* Texas A&M Agrilife Extension, 8/17.
56. https://texnat.tamu.edu/files/2021/10/Diseases-Chupacabra-2017.pdf
57. "Chupacabra in the Carolinas? Or a Coyote with Mange? We Asked an Expert," Drew Tripp, ABC4 News. August, 8, 2017/
58. "From Spooky Lore to Science Fact: Unmasking the 'Chupacabra.'"

Sarah Fuller, *Agrilife Today*, October 15, 2024.

59. "Are the Strange Creatures Found around Cuero the Legendary Chupacabra?" Kristen Cabrera, *Texas Standard*, November 1, 2023.
60. "Chupacabra Caught on Tape," KFDA News Channel 10, August 12, 2008. https://www.youtube.com/watch?v=7p1YCwf9IXg
61. https://civicscience.com/u-s-belief-in-sasquatch-has-risen-since-2020/
62. https://thehill.com/blogs/blog-briefing-room/4400922-americans-ghosts-aliens-devil-survey/
63. https://assets.realclear.com/files/2024/01/2334_RCORTopline-Jan92024.pdf
64. "Huge Footprints Found on Wilderness Road," *Eureka Humboldt Standard*, October 6, 1958.
65. "Bigfoot Fans Offered Substitute Silver Object," *Siskiyou Daily News*, October 10, 1958.
66. "2 Men See Bigfoot — Mystery Deepens," *Eureka Humboldt Standard*, October 15, 1958.
67. "Ray Wallace, 84: Took Bigfoot Secret to Grave — Now His Kids Spill It," *Los Angeles Times*, December 6, 2002
68. https://www.news.com.au/technology/science/anim.als/bob-gimlin-explains-why-releasing-his-bigfoot-footage-was-one-big-mistake-he-wished-he-could-undo/news-story/4dc66f0e7adaf352fc19a5fe0262cb6a
69. https://nypost.com/2023/10/11/bigfoot-spotted-in-colorado-in-broad-daylight-see-the-video/
70. "Bigfoot Expert Weighs in on Colorado Footage, Notices One Surprising Detail," *New York Post*, October 19, 2023. https://nypost.com/2023/10/19/bigfoot-expert-weighs-in-on-colorado-footage-notices-one-surprising-detail/
71. "Man Apparently Attempting Bigfoot Hoax Killed on Montana Highway," Reuters, August 28, 2012. https://www.reuters.com/article/lifestyle/man-apparently-attempting-bigfoot-hoax-killed-on-montana-highway-idUSBRE87R1B7/
72. "Montana Man Told Police a Hunter 'Mistook Him for Bigfoot' and Shot at Him, Cops say," *Idaho Statesman*, December 19, 2018.

Photo Sources

Aesopposea (Wikicommons): p. 172.
Kim Alaniz: p. 49.
Gray Barker: p. 183.
H. M. Bec: p. 130.
Gian Bernal: p. 129.
Stara Blazkova: p. 65.
Cbarry123 (Wikicommons): p. 96.
Centers for Disease Control and Prevention: pp. 94, 152.
Charlotte (Wikicommons): p. 147.
Chern (Wikicommons): p. 90.
Cpt. Muji (Wikicommons): p. 148.
Richie Diesterheft: p. 178.
Falmouth Packet: pp. 43, 44.
FX: p. 106.
Eric Gaba: p. 48.
German Historical Museum: p. 68.
Gourami Watcher (Wikicommons): p. 5.
Rita Greer: p. 112.
Herzog August Bibliothek Wolfenbüttel: p. 115.
Illustrated London News Ltd./Mary Evans Picture Library: p. 53.
Elizabeth K. Joseph: p. 234.
KaOokami (Wikicommons): p. 10.
Anthony Karen: p. 147.
Jean-Noël Lafargue: p. 144.
Library of Congress: pp. 67, 194, 247.
Los Angeles County Museum of Art: p. 8.
Olaus Magnus (Wikicommons): p. 34.
R. H. Mathews: p. 83.
Megamoto85 (Wikicommons): p. 16.
Ad Meskens: p. 63.
Museu Nacional d'Art de Catalunya: p. 202.
NASA/JPL-Caltech: p. 51.
National Library of Medicine: p. 102.
National Portrait Gallery: p. 199.
NTNU University Museum, Norway: p. 39.
Roger Patterson and Robert Gimlin: p. 228.
Philadelphia Bulletin: p. 204.
Geoff Pick: p. 17.
Rawdonfox (Wikicommons): p. 117.

San Antonio Light: p. 56.
Scribd.com: p. 153.
Scyrene (Wikicommons): p. 72.
Shutterstock: pp. 14, 18, 20, 21, 22, 23, 25, 26, 29, 30, 35, 42, 45, 58, 60, 74, 89, 100, 104, 105, 111, 124, 143, 149, 159, 161, 168, 175, 182, 184, 192, 193, 197, 206, 210, 212, 213, 215, 217, 220, 221, 223, 227, 231, 238, 239, 241, 243, 244, 246, 249, 252, 254, 256.
Sonja (Wikicommons): p. 188.
Tim Starling: p. 82.
State Library of Victoria: p. 85.
Timeinc.com: p. 140.
Caroline Toms: p. 224.
United Artists: p. 78.
Mel. White: p. 137.
Mark Edward Wilson: p. 71.
Don Woods: p. 167.
Public domain: pp. 3, 4, 9, 12, 75, 93, 99, 118, 121, 122, 127, 180, 201.

Further Reading

Readers seeking further information on some of the cases, locations and incidents contained in this book may find the following books to be useful.

Barker, Gray. *The Silver Bridge: The Classic Mothman Tale.* Seattle, WA: Metadisc Books, 2008.

Brickley, Lee. *UFOs, Werewolves & the Pig-Man: Exposing England's Strangest Location—Cannock Chase, England?* Yam Yam Books, 2013.

Derenberger, Woodrow W., and Harold W. Hubbard. *Visitors from Lanulos: My Contact with Indrid Cold.* Point Pleasant, WV: New Saucerian Books, 2014.

Keel, John A. *The Mothman Prophecies: A True Story*. United States: Tor Books, 2024.

Long, Greg. *The Making of Bigfoot: The Inside Story*. Amherst, NY: Prometheus Books, 2004.

Mckee, Gabriel. *The Saucerian: UFOs, Men in Black, and the Unbelievable Life of Gray Barker*. Cambridge, MA: MIT Press, 2025.

Meldrum, D. Jeffrey. *Sasquatch: Legend Meets Science.* New York: Forge, 2007.

Naish, Darren. *Hunting Monsters: Cryptozoology and the Reality behind the Myths.* London: Sirius, 2017.

Redfern, Nick. *The Bigfoot Book: The Encyclopedia of Sasquatch, Yeti and Cryptid Primates*. Detroit: Visible Ink Press, 2025.

Redfern, Nick, and Brad Steiger. *Werewolf Stories: Shape-shifters, Lycanthropes, and Man-Beasts*. Detroit: Visible Ink Press, 2023.

Regal, Brian, and Frank J. Esposito. *The Secret History of the Jersey Devil: How Quakers, Hucksters, and Benjamin Franklin Created a Monster*. Baltimore: Johns Hopkins University Press, 2019.

Ronson, Jon. *The Men Who Stare at Goats*. London: Picador, 2024.

Schlosser, S. E., and Paul G. Hoffman. *Spooky New Jersey: Tales of Hauntings, Strange Happenings, and Other Local Lore.* Guilford, CT: Globe Pequot, 2017.

Steiger, Brad. *The Werewolf Book: The Encyclopedia of Shape-shifting Beings.* Detroit: Visible Ink Press, 2014.

Warren, E., L. Warren, B. Ramsey, and R. D. Chase. *Werewolf: A True Story of Demonic Possession*. Graymalkin Media, 2014.

White, Rupert, and Tony Shiels. *Monstermind: The Magical Life and Art of Tony "Doc" Shiels*. Antenna Publications, 2015.

Witchell, Nicholas. *The Loch Ness Story*. Harmondsworth: Penguin Books, 1976.

Index

A

Adam, 126–27, 127 (ill.)
Adamski, George, 161
Alford, David, 24
Alfred, Lord Tennyson, 37–38
Alnwick Castle, 109–14, 111 (ill.)
Angrboda, 9
Arnold, Kenneth, 168, 232
Ashmore, Kelly, 19
Aswang, 130, 130 (ill.)
Australia
  Bunyip, 85 (ill.), 85–87
  Moolyewonk, 81–83, 82 (ill.)
  Yowie, 83 (ill.), 83–85

B

Bandit (German Shepherd), 184–86
Barker, Gray, 160–61, 162, 168, 183 (ill.), 183–87
Báthory, Elizabeth, 122 (ill.), 122–23
Batman, 177
bats, 99–101, 100 (ill.)
Battle of Point Pleasant, 171–73, 172 (ill.)
Belford, Tony, 23–24
Bell, Melissa, 153
Bemis, Jess, 221–22
Berlitz, Charles, 34
Bermuda Triangle, 34–36, 35 (ill.)
Berry, Matt, 106 (ill.)
berserker, 10, 10 (ill.)
Bigfoot Discovery Museum (Felton, CA), 233, 234 (ill.)
Bigfoot Field Researchers Organization (BFRO), 226–27
Bigfoot/Sasquatch, 223 (ill.)
  belief in, 219–20
  Crew, Gerry, 222, 224 (ill.), 224–27
  elephantitis, 222–23
  Genzoli, Andrew, 221–22
  Megargle and Morgan, 237–42
  Parker video, 233–34
  Patterson-Gimlin film, 228 (ill.), 228–32, 231 (ill.), 233, 248
  Squatching, 242–59
  Tenley, Randy Lee, 235
black bears, 246, 246 (ill.)
Black, David, 205–6
Black-Eyed Kids (BEKs), 15–17, 16 (ill.)
Bogart, Humphrey, 11
Boleskine House, 74–75
Bonaparte, Joseph, 202 (ill.), 202–3
Bouyer, Frederic, 38
Boyd, Alastair, 63
Boyle, Danny, 152
Bram Stoker's Dracula (1992), 121, 122
Brickley, Lee, 17–19, 20
Brode, Noah, 219
Bronson, Deming "Dick," 1
Brown, Edwin, 96, 97
Brown, George, 96
Brown, Mary, 95–96
Brown, Mary Olive, 95–96
Brown, Mercy, 95–98, 96 (ill.)
Browning, Tod, 99
bullying, 103

Bunyip, 85 (ill.), 85–87
Butfiloski, Jay, 215

C

Cabrera, Kristen, 216
Camacho, Victor, 136
Canion, Phylis, 216–17
Cannock Chase, 14 (ill.), 14–20
Carpenter, John, 165
Centers for Disease Control and Prevention (CDC), 152 (ill.), 153
Chambers, Maurice, 63
Chaney, Lon, Jr., 12 (ill.), 13
Charleston, L. J., 181
Chase, Robert David, 27
Chedipe, 123–25, 124 (ill.)
Chernobyl nuclear facility (Ukraine), 181–82, 182 (ill.)
Chicxulub Crater, 50–52, 51 (ill.)
Chupacabra, 209–17, 210 (ill.), 212 (ill.), 213 (ill.), 215 (ill.)
Clarke, Dave, 45
Clooney, George, 76
Cockrell, Robert, 158–60, 161–62
Cold, Ingrid, 186–87
Concodes, Lara Mae, 131
CONPLAN 8888: Counter-Zombie Dominance, 153 (ill.), 153–56
Coppola, Francis Ford, 122
Cornstalk, Chief, 172 (ill.), 172–73
Coyne, Joseph R., 204
Craven, Wes, 151
Crew, Gerry, 222, 224 (ill.), 224–27
Crowley, Aleister, 74–75, 75 (ill.)
cryptids, 158
Cuyos, Jucell Marie P., 131

D

Dames, Ed, 76
Davis, Wade, 148 (ill.), 148–51
The Day the Earth Stood Still (1951), 165
Decatur, Stephen, 199 (ill.), 199–200
Del Valle, Fernando, 209
Demetriou, Natasia, 106 (ill.)
Derenberger, Taunia, 187
Derenberger, Woodrow "Woody," 186–87
digitally manipulated imagery, 73, 74 (ill.)
Dinsdale, Tim, 71, 72–73, 232
Dracula, 98–100, 99 (ill.), 100
Dracula 2000 (2000), 126
Dunn, Matthew, 230

E

elephantitis, 222–23
emergency rooms and full moon, 21–22
Esposito, Frank J., 196
eternal life, 103–4
Eve, 127
Expedition Bigfoot, 243

F

Fallout 76 (video game), 168–69
Fenrir, 9, 9 (ill.)
Finding Bigfoot, 243
Fisher, G. Bailey, 165
Fisher, Terry, 24
Flatwoods Monster, 165–69, 166 (ill.), 168 (ill.)
Flückinger, Johannes, 114, 120
flying vampires, 128–32, 129 (ill.), 130 (ill.)
Fort, Charles, 180
Forteana, 180
Francis Scott Key Bridge collapse (Baltimore, MD), 188–89
Franklin, Benjamin, 196
Freki, 9
Fresno Nightcrawlers, 135–38, 137 (ill.)
Fukushima, Japan, nuclear accident (2011), 182
full moon, 21 (ill.), 21–22

G

Gambino, Emanuel, 191
Garland, Alex, 152
Genzoli, Andrew, 221–22

Geoffreys, Stephen, 103
George III, 91
Gere, Richard, 180
Gerhard, Ken, 256–57
Geri, 9
giant squid, 39, 39 (ill.)
Gilroy, Rex, 81–83
Gimlin, Bob, 228–32
Goat Sucker. *See* Chupacabra
Goebbels, Joseph, 67, 68
Goodall, Jane, 255
Grafton Monster, 158–63, 159 (ill.), 161 (ill.)
Grant, Arthur, 56, 56 (ill.)
Gray, Hugh, 52–55, 53 (ill.)
Guercio, Gino del, 149
Guillén, Harvey, 106 (ill.)

H–I

Haiti and zombies, 143–52, 144 (ill.), 147 (ill.)
Hardman, Mathew, 133–34
Hardy, Dorothy, 9 (ill.)
Harrison, Vernon, 71
Harryhausen, Ray, 36–37
Hawkesbury River Monster, 81–83
Henke, Scott, 213
Hensley, Terry, 213
Heymann, Philip B., 211
Hieronymus, Bob, 230
Hines, Terence, 151
Hodag, 1–5, 3 (ill.), 4 (ill.), 5 (ill.)
Holliday, John Henry "Doc," 92
Holmes, John, 46
Hurt, John, 4
Hutchinson, Mrs. Earl, 167
In Search of..., 157
Indian vampires, 123–25, 124 (ill.)
It Came from Outer Space! (1953), 165

J–K

Jersey Devil, 204 (ill.)
  Bonaparte, Joseph, 202–3
  Decatur, Stephen, 199–200
  Kidd, William, 201–2
  Leeds Devil, 192–99, 193 (ill.), 194 (ill.)
  Mothman, 204
  photo and video of, 205–6, 206 (ill.)
  sports teams named after, 207
Kahn, Ali, 152 (ill.)
Kaza, Cindy, 34
Keel, John, 161, 179–80, 180 (ill.), 183–84, 187, 204
Keigh-tugh-qua, 172
Kidd, William, 201 (ill.), 201–2
Kilmer, Val, 92
King Kong, 77
Kirkman, Robert, 139
Kraken, 36–40, 37 (ill.)
Krampus, 29 (ill.), 29–32, 30 (ill.)

L

Lee, Christopher, 78
Leeds, Daniel, 195
Leeds Devil, 192–99, 193 (ill.), 194 (ill.)
Leeds, Mother, 192–93, 194–95, 198
Leeds, Titan, 195–96
Lemon, Eugene, 166
Lennox, Annie, 11
Lewis, Charles, 172
Leyshon, Mabel, 133–34
Lilith, 125–27, 127 (ill.)
Linney, Laura, 180
Loch Ness, 59, 60 (ill.), 158
Loch Ness Monster, 65 (ill.)
  description and history of loch, 47–52, 48 (ill.)
  digitally manipulated imagery, 73, 74 (ill.)
  downed blimp explanation, 66, 67 (ill.)
  ghost, 76
  Grant sighting, 56, 56 (ill.)
  Gray photograph, 52–55, 53 (ill.)
  MacNab sighting, 69–70
  Morgawr, 41, 43
  paranormal explanation, 74–76
  Shiels photograph, 70–73
  skepticism and explanations, 76–79
  Spicer sighting, 57–58
  Surgeon's Photograph, 61–66, 63 (ill.)

Wetherell sighting, 60–61
World War II years, 67–69
Loki, 9
Long, Greg, 230
The Lost Boys (1987), 102–3
Lugosi, Béla, 98–99, 99 (ill.), 144
Lussier, Patrick, 126
lycanthropy, 7, 12–13, 25
Lycaon, King, 8 (ill.)

M

MacFarlane-Barrow family, 67, 69
MacNab, Peter, 69–70
Magnus, Olaus, 34 (ill.)
Mallette, Steve, 175
Mallettes, 174–75, 184, 185
Manananggal, 128–32, 129 (ill.)
mange, 213 (ill.), 213–14
Martelle, Scott, 226
Martin, David, 63
Martin, Emily, 206
Mary F, 42–43, 43 (ill.), 44 (ill.)
Matedios, Efren, 131
Maxwell, Robert, 181–82
May, Edward, 166
May, Freddie, 166
May, Kathleen, 166
Mays, John, 32
McGrath, Terence, 66
McGregor, Ewan, 76
McKee, Gabriel, 161
McKenna, Robert, 26
Megargle, Alan, 237–42, 244–45, 250, 252–53
Meldrum, Jeff, 255
Mitchell, Alex, 233
Moolyewonk, 81–83, 82 (ill.)
Morgan, Jesse, 237–42, 244–45, 250, 252, 258
Morgawr, 41–46, 42 (ill.), 43 (ill.), 44 (ill.), 45 (ill.)
Mothman, 175 (ill.)
Barker, Gray, 160–61, 183–87
foreign sightings, 181–82, 182 (ill.)
Jersey Devil, 204
Point Pleasant, West Virginia, 157–58, 171–81
Mothman Festival, 188, 189 (ill.)
The Mothman Prophecies (Keel), 180, 180 (ill.), 183–84, 187
Mountain Monsters, 243
Mussolini, Benito, 68, 68 (ill.)
Myers, Daphne, 247
Myers, Jim, 247

N–O

Naish, Darren, 72, 72 (ill.)
Narcisse, Angelina, 147
Narcisse, Clairvius, 147–48, 149, 151
Neeson, Liam, 36
Nessie. *See* Loch Ness Monster
New Jersey Air National Guard, 206–7
New Jersey Devils, 207
New Jersey Pine Barrens/Pinelands, 191–92, 192 (il.), 193
Newton, Isaac, 11
Nickell, Joe, 167
Night of the Living Dead (1968), 139, 140 (ill.), 141
nightcrawlers, 135–38, 137 (ill.)
Nimoy, Leonard, 157
Novak, Kayvan, 106 (ill.)
Odin, 9, 9 (ill.)
Oldman, Gary, 122

P

Page, Jimmy, 75
Paole, Arnod, 114–20, 115 (ill.)
Park County, Colorado, 242
Parker, Hayley, 19
Parker, Shannon, 233
Parker, Stetson, 233
Partridge, Newell, 184–85
Pasteur, Louis, 101–2, 102 (ill.)
Patterson, Roger, 228–32, 248
Patterson-Gimlin film, 228 (ill.), 228–32, 231 (ill.), 233, 248
Peters, Tommy, 162
plesiosaur, 48–52, 49 (ill.), 74, 76
Point Pleasant, West Virginia, 157–58, 171–81, 178 (ill.), 178–79
Pontoppidan, Erik, 37
porphyria, 90 (ill.), 90–92
Poseidon, 36
The Private Life of Sherlock Holmes (1970), 78 (ill.), 78–79

Proksch, Mark, 106, 106 (ill.)
Pules, Marcus, 182
Pulme, Robert, 16

R

rabies, 100–102
Rage (bioweapon), 152
Ragsdale, William, 103
Ramsey, Bill, 22–27
Reed, Daniel A., 161–62
Regal, Bryan, 196
REM-pod, 253–54, 254 (ill.), 257–58
Rhinelander, Wisconsin, 1–5, 4 (ill.), 5 (ill.)
Rice, Anne, 107
Romero, George A., 139, 141
Round Rock Chupacabras, 207
Rugg, Michael, 233–34, 234 (ill.)
Ryan, Mike, 4

S

sanguinarians, 105
Santa Claus, 29, 32
Sarandon, Chris, 103
Sargent, Denny, 8–9
Sasquatch. *See* Bigfoot/Sasquatch
Sasquatch Outpost (Bailey, CO), 247 (ill.), 247–50
Scarberrys, 174–75, 184, 185
Schlosser, S. E., 203
sea monsters, 33–34, 34 (ill.)
Seabrook, W. B., 144
Seattle Kraken, 207
Shaun of the Dead (2004), 141
Shepard, Eugene, 3–4 (ill.), 4 (ill.)
Shiels, Tony "Doc," 43–46, 70–73, 71 (ill.)
Silver Bridge (Point Pleasant, WV), 178 (ill.), 178–79
The Silver Bridge (Barker), 183–87, 184 (ill.)
Slide Rock Bolter, 225
Space Wolves, 11
Spicer, George, 57–58
Spurling, Christian, 63, 65, 66
Squatching, 242–59
squid, giant, 39, 39 (ill.)
Stafford, Thomas F., 167
Steenstrup, Japetus, 39
Stephens, Robert, 78
Stewart, Doug, 214–15
Stoker, Bram, 98, 121
Surgeon's Photograph, 61–66, 63 (ill.)

T–U

Taylor, Erin, 242, 250
Tenley, Randy Lee, 235
Tepes, Vlad, 121 (ill.), 121–22
tetrodotoxin, 149 (ill.), 149–51
The Thing, 165
The Thing from Another World (1951), 165
Titmus, Robert, 225
Tomeček, John M., 213, 215–16
touch coins, 94
transfiguration, 24
tuberculosis, 92–95, 93 (ill.), 94 (ill.)
Turner, W. R., 60
UFOs, 167–68
unibrow, 13–14

V

vampires
  in Africa, 132–33
  Alnwick Castle, 109–14
  Báthory, Elizabeth, 122 (ill.), 122–23
  bats, 99–101, 100 (ill.)
  blood consumption, 105–7
  Brown, Mercy, 95–98, 96 (ill.)
  bullying, 103
  destruction and hunting of, 116–20, 117 (ill.), 118 (ill.)
  Dracula, 98–100, 99 (ill.)
  eternal life, 103–4
  flying, 128–32, 129 (ill.), 130 (ill.)
  Indian, 123–25, 124 (ill.)
  lifestyle, 104–8
  Lilith, 125–27, 127 (ill.)
  Lugosi, Béla, 98–99, 99 (ill.)
  Paole, Arnod, 114–20
  porphyria, 90 (ill.), 90–92
  rabies, 100–102
  stereotypes, 89–90

tuberculosis, 92–95
Vlad the Impaler, 121 (ill.), 121–22
in Wales, 133–34
Verne, Jules, 39
Vlad the Impaler, 121 (ill.), 121–22
voodoo, 146, 146 (ill.)

W

Wakwaks, 128
The Walking Dead, 139
Wallace, Michael, 226
Wallace, Raymond, 224, 225–27, 227 (ill.), 232
Ward, Burt, 177
Warhammer 40,000 (game), 11
Warren, Ed, 24, 25, 27
Warren, Lorraine, 24, 25, 27
Watson, Roland, 54
Wayland, Tobias, 171
werewolves, 7–9, 8 (ill.), 11–14, 17–20, 20 (ill.), 22 (ill.), 22–27
West, Adam, 177
Wetherell, Ian, 63
Wetherell, Marmaduke A., 60–61, 63, 64, 65
What We Do in the Shadows (2014), 106, 106 (ill.)
White Zombie (1932), 144
Whitehall, New York, 238, 238 (ill.), 239 (ill.)
Wilder, Billy, 78
William of Newburgh, 109–14
Wilson, Robert, 61–66, 63 (ill.), 64, 65
wolf pelts, 10, 10 (ill.)
wolves, 8–11
Wolves of Fenris, 11
the Woo, 257
World War I, 14–15

Y–Z

Ybarra, Sylvia, 209–10
Yowie, 83 (ill.), 83–85
Zeus, 8 (ill.), 36
zombies
background, 143–52, 144 (ill.), 146 (ill.), 149 (ill.)
disaster preparedness, 153 (ill.), 153–56
in Haiti, 143–52, 144 (ill.), 147 (ill.)
pop culture, 139–43, 140 (ill.), 143 (ill.)
tetrodotoxin, 149 (ill.), 149–51

Read more about

Bigfoot in . . .

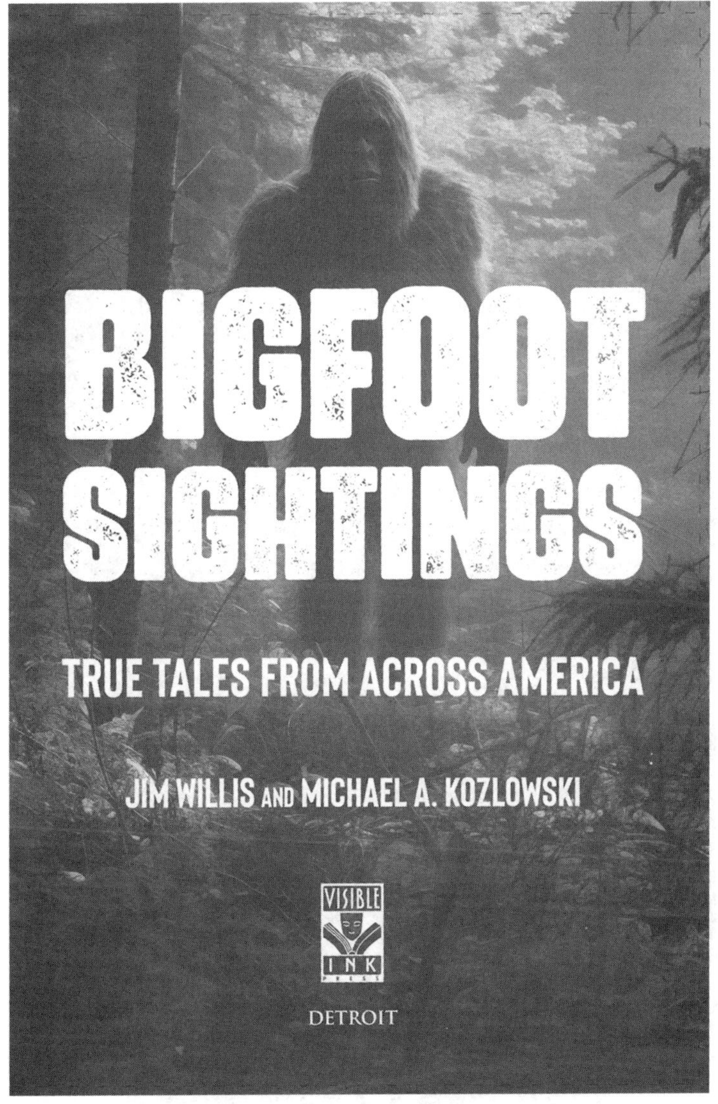

IBSN: 978-1-57859-869-4

And if you enjoy a good ghost story . . .

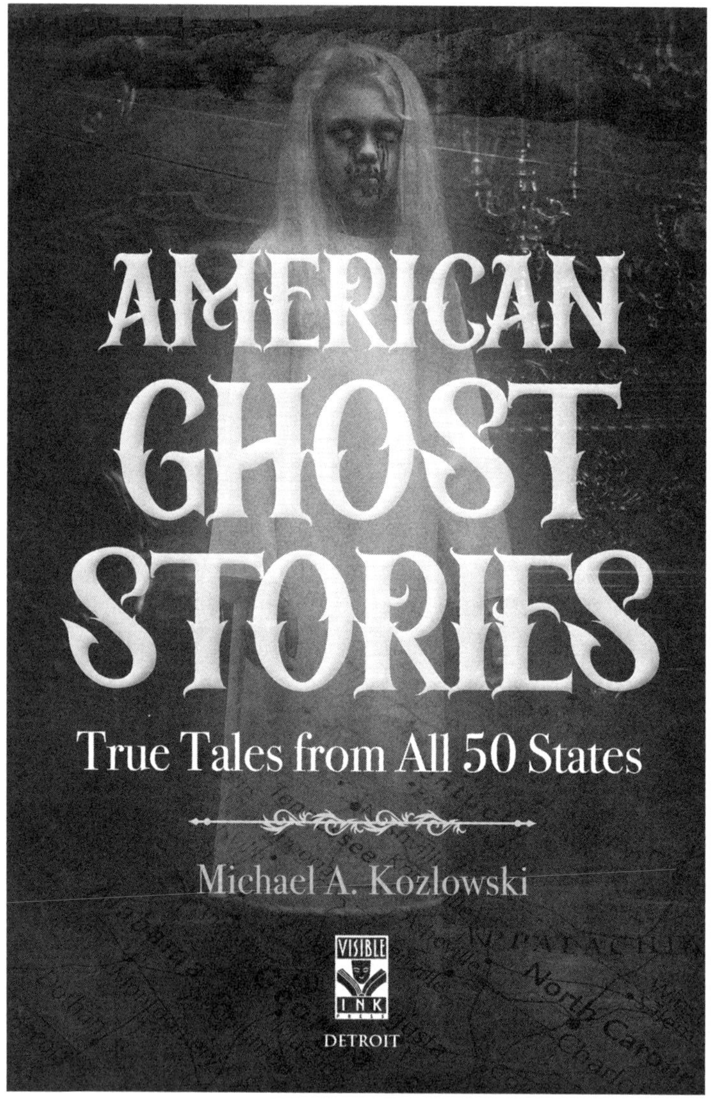

ISBN: 978-1-57859-799-4

And even more ghost stories . . . !

ISBN: 978-1-57859-812-0

More monsters from Richard Estep . . .

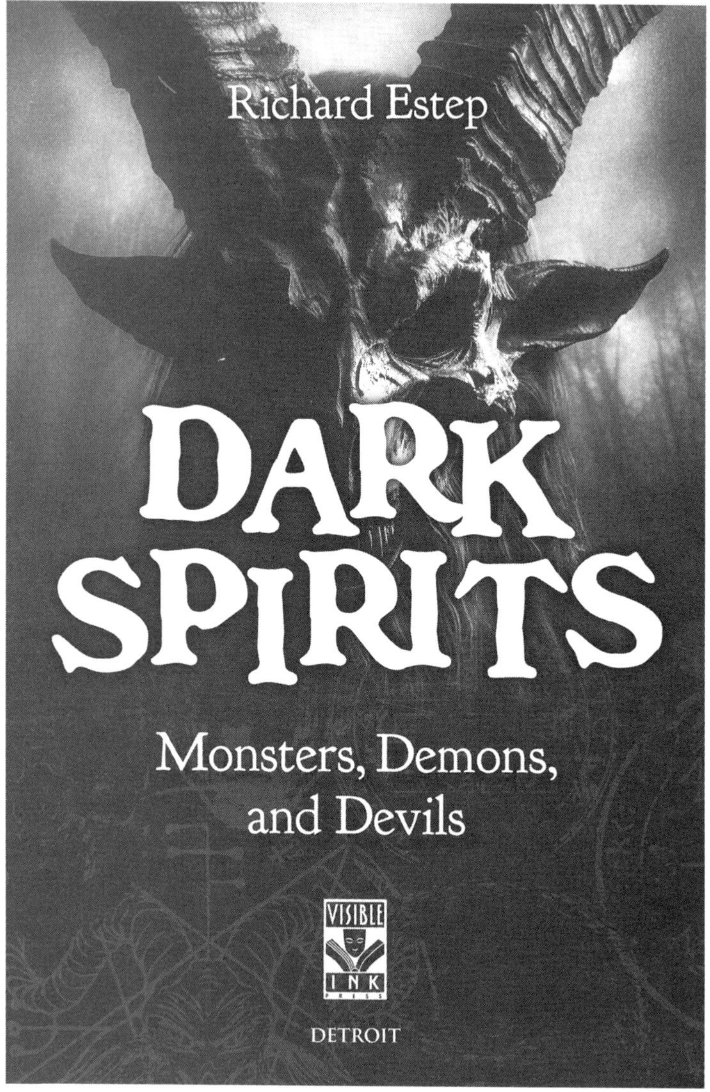

ISBN: 978-1-57859-847-2